P9-DGS-598

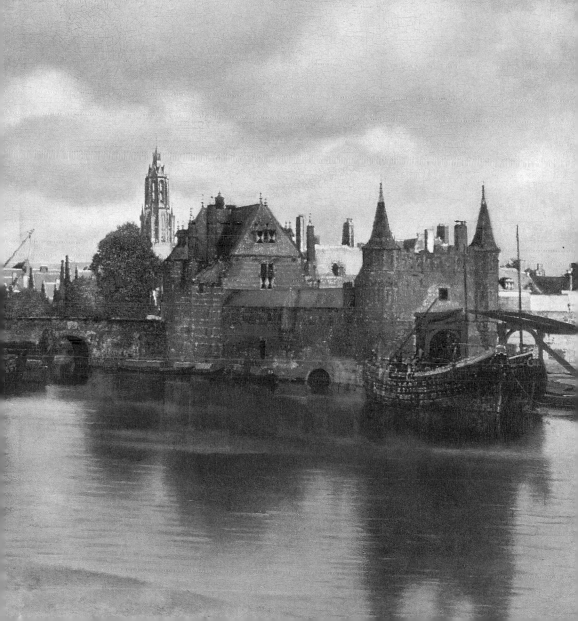

VERMEER'S HAT

VERMEER'S HAT

*The Seventeenth Century and the Dawn
of the Global World*

TIMOTHY BROOK

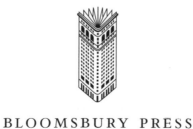

BLOOMSBURY PRESS

Published by Bloomsbury Press, New York and London
Distributed to the trade by Macmillan

Art credits
View of Delft © Royal Picture Gallery Mauritshuis, The Hague. *Officer and
Laughing Girl* © The Frick Collection, New York. *Young Woman Reading a Letter
at an Open Window* © Staatliche Kunstsammlungen, Gemäldegalerie, Dresden.
The Geographer Photo © Städel Museum—ARTOTHEK. Lambert van
Meerten plate reproduced by kind permission of Gemeente Musea Delft.
Woman Holding a Balance © Board of Trustees, National Gallery of Art, Washington, D.C.
The Game of Cards, Gift of Mr. and Mrs. John S. Newberry, photograph 1995, The Detroit
Institute of Arts. Figure of Kuan Yü, The Avery Brundage Collection. © Asian Art
Museum of San Francisco. Used by permission.

Maps by Eric Leinberger

LIBRARY OF CONGRESS CATALOGING IN PUBLICATION DATA

Brook, Timothy, 1951–
Vermeer's hat: the seventeenth century and the dawn of the global world / Timothy Brook.
p. cm.
Includes bibliographical references and index.
ISBN-13: 978-1-59691-444-5
ISBN-10: 1-59691-444-0
1. Civilization, Modern—seventeenth century.   2. Culture and globalization.   3. Vermeer,
Johannes, 1632–1675—Themes, motives.   I. Title.
CB401B76 2008
909'.6—dc22
2007015767

ISBN-10 1-59691-444-0
ISBN-13 978-1-59691-444-5

First U.S. Edition 2008

1 3 5 7 9 10 8 6 4 2

For Fay

Our arrivals at meaning and at value are momentary pauses in the ongoing dialogue with others from which meaning and value spring.

—Gary Tomlinson, *Music in Renaissance Magic*

CONTENTS

ILLUSTRATIONS

MAPS

The View from Delft

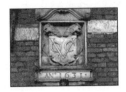

THE SUMMER I was twenty, I bought a bicycle in Amsterdam and cycled southwest across the Low Countries on what would be the final leg of a journey that took me from Dubrovnik on the Adriatic to Ben Nevis in Scotland. I was on my second day out, pedaling across the Dutch countryside, when the light began to fade and the late-afternoon drizzle blowing in off the North Sea turned the road under my tires slick. A truck edged me too close to the verge, and my bicycle went over into the mud. I was not hurt, but I was soaked and filthy and had a bent fender to straighten. Without the shelter of a bridge, which was my usual hobo's recourse in bad weather, I knocked at the door of the nearest house to ask for a few moments out of the rain. Mrs. Oudshoorn had watched my spill from her front window, which is where I guessed she spent many a long afternoon, so I was not altogether a surprise when she opened her door a crack and peered out at me. She hesitated for a brief moment, then put caution aside and opened the door wide so that this bedraggled young Canadian could come inside.

All I wanted was to stand for a few minutes out of the rain and pull myself together, but she wouldn't hear of it. She poured me a hot bath, cooked me dinner, gave me a bed to sleep in, and pressed on me several of her dead husband's things, including a waterproof coat. The next morning, as sunlight poured over her kitchen table, she fed me the best breakfast I ever had eaten and chuckled slyly about how angry her son would be if he ever found out she'd taken in a complete

stranger, and a man at that. After breakfast she gave me postcards of local sites to take as mementos and suggested I go see some of them before climbing back on my bicycle and getting back on the road. The
sun was shining that Sunday morning, and there was nowhere I had to
be, so out I went for a stroll and a look. Her town has stayed with me
ever since. Mrs. Oudshoorn gave me more than the hospitality of her
home. She gave me Delft.

"A most sweet town, with bridges and a river in every street," is
how the London diarist Samuel Pepys described Delft when he visited in May 1660. The description perfectly fit the town I saw, for
Delft has remained largely as it looked in the seventeenth century. Its
cobbled streets and narrow bridges were dappled that morning by
galleon-shaped clouds scudding in from the North Sea a dozen kilometers to the northwest, and the sunlight reflecting off the canals lit
up the brick façades of the houses. Unlike that far grander canal city,
Venice, which Italians built up from the surface of the sea on wooden
pilings driven into tidal sandbars, the Dutch built Delft below sea
level. Dikes held back the North Sea, and water sluices were dug to
drain the coastal fens. This history resides in its name, *delven* being the
Dutch word for digging. The main canal running the length of the
western part of the town is still called the Oude Delft, the Old Sluice.

Memories of the seventeenth century are peculiarly present in the
two great churches of Delft. On the Great Market Square is Nieuwe
Kerk, the New Church, so named because it was founded two centuries after the Oude Kerk, the Old Church on the Oude Delft canal.
Both great buildings were built and decorated as Catholic churches,
of course (the Old Church in the thirteenth century, the New
Church in the fifteenth), though they did not remain so. The light
coming through the clear glass in the windows and illuminating their
interiors bleaches out that early history in favor of what came later:
the purging of Catholic idolatry, including the removal of stained
glass in the 1560s, which was part of the Dutch struggle for independence from Spanish rule, and the fashioning of Protestant gathering
places of almost civil worship. The floors of both churches belong

quite securely to the seventeenth century, for they are covered with inscriptions marking the graves of the wealthier citizens of seventeenth-century Delft. People in those days hoped to be buried as close as possible to a holy place, and better than being buried beside a church was to be interred underneath it. Many of the numerous paintings done of the interiors of these two churches show a lifted paving stone, occasionally even gravediggers at work, while other people (and dogs) go about their business. The churches kept registers of where each family had its grave, but most of the graves bear no written memorial. Only those who could afford the cost had the stones laid over them inscribed with their names and deeds.

It was in the Old Church that I came upon one stone inscribed neatly and sparely: JOHANNES VERMEER 1632–1675. I had stumbled upon the last remains of an artist whose paintings I had just seen and admired in the Rijksmuseum, the national museum in Amsterdam, a few days earlier. I knew nothing about Delft or Vermeer's connection to the town. Yet suddenly there he was in front of me, awaiting my notice.

Many years later I learned that this paving stone had not been placed over his grave when he died. At that time, Vermeer was not a person of sufficient importance to deserve an inscribed gravestone. He was just a painter, an artisan in one of the fine trades. It is true that Vermeer was a headman of the artisans' guild of St. Luke, and that he enjoyed a position of honor in the town militia—though that was a distinction he shared with some eighty other men in his neighborhood. Even if there had been money on hand when he died, which there wasn't, this status did not justify the honor of an inscription. Only in the nineteenth century did collectors and curators come to think of Vermeer's subtle and elusive paintings as the work of a great artist. The stone there now was not laid until the twentieth century, put down to satisfy the many who, unlike me, knew he was there and came to pay their respects. This slab does not actually mark the place where Vermeer was buried, though, since all the paving stones were taken up and relaid when the church was restored following the great fire of 1921. All we know is that his remains are down there somewhere.

Nothing else of Vermeer's life in Delft has survived. We know that he grew up in his father's inn off the Great Market Square, and that he lived most of his adult life in the house of his mother-in-law, Maria Thins, on the Oude Langendijck, or Old Long Dike. This was where he surrounded himself with an ever-growing brood of little children downstairs; painted most of his pictures upstairs; and died suddenly at the age of forty-three, his debts mounting and his wellspring of inspiration gone dry. The house was pulled down in the nineteenth century. Of Vermeer's life in Delft, nothing tangible is left.

The only way to step into Vermeer's world is through his paintings, but neither is this possible in Delft. Of the thirty-five paintings that still survive (a thirty-sixth, stolen from the Isabella Stewart Gardner Museum in Boston in 1990, is still missing), not one remains in Delft. They were sold after he died or carted to auctions elsewhere, and now are dispersed among seventeen different galleries from Manhattan to Berlin. The three closest works are in the Mauritshuis, the royal picture gallery in The Hague. These paintings are not far from Delft—The Hague was four hours away by river barge in the seventeenth century but is now only ten minutes by train—but they are no longer where he painted them. To view a Vermeer, you have to be somewhere other than Delft. To be in Delft, you have to forego the opportunity to look at a Vermeer.

Any number of reasons could be introduced to explain why Vermeer had to have come from Delft, from local painting traditions to the character of the light that falls on the town. But these reasons do not allow us to conclude that Vermeer would not have produced paintings just as remarkable had he lived somewhere else in Holland. Context is important, but it doesn't account for everything. By the same token, I could put forward any number of reasons to explain why a global history of the intercultural transformations of seventeenth-century life must start from Delft. But they wouldn't convince you that Delft was the only place from which to begin. The fact of the matter is that nothing happened there that particularly changed the course of history, except possibly art history, and I won't try to claim otherwise. I start from Delft simply because I happen to have fallen off my bike there, because Vermeer happened to have lived there, and because I happen to enjoy looking at his paintings. So long as Delft does not block our view of the seventeenth-century world, these reasons are as good as any for choosing it as a place to stand and consider the view.

Suppose I were to choose another place from which to tell this story: Shanghai, for instance, since my travels took me there several years after that first visit to Delft and led to my becoming a historian of China? It would suit the design of this book, in fact, since Europe and China are the two poles of the magnetic field of interconnection that I describe here. How much would choosing Shanghai over Delft change the story I am about to tell? It's possible it would not change a great deal. Shanghai was actually rather like Delft, if we want to look for similarities below the obvious differences. Like Delft, Shanghai was built on land that had once been under the ocean, and it depended on water sluices to drain the bogs on which it rests. (The name Shanghai, which could be translated as On the Ocean, is in fact an abbreviation of Shanghaibang, Upper Ocean Sluice.) Shanghai similarly was a walled city (though it was walled only in the mid-sixteenth century to protect it against raiders from Japan). It was crisscrossed with canals and bridges and had direct water access to the ocean. The marketing center for a productive agricultural economy built on the reclaimed land, it too anchored an artisanal network of commodity production in the surrounding countryside (cotton textiles in this instance). Shanghai did not have the urban bourgeoisie whom (and for whom) Vermeer painted, nor perhaps quite the same level of cultivation and sophistication. Its most prominent native son (and Catholic convert) Xu Guangqi complained in a letter of 1612 that Shanghai was a place of "vulgar manners." Yet Shanghai's wealthy families engaged in practices of patronage and conspicuous consumption, which included buying and showing paintings, that seem rather like what the merchant elite of Delft were doing. An even more striking coincidence is that Shanghai was the birthplace of Dong Qichang—the greatest painter and calligrapher of his age—who transformed painting conventions and laid the foundations of modern Chinese art. It makes no sense to call Dong the Vermeer of China, or Vermeer the Dong of Holland; but the parallel is too curious to leave unmentioned.

The similarities between Delft and Shanghai may seem superficial when we consider their differences. There was, first of all, the difference of scale: Delft at mid-century had only twenty-five thousand residents, ranking sixth among Dutch cities, whereas Shanghai before the famines and disorder of the 1640s administered an urban population well over twice that number and a rural population of half a million. More significant were the differences in their political contexts: Delft was an important base for a newly emerging republic that had thrown off the Hapsburg empire of Spain, whereas Shanghai was an administrative seat within the secure control of the Ming and Qing empires.[1] Delft and Shanghai must also be distinguished in terms of the state policies that regulated interactions with the outside world. The Dutch government was actively engaged in building trade networks stretching around the globe, whereas the Chinese government maintained an on-again, off-again policy of restricting foreign contact and trade (a policy that was much debated within China). These differences are significant, but if I treat them lightly, it is because they do not much affect my purpose, which is to capture a sense of the larger whole of which both Shanghai and Delft were parts: a world in which people were weaving a web of connections and exchanges as never before. This story stays largely the same, regardless of where one begins telling it.

Choosing Delft over Shanghai has something to do with what has survived. When I fell off a bicycle in Delft, I stepped into a memory of the seventeenth century. Not so when you fall off a bicycle in Shanghai. The past there has been so thoroughly obliterated by first colonialism, then state socialism, and most recently global capitalism, that the only doors that actually open onto the Ming dynasty are on library shelves. A wisp of memory lingers in the little streets around Yuyuan, the Garden of Ease in the heart of what used to be the old city. This garden was founded at the end of the sixteenth century as a retirement gift for the builder's father, but around it grew up a small public gathering area where, among other things, artists came to hang their works to sell. But the area has been so thoroughly built up in the intervening centuries that there is little to betray what might have existed in the Ming dynasty.

But I start my story in Delft rather than Shanghai for a particular reason: the extraordinary portfolio of paintings of Delft by Johannes Vermeer. Dong Qichang left no such portfolio of paintings of Shanghai, from which he fled as soon as he could afford to move to the prefectural capital. Vermeer stayed home, and painted what he saw. When we run our eyes over his canvases, we seem to enter a lived world of real people surrounded by the things that gave them a sense of home. The enigmatic figures in his paintings carry secrets we will never know, for it is their world and not ours. Yet he paints them in a way that seems to give us the sensation we have entered an intimate space. It is all "seems," though. Vermeer had such control of painting technique that he could fool the eye into believing that the canvas was a mere window through which the viewer can look straight into the places he paints as though they were real. The French call such deception in painting trompe l'oeil, fool the eye. In Vermeer's case, the places were real, but perhaps not quite in the way he painted them. Vermeer was not a photographer, after all. He was an illusionist drawing us into his world, the world of a bourgeois family living in Delft in the middle of the seventeenth century. Even if Delft didn't quite look like this, though, the facsimile is close enough for us to enter that world and think about what we find.

We will linger over five Vermeer paintings in this book, plus a canvas by his Delft contemporary Hendrik van der Burch and a painting on a delftware plate, looking for signs of Delft life. I have chosen these seven paintings not just for what they show, but for the hints of broader historical forces that lurk in their details. As we hunt for these details, we will discover hidden links to subjects that aren't quite stated and places that aren't really shown. The connections these details betray are only implied, but they are there.

If they are hard to see, it is because these connections were new. The seventeenth century was not so much an era of first contacts as an age of second contacts, when sites of first encounter were turning into places of repeated meeting. People were now regularly arriving from elsewhere and departing for elsewhere, and as they were carrying things with them—which meant that things were ending up in places other than where they were made, and were being seen in these new locations for the first time. Soon enough, though, commerce took over. Moving things were no longer accidental travelers but commodities produced for circulation and sale, and Holland was a one place where these new commodities converged. In Amsterdam, the focal point of their convergence, they caught the attention of the French philosopher René Descartes. In 1631, Descartes was in the midst of a long exile in the Netherlands, his controversial ideas having driven him from Catholic France. He described Amsterdam that year as "an inventory of the possible." "What place on earth," he asked, "could one choose where all the commodities and all the curiosities one could wish for were as easy to find as in this city?" Amsterdam was a particularly good place to find "all the commodities and all the curiosities one could wish for," for reasons that will become clear as we proceed. Such objects came to Delft in lesser numbers, but still they came. A few even ended up in the household that Vermeer shared with his mother-in-law, Maria Thins, to judge from the inventory of possessions that his wife, Catharina Bolnes, drew up in the course of filing for bankruptcy after he died. Vermeer was not wealthy enough to own many nice things, but those he did acquire reveal something about his place in the world. And where we will see them in action is in his paintings.

To bring to life the stories I want to tell in this book, I will ask that we examine paintings; or more exactly, objects in paintings. This method requires suspending some of the habits we have acquired when it comes to looking at pictures. Chief among these habits is a tendency to regard paintings as windows opening directly onto another time and place. It is a beguiling illusion to think that Vermeer's paintings are images directly taken from life in seventeenth-century Delft. Paintings are not "taken," like photographs; they are "made," carefully and deliberately, and not to show an objective reality so much as to present a particular scenario. This attitude affects how we look at things in paintings. When we think of paintings as windows, we treat the objects in them as two-dimensional details showing either that the past was different from what we know today, or that it is the same, again as though a photograph had been taken. We see a seventeenth-century goblet and think: That is what a seventeenth-century goblet looks like, and isn't it remarkably like/unlike (choose one) goblets today? We tend not to think: What is a goblet doing there? Who made it? Where did it come from? Why did the artist choose to include it instead of something else, a teacup, say, or a glass jar?

As we gaze at each of the seven paintings on which this book has been draped, I want us to ask just these sorts of questions. We can still enjoy the pleasures of the surface, but I also want us to duck past the surface and look hard at the objects as signs of the time and place in which the painting was made. Such signs slipped into the picture as it was being painted largely unawares. Our task is to coax them out, so that we can in effect use the painting to tell not just its own story, but our own. Art critic James Elkins has argued that paintings are puzzles that we feel compelled to solve in order to ease our perplexities about the world in which we find ourselves, as well as our uncertainties as to just how it is that we found ourselves here. I have recruited these seven Dutch paintings for such service.

If we think of the objects in them not as props behind windows but as doors to open, then we will find ourselves in passageways leading to discoveries about the seventeenth-century world that the paintings on their own don't acknowledge, and of which the artist himself was probably unaware. Behind these doors run unexpected

corridors and sly byways linking our confusing present—to a degree
we could not have guessed, and in ways that will surprise us—to a
past that was far from simple. And if there is one theme curving
through seventeenth-century Delft's complex past that every object
we examine in these paintings will show, it is that Delft was not alone.
It existed within a world that extended outward to the entire globe.

LET US BEGIN WITH *View of Delft* (see plate 1). This painting is unusual in the Vermeer oeuvre. Most Vermeers are staged in interior
rooms engagingly decorated with discrete objects from the artist's family life. *View of Delft* is quite different. One of just two surviving outdoor scenes, it is his only attempt to represent a large space. Objects,
even people, dwindle in scale and significance when set against the
wide panorama of buildings and the vast sky above. The painting is
anything but a generic landscape, however. It is a specific view of Delft
as it appears from a vantage point just outside the south side of the
town looking north across the Kolk, Delft's river harbor. Across the tri-
angular surface of the water in the foreground stand the Schiedam and
Rotterdam gates, which flank the mouth of the Oude Delft where it
opens into the Kolk. Beyond the gates is the town itself. Our attention
is drawn to the sunlit steeple of the New Church. The steeple is visibly
empty of bells, and as it is known that the bells started to be mounted
in May 1660, we can date the painting to just before that moment.
There are other towers on the skyline. Moving leftward, we see the
cupola atop the Schiedam Gate, then the smaller conical tower of the
Parrot Brewery (Delft had been a center of beer making in the sixteenth century). And poking just into view beside that we see the top
of the steeple of the Old Church. This is Delft in the spring of 1660.

I encountered the painting for the first time on a visit to the Mauritshuis thirty-five years after I landed in Delft. I went expecting to
see *Girl with a Pearl Earring* and I did. I knew that there were other
Vermeers on display as well, though I did not know which ones until
I turned into the corner room on the top floor and found myself fac-
ing his *View of Delft*. The painting was larger than I expected, busier

and far more complex in its modulation of light and shade than re-
productions revealed. As I was trying to decipher the buildings in the
painting based on what I knew from seventeenth-century maps, it
dawned on me that Delft was ten minutes away by train. Why not
compare Vermeer's rendition with real life, especially if the seventeenth century were still as present as I suspected? I rushed downstairs
to the gift shop, bought a postcard of the painting, and hurried to the
station. The train pulled out four minutes later, and in no time I was
back in Delft.

I was able to walk right to the spot where Vermeer composed the
picture, though the knoll of the small park that now stands in the
foreground wasn't quite high enough for me to set the scene exactly
according to his perspective. He must have painted it from a second-
story window. Still, only a small adjustment was needed to transcribe the painting onto Delft as it looks today. The vicissitudes of
time and city planning have decayed much of the original scene. The
Schiedam and Rotterdam gates are gone, as is the Parrot Brewery.
The city wall has been replaced by a busy road. But the spires of both
the New Church and the Old Church continue to stand in the very
places where Vermeer put them. It wasn't Delft in 1660, but it was
close enough for the picturesque scene in *View of Delft* to tell me
where I was. Looking at the painting now, the first door opens easily.
This is Delft as it looked from the south. Is there a second door? Yes;
in fact there are several.

The first place we will look for a second door is in the harbor. The
Kolk handled boats traveling to and from Delft on the Schie Canal,
which ran southward to Schiedam and Rotterdam on the Rhine.
Tied up at the quay in the foreground to the left is a passenger barge.
Built long and narrow in order to pass easily through canal locks,
horse-drawn barges like this operated on fixed schedules and linked
Delft to cities and towns throughout southern Holland. Several people have gathered on the quay near the barge. Their dress and de-
meanor suggest that they will take their places among the eight
first-class passengers who paid to sit in the cabin at the back of the

barge, rather than jostle in among the twenty-five second-class passengers in the front. A hint of breeze ruffles the water, but otherwise
nothing is moving. On the other two sides of the harbor, all the boats
are tethered or out of commission. The only suggestions of restlessness are the jagged skyline of buildings and the shadow cast by the
huge cumulus cloud hanging at the top of the painting. But the over-
all effect is one of perfect tranquility on a lovely day. There are other
boats tethered around the Kolk: small cargo transports tied up be-
neath the Schiedam Gate, and another four passenger barges tethered
beside the Rotterdam Gate. The two I want to draw our attention to,
however, are the wide-bottomed vessels moored to each other at the
right-hand side of the painting. This stretch of the quay in front of
the Rotterdam Gate was the site of the Delft shipyard. The back
masts of these two vessels are missing, and their front masts partially
struck, which indicates that they are there for refitting or repair.
These are herring buses, three-masted vessels built to fish for herring
in the North Sea. Here is another door to the seventeenth-century
world, but it requires some explaining to open.

If there is one overwhelming condition that shaped the history
of the seventeenth century more than any other, it is global cooling.
During the century and a half between 1550 and 1700, temperatures
fell all over the world, not continuously or consistently, but they fell
everywhere. In Northern Europe, the first really cold winter of what
has come to be called the Little Ice Age was the winter of 1564–65.
In January 1565, the great painter of the common people of the Low
Countries, Pieter Bruegel the Elder, did his first winter landscape
showing hunters in the snow and people playing on the ice. Bruegel
may have thought he was painting an anomaly that would not return,
but it did. He painted several more winter scenes in the following
years, starting the fashion for winterscapes. Vermeer never painted
skating scenes, but we know he went out in them, as he bought an
iceboat rigged with a sail from a Delft sail maker in 1660, for which
he agreed to pay the considerable sum of eighty guilders. His timing
was not great, for the canals of Holland failed to freeze for the next

two winters. Then the cold returned. Temperatures elsewhere declined too. In China, heavy frosts between 1654 and 1676 killed orange and mandarin groves that had been producing fruit for centuries. The world would not always be this cold, but this was the condition under which life was lived in the seventeenth century.

Cold winters meant more than ice sailing. They meant shorter growing seasons and wetter soil, rising grain prices, and increasing sickness. A fall in spring temperature of just half a degree centigrade delays planting by ten days, and a similar fall in the autumn cuts another ten days off the harvest. In temperate climates, this could be disastrous. According to one theory, cold weather could induce another evil consequence, plague. All over the world in the century from the 1570s to the 1660s, plague stalked densely populated societies. Plague struck Amsterdam at least ten times between 1597 and 1664, on the last occasion killing over twenty-four thousand people. Southern Europe was hit even harder. In one outbreak in 1576–77, Venice lost fifty thousand people (28 percent of its population). A second great epidemic in 1630–31 killed another forty-six thousand (a proportionately higher 33 percent of the then-diminished population). In China, a harsh run of cold weather in the late 1630s was followed by a particularly virulent epidemic in 1642. The disease raced down the Grand Canal with shocking speed, annihilating whole communities and leaving the country vulnerable first to peasant rebels, who captured Beijing in 1644, and then to the armies of the Manchus, who founded a dynasty (the Qing) and ruled China for the next three centuries.

Cold and plague dented the rate at which the world's population was growing, but in retrospect it looks now as though humankind was only preparing for the leap that started around 1700 and still keeps us in midair. Humankind had already broken the limit of half a billion before the seventeenth century began. We were well past six hundred million by the time it ended. Johannes Vermeer and Catharina Bolnes made their little contribution to world population growth, though it was not easy. They buried at least four of their children, three of them in the family grave in the Old Church. There is no record of what they died of, though one suspects plague would have been mentioned, had that been the cause of death. But losses in the family were outweighed by gains, for another eleven children survived to adulthood. Five or six had already been born by the time Vermeer bought the iceboat; perhaps he bought it for their pleasure as well as his own. In the long term, though, only four of his children married and had children. In many families, if not Vermeer's, those who failed to marry were propelled out of their home communities in search of employment and survival. The young men became the sailors who manned the ships, the employees and bondsmen who staffed the wharves and warehouses handling the new global trade, and the soldiers who filled the armies and protected the trade. The same young men also supplied the crews of the pirate ships that preyed on the growing maritime traffic. The young women became maids and prostitutes.

In *View of Delft*, the herring buses are a sign of this history. One benefit that the Dutch gained from global cooling was the southward movement of fish stocks in the North Sea. Colder winters meant that Arctic ice moved farther south, causing major freeze-ups along the coast of Norway, where the herring fishery had traditionally been based. The fishery moved south toward the Baltic Sea, and there it came under the control of Dutch fishermen. This is why we see herring buses moored outside Delft. One of the founding scholars of climate history has even proposed that the prosperity the Dutch enjoyed in the first half of the seventeenth century—the very prosperity that Vermeer captures in his domestic interiors—occurred because of this resource windfall. The herring catch gave the Dutch a stake they could then invest in other ventures, especially in shipping and maritime trade. Those two herring boats are Vermeer's evidence of climate change.

View of Delft has another door we can open onto the seventeenth century. Look again at the steeple of the Old Church next to the Parrot Brewery tower, and we see a long roof that runs in an unbroken line to the left side of the canvas. (Had Vermeer continued the painting a little farther to the left, he would have had to include the great windmill at the corner of the city wall that pumped water out of the canal, which would have altered the structure of the painting.) Earlier commentators have accused Vermeer of simplifying the skyline in order not to detract from other elements in the painting. When I went to stand on the far side of the Kolk, I looked for that roofline. The roofs I saw were not composed in quite the way Vermeer painted them, but despite the architectural adding and subtracting that has gone on since 1660, I could see what he was painting: the roof of a large warehouse complex stretching the entire block from the Oude Delft to the moat on the city's west side. It was the warehouse of the Oost-Indisch Huis, East India House, as I was able to determine by walking up the Oude Delft and checking the house fronts. This was the home of the Delft Chamber of the Dutch East India Company (Verenigde Oostindische Compagnie), the center of a vast web of international trade connecting Delft to Asia.

The Dutch East India Company—the VOC, as it is known—is to corporate capitalism what Benjamin Franklin's kite is to electronics: the beginning of something momentous that could not have been predicted at the time. The world's first large joint-stock company, the VOC was formed in 1602 when the Dutch Republic obliged the many trading companies popping up to take advantage of the Asian trade boom to merge into a single commercial organization. The stick was monopoly. Commercial ventures that did not join the VOC would not be allowed to trade in Asia. The carrot was unlimited profits in which the state would not interfere, other than to expect a modest tax dividend. The merchants grudgingly went along with the arrangement, and the VOC emerged as a federation of six regional chambers: the Amsterdam Chamber, which contributed half the capital, the Hoorn and Enkhuizen chambers in north Holland, Middelburg in the Rhine estuary (Zeeland) in the south, and Rotterdam and Delft in the heart of Holland. What at first sight looked like an unworkable compromise—separate chambers controlled their own capital and operations while adhering to uniform guidelines and policies—turned out to be a brilliant innovation. Only a unique federal state such as the Dutch Republic could have dreamed up a federal company structure. The VOC combined flexibility with strength, giving the Dutch a huge advantage in the competition to dominate maritime trade to Asia.

Within a few decades, the VOC proved itself to be the most powerful trading corporation in the seventeenth-century world and the model for the large-scale business enterprises that now dominate the global economy. Its monogram also became the best-known company trademark of that age, possibly in fact the first global logo. The company-wide monogram consisted of the company's three initials with a *V* (Verenigde) in the middle and an *O* (Oostindische) and a *C* (Compagnie) overlapping its two antennae. It was left for each chamber to add its own initial by placing it above or below the *VOC* initials. The Delft Chamber placed its *D* (Delft) over the bottom point of the *V*, producing a monogram that can still be seen today on the façade of the former Delft Chamber offices on the west side of the Old Delft Canal. The chamber acquired this building in 1631. Over time it added other buildings to it, each decorated with the same monogram. The original buildings have long since been converted into private apartments—the VOC went bankrupt in the 1790s and was disbanded in 1800—but its logo is still there to remind us of this history. Universally familiar to the Dutch, it gives the long-defunct company a virtual presence in the Netherlands even today.

Everyone in seventeenth-century Delft would have known where the Delft Chamber was located. The VOC was too important to the Delft economy for this not to be common local knowledge. If any of them stood with me on the far side of the harbor from the point at which the Old Delft Canal passed under the Capels Bridge between the Schiedam and Rotterdam gates and emptied into the Kolk, they could have pointed out the red tiled roofs of the VOC warehouse and office complex without difficulty. So too they could have turned to point south down the canal in the direction of Delfshaven, Schiedam, and Rotterdam, the town's maritime ports on the mouth of the

Rhine. This stretch of Delft constituted the town's commercial face, the place from which its citizens traded with the world. Once we have noticed the VOC's presence, *View of Delft* begins to strike us as less merely decorative, less casual in its choice of subject, more intentional.

Despite the VOC's visibility in the painting, as in Delft, there is no evidence that Vermeer himself had a personal connection with his subject. His grandfather was almost bankrupted speculating in VOC shares in the Company's early years, after which the family had nothing to do with it. But no Delft family could truly escape the VOC. Vermeer's father, Reynier Vos (the family had not yet adopted the surname Vermeer at the time Reynier was born), an art dealer and innkeeper, may not have worked for the Company, but his trade depended on serving those who passed through Delft, and most of those came on Company business. So too a painter could well find himself within the orbit of the VOC. In Amsterdam, for instance, Rembrandt van Rijn collected fat fees to paint the portraits of VOC directors. But Vermeer didn't do portraits on commission, so far as we know. Delft may have been a Company town, but Vermeer never became a Company painter.

Though Vermeer never worked for the VOC, tens of thousands of Dutch people did. A team of Dutch historians has estimated that in the company's first ten years of operations, which almost coincides with the first decade of the seventeenth century, eighty-five hundred men left the Netherlands on VOC ships. In every decade that followed, that total progressively increased. By the 1650s, over forty thousand were departing every ten years. Close to a million people made the sea journey from Holland to Asia during the two centuries between 1595 and 1795. Most were young men who preferred a post with the East India Company to staying and making do with crowded homes and limited patrimonies. Asia for them represented the hope of making better lives elsewhere. At least three of Vermeer's cousins were among these VOC out-migrants. According to the will of his father's brother, Dirck van der Minne, in 1675, a cousin named

Claes was working as a "surgeon in the East Indies" and two first cousins once removed, Aryen and Dirck Gerritszoon van Sanen, Claes's nephews, were "both in the East Indies" at the time the will was read.

Not all this million passed through Delft on their way to the East but many thousands did, making their way down the canal to Rotterdam on the mouth of the Rhine. Vermeer would have encountered them while he was a child in his father's inn and heard the boasts of those going out East and the tall tales of those coming home. To go was not always to come back. Indeed, the odds were against it. Of every three men who took ship to Asia, two did not return. Some died on the journey out, and many more succumbed to diseases against which they had no immunities after they arrived. But mortality was not the only factor that kept men from returning. Many chose to stay in Asia, some to avoid paying the cost of success or the shame of failure when they got home, others because they were able to make new lives in the places where they ended up and had no desire to return to what they had left behind. Despite the heavy toll of mortality on the company's men, the VOC prospered, and with it the Netherlands.

THE EUROPEAN CAPACITY TO MOUNT and sustain commercial operations on a global scale depended in no small part on new technologies accompanying maritime trade. The English polymath Francis Bacon in 1620 selected for special notice three "mechanical discoveries" that, in his view, "have changed the whole face and state of things throughout the world." One such discovery was the magnetic compass, enabling navigators to sail out of sight of land and still guess where they were. Another was paper, which permitted merchants to keep the detailed records needed for multiple transactions and sustain the heavy correspondence that trade over long distances demands. The third discovery was gunpowder. Without the rapid advances arms manufacturers made in ballistics technology in the sixteenth and seventeenth centuries, European traders abroad would have been hard pressed to overwhelm local opposition to unwanted trade arrangements and protect the spoils of commerce. The VOC took advantage of all three innovations to build a network of trade that stretched all the way to East Asia. "No empire, no sect, no star," Bacon asserted, "seems to have exerted greater power and influence on human affairs" than these three inventions.

Bacon, famously unaware that all three discoveries came from China, noted that they were of "obscure and inglorious" origin. Had he been told their origin was Chinese, he would not have been surprised. Thanks to Marco Polo's colorful descriptions in his *Travels* of the Mongol court in the later part of the fourteenth century, China held a powerful place in the popular imagination. Europeans thought of it as a place of power and wealth beyond any known scale. This idea led many to believe that the quickest route to China must also be the quickest route to their own wealth and power, and to pursue the search for that route. The quest to get to China was a relentless force that did much to shape the history of the seventeenth century, not just within Europe and China, but in most of the places in between. This is why China lurks behind every story in this book, even those that don't at first glance seem to have anything to do with it. The lure of China's wealth haunted the seventeenth-century world.

The explosion of seventeenth-century migration was prefaced by an attraction for China that already had begun to shape European choices in the sixteenth century. The sixteenth was a century of discoveries and violent encounters, of windfalls and errors, of borders crossed and borders closed, creating a web of connections that spread in all directions. The seventeenth century was something different. First encounters were becoming sustained engagements; fortuitous exchanges were being systematized into regular trade; the language of gesture was being supplanted by pidgin dialects and genuine communication. Running through all these changes was the common factor of mobility. More people were in motion over longer distances and sojourning away from home for longer periods of time than at any other time in human history. More people were engaging in transactions with people whose languages they did not know and whose

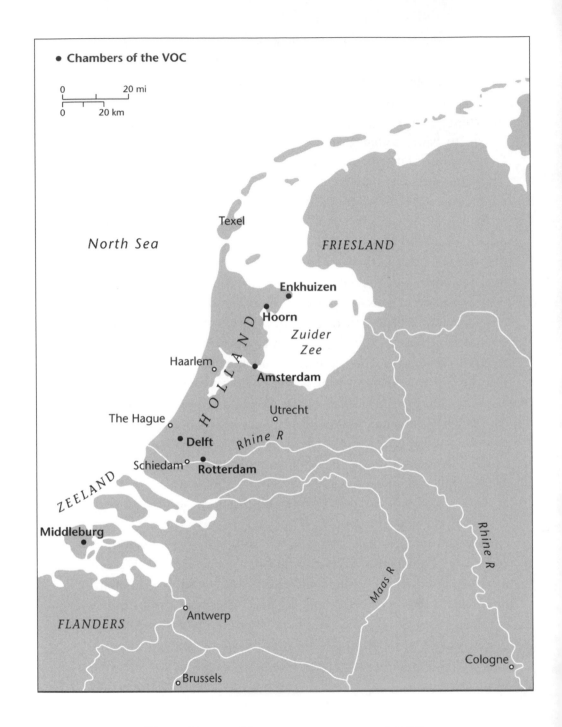

North Sea

Texel

FRIESLAND

Enkhuizen

Hoorn

Zuider Zee

Haarlem

H O L L A N D

Amsterdam

The Hague

Utrecht

Rhine R

Delft

Schiedam

Rotterdam

ZEELAND

Middleburg

Maas R

Rhine R

FLANDERS

Antwerp

Cologne

Brussels

THE LOW COUNTRIES ca. 1650

cultures they had never experienced. At the same time, more people were learning new languages and adjusting to unfamiliar customs. First contacts for the most part were over. The seventeenth was a century of second contacts.

With second contacts, the dynamic of encounter changes. Interactions become more sustained and likelier to be repeated. The effects they produce, however, are not simple to predict or understand. At times they induce a thorough transformation of everyday practices, an effect that Cuban writer Fernando Ortiz has called "transculturation." At other times they provoke resistance, violence, and a loss of identity. In the seventeenth century, most second contacts generated effects that fall between these two extremes: selective adjustment, made through a process of mutual influence. Rather than complete transformation or deadly conflict, there was negotiation and borrowing; rather than triumph and loss, give and take; rather than the transformation of cultures, their interaction. It was a time when people had to adjust how they acted and thought in order to negotiate the cultural differences they encountered, to deflect unanticipated threats and respond cautiously to equally unexpected opportunities. It was a time not for executing grand designs, but for improvising. The age of discovery was largely over, the age of imperialism yet to come. The seventeenth century was the age of improvisation.

The changes this impulse toward improvisation evoked were subtle but profound. Consider again Dong Qichang, the artist from Shanghai to whom I have referred. Dong Qichang's was the first generation in China to see European prints. Jesuit missionaries brought some to China to convey their message in visual form and help converts imagine the life of Christ. In Dong's own painting, 1597 marks a major shift in style that set the foundations for the emergence of modern Chinese art. It has been suggested that the visual devices in European prints may have impelled him toward this new style. Or take our artist from Delft. Vermeer was among the first generations of Dutch painters to see Chinese painting, rarely on silk or paper, more commonly on porcelain. It has been suggested that his use of "Delft

blue," his preference for off-white backgrounds to set off blue materials, his taste for distorting perspective and enlarging foregrounds (he
does both in *View of Delft*), and his willingness to leave backgrounds
empty betray a Chinese influence. Given what little we know of Vermeer, and how well we know it, it is unlikely that evidence will ever
come to light that allows this suggestion to be proven or disproven. It
is simply an idea of influence, but something that would have been an
impossibility a generation earlier. Hints of intercultural influence of
this sort, so fine as to be almost imperceptible, are just what we should
learn to expect as we go back into the seventeenth century.

Seen in this way, the paintings into which we will look to find
signs of the seventeenth century might be considered not just as
doors through which we can step to rediscover the past, but as mirrors reflecting the multiplicity of causes and effects that have produced the past and the present. Buddhism uses a similar image to
describe the interconnectedness of all phenomena. It is called Indra's
net. When Indra fashioned the world, he made it as a web, and at
every knot in that web is tied a pearl. Everything that exists or has
ever existed, every idea that can be thought about, every datum that
is true—every dharma, in the language of Indian philosophy—is a
pearl in Indra's net. Not only is every pearl tied to every other pearl
by virtue of the web on which they hang, but on the surface of every
pearl is reflected every other jewel in the net. Everything that exists
in Indra's web implies all else that exists.

Vermeer would have appreciated the metaphor. He loved to put
curved surfaces into his paintings and use them to reflect everything
around them. Glass spheres, brass utensils, pearls—like the lenses he
probably used to help him paint—were suitable for revealing realities
beyond what was immediately there. In no less than eight of his pictures, Vermeer paints women wearing pearl earrings. And on these
pearls he paints faint shapes and outlines hinting at the contours of
the rooms they inhabit. No pearl is more striking than the one in the
Girl with a Pearl Earring. On the surface of that large pearl—so large it
was probably not a real pearl at all, but a glass teardrop varnished to

give it a pearly sheen—we see reflected her collar, her turban, the window that illuminates her off to the left, and, indistinctly, the room where she sits.[2] Look closely at one of Vermeer's pearls, and his ghostly studio floats into view.

This endless reflectivity, writ large, nods toward the greatest discovery that people in the seventeenth century made: that the world, like this pearl, was a single globe suspended in space. It was their burden to confront the idea of the world as an unbroken surface on which there is no place that cannot be reached, no place that is not implied by every other place, no event that belongs to any world but the one they now had to share. It was their burden as well to inhabit a reality imbued with a permanent restlessness, where people were in constant motion and things might travel half the globe just so that a buyer here could obtain what a maker there had made. These burdens forced people to think about their lives in fresh and unfamiliar ways. For some, such as Song Yingxing, the author of China's first encyclopedia of technology, *Exploitation of the Works of Nature* (1637), this mobility was a sign of living in more open and better times. "Carriages from the far southwest may be seen traversing the plains of the far northeast," he enthuses in the preface to his encyclopedia, and "officials and merchants from the south coast travel about freely on the North China Plain." In the old days, you "had to resort to the channels of international trade to obtain a fur hat" from foreign lands, but now you could get one from your haberdasher down the street.

For others, the emerging global mobility did not just redefine their idea of the world, but widened horizons and opened opportunities that would not have existed a few decades earlier. However much pleasure Song Yingxing gained from knowing that a new and wider world existed, he was fated to spend his life tucked away in the interior of China as an armchair surveyor of the world—so far from the ocean that he may never have even seen it, let alone sailed on it. Had the Chinese encyclopedist had the opportunities of a Dutchman of his generation, however, he might well have been someone like Willem Cornelisz Schouten. Schouten hailed from the Dutch port of

Hoorn, home to many of the first generation of Dutch sea captains. He first circumnavigated the globe between 1615 and 1617, and then was back in Asian waters with the VOC in the 1620s. Schouten did not survive the long sea journey home across the Indian Ocean in 1625, however. He died of unrecorded causes just before his ship reached Antongil Bay on the east coast of Madagascar, and was buried there. An anonymous epitaph in verse epitomizes him as personifying the spirit of his age.

> In this our western world, where he was born and bred,
> Brave Schouten could not rest; his inmost soul afire
> Urged him to seek beyond, to voyage and strive ahead.

The poet could have bemoaned brave Schouten's death as a failure to return home to Hoorn, but he doesn't. Instead, he celebrates this sailor's death as a great success, the culmination of the global life he had chosen to live.

> 'Tis meet then that he lies i' the world of his desire,
> Safe after all his travels. Oh great and eager mind,
> Repose in blessed peace!

Dying abroad in the seventeenth century was not banishment from home for Schouten, but permanent residence in the world he desired. The only final end for Schouten, should he ever tire of Madagascar, was not Hoorn but heaven.

> . . . Yet if they soul refuse
> In narrow Antongil for e'er to stay confined,
> Then (as in earthly life so fearless thou didst choose
> The unknown channel 'twixt the seas of East and West,
> Outstripping the sun's course by a whole day and night),
> Ascend thou up, this time surpassing the sun's height,
> And find in heaven with God hope and eternal rest.

The commanding passion of the seventeenth century, on both sides of the globe, was to navigate "the unknown channel 'twixt the seas of East and West"; to reduce that once unbridgeable distance through travel, contact, and new knowledge; to pawn one's place of birth for the world of one's desire. This was the fire within seventeenth-century souls. Not everyone was thrilled with the disorder and dislocation that the passions of great and eager minds produced. One Chinese official complained in 1609 that the end result of this whirlwind of change was simply that "the rich become richer and the poor, poorer." Even Willem Schouten may have had his doubts about the whole business as he lay in his hammock and drifted into death. But enough people were drawn into the vortex of movement to believe that they too could outstrip the sun's course. Their world—and it was fast becoming our world—would never be the same. No surprise, then, that artists as homebound as Johannes Vermeer were catching glimpses of the change.

Vermeer's Hat

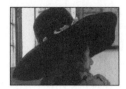

V ERMEER MUST HAVE owned several hats. No document mentions this, but no Dutchman of his generation and status went out in public bareheaded. Take a look at the people in the foreground of *View of Delft*, and you will see that everyone, male and female, has a hat or head covering. A poor man made do with wearing a slouch cap known as a *klapmuts*, but the better sort flaunted the kind of hat we see in *Officer and Laughing Girl* (see plate 2). We should not be surprised to see the officer wearing his lavish creation indoors. When Vermeer painted a man without a hat, he was someone at work: a music teacher or a scientist. A courting man did not go hatless. The custom for men to remove their hats when entering a building or greeting a woman (a custom generally forgotten today) was not yet being observed. The only person before whom a European gentleman bared his head was his monarch, but as Dutchmen prided themselves in bowing to no monarch and scorned those who did, their hats stayed on. Vermeer himself wears hats in the two scenes into which he painted himself. In his cameo appearance as a musician in *The Procuress*, he wears an extravagant beret that slouches almost to his shoulder. In *The Art of Painting* ten years later, he wears a much smaller black beret, even then the distinguishing badge of the artist.

Vermeer had other social roles to play, and so needed other costumes in which to play them. He enjoyed the gentlemanly prestige of being a "marksman" in the Delft militia, though there is no evidence he knew how to use a firearm. A pike, breastplate, and iron helmet appear in the inventory of his possessions that wife Catharina Bolnes drew up after his death as a deposition in her application for bankruptcy, but there is no gun, and no military costume. To judge from the many portraits from the period showing Dutch gentlemen in such costume, he would have needed a grand felt hat of just the sort the soldier in *Officer and Laughing Girl* is wearing. A beret would have been considered flippant, and an iron helmet was uncomfortable to wear and only donned for combat. Being a militiaman involved a certain social distinction that one had to maintain by dressing properly, so Vermeer must have owned a hat like the one we see in *Officer and Laughing Girl*.

What we don't know is whether he owned that particular hat. There is no sign of one in the posthumous inventory, but as hats of this sort were expensive and Catharina was desperately short of cash, she might well have sold it in the two and a half months between his death and her filing for bankruptcy protection. What we do know is that there was a hatter in the family. Dirck van der Minne, the uncle who had a son and two grandsons in the East Indies when his will was read in 1657, was a felt maker and hatter. Perhaps Uncle Dirck made hats for Vermeer. Perhaps we are looking at one of them in *Officer and Laughing Girl*.

The hat will be the door inside this painting that we will open, but let us briefly consider the painting itself. What do we see? An exuberantly dressed officer in scarlet tunic, larger than life (the effect of a trick of visual distortion that Vermeer liked to play), wooing a beautiful young woman (my guess is that we are looking at Catharina). The content of the scene might seem highly individual, but it belongs firmly to the era in which Vermeer painted it, for it presents an almost generic account of the new rules governing how young men and women in polite Dutch society courted in the late 1650s.

A few decades earlier, officers did not have the opportunity to sit bantering like this with women of higher station. Custom did not tolerate private meetings between wooer and wooed. During Vermeer's lifetime, the rules of courtship shifted, at least in urban Holland.

Civility pushed aside military prowess as the way to win a woman. Romance took over from cash-in-hand as the currency of love, and the home became the new theater for acting out the tension between the genders. Men and women still negotiated over sex and companionship—this is exactly what the officer and the laughing girl are doing—but the negotiation was now disguised as banter, not barter, and its object was marriage and a solid brick house with leaded window panes and expensive furnishings, not an hour in bed.

As the new emblems of bourgeois life crowded out cash, and politesse replaced rowdiness, the interactions of men and women became more restrained, more subtle and refined. And so the artists who painted scenes of flirtation no longer set them within lively brothels, as they did earlier in the seventeenth century, but within domestic interiors. Vermeer lived at the cusp of this shift in gender relations, and of the painterly conventions that went along with them. *Officer and Laughing Girl* shows him working out the consequences of this shift.

Soldiers who fought in the long Dutch war of independence against Spain might once have claimed women as the spoils of war, but that age was finished. This may be why Vermeer has hung *The New and Accurate Topography of All Holland and West Friesland* on the back wall of the room behind the conversing couple. The map originated from a piece of commissioned propaganda celebrating the Dutch struggle for independence prior to the truce of 1609, but that war was now well in the past.[1] Officers no longer had the same battlefield role to play and could not claim quite the same authority and respect. This reversal in the prestige of soldiering may be what Vermeer is alluding to by reversing the color scheme on the map, making the land blue and the water brown. Land and sea have traded places; so too soldiers and civilians face each other in a different social order. So too, perhaps, men and women have changed roles, for despite the swagger of the officer in the picture, it is he who implores and she who controls the terms of the bargain of marriage that they might make. These reversals were part of the larger transition that Dutch society was undergoing in Vermeer's time: from military to civil society, from monarchy to republicanism, from Catholicism to Calvinism, merchant house to corporation, empire to nation, war to trade.

The door we go to in this painting is not the map, however, but the hat, for on the other side of that door lies the passageway that leads out into the wider world. At the end of the passageway we find ourselves at a place now known as Crown Point on Lake Champlain on the morning of 30 July 1609.

"They gazed at me and I at them," Samuel Champlain wrote, recalling the moment when he stepped forward from the ranks of his Native allies with an arquebus in his hands. Champlain was the leader of a French mission on the St. Lawrence River seeking to probe the Great Lakes region for a northwest passage to the Pacific. Arrayed against him were dozens of Mohawk warriors in wooden armor. Three chiefs stood at the front. They froze at the sight of him, then began to advance. As soon as they raised their bows, Champlain wrote, "I levelled my arquebus and aimed straight at one of the three chiefs." The wooden slats of their armor were poor protection from gunfire. "With this shot two fell to the ground and one of their companions was wounded, who died of it a little later."

There had been four lead balls in the chamber of Champlain's arquebus. At a distance of thirty meters there was no guarantee that even one would find its mark, but somehow three of them did. When the three Mohawk chiefs fell, two of them dead on the spot, the warriors behind them froze in shock. A shout of jubilation went up behind Champlain. His allies' cry was "so loud that one could not have heard it thunder." Champlain needed this confusion, as it took a full minute to reload an arquebus, during which time he was exposed to return fire from the other side. Before the attackers had time to recover, one of the two French arquebusiers Champlain had sent into the woods fired at their flank through the trees. The shot, reports Champlain, "astonished them again. Seeing their chiefs dead, they lost courage and took to flight, abandoning the field and their fort, and fleeing into the depth of the forest."

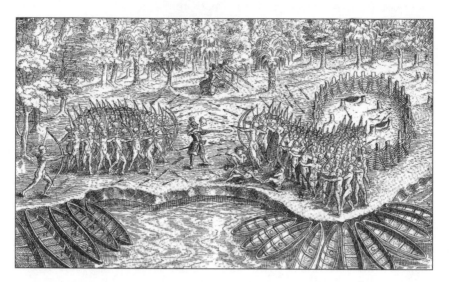

Samuel Champlain firing at Mohawk warriors on the shore of Lake Champlain, 1609. From Samuel Champlain, *Les Voyages du Sieur de Champlain*.

Champlain's Native allies joined in the assault. A volley of arrows streaked over his head, striking some of the enemy archers and giving him the cover he needed to reload. He fired again into the backs of the retreating Mohawks, killing several more. The battle was over barely minutes after it had begun. Champlain's allies scalped the dozen dead Mohawks for tokens of victory they could take back to their villages, where they would be greeted by the women swimming out to the canoes and hanging the scalps around their necks. They captured another dozen Mohawks to take north as replacements for the young males whose ranks the intertribal war was constantly thinning on both sides. Some of Champlain's allies had been hit, but none fatally. The contest had been lopsided—death and defeat on one side, a few arrow wounds on the other—and the victory complete.

What happened that morning was a turning point—Métis historian Olive Dickason has declared it to be *the* turning point—in the history of the European-Native relationship: the beginning of the long, slow destruction of a culture and a way of life from which neither side has yet recovered. How did all this come about?

Samuel Champlain was part of the first wave of incursions by Europeans into the North American continent. He made his initial journey up the St. Lawrence River into the Great Lakes system—a region he called Canada—in 1603 as a member of a French expedition to establish trading alliances. The most important person he met on that voyage was Anadabijou, chief of a tribe the French called the Montagnais.[2] Five thousand Montagnais lived at that time along the north shore of the St. Lawrence River around Tadoussac, where the Saguenay River flows into the St. Lawrence. The Saguenay was an important trade route even before the French arrived on the scene, but their manufactured goods, especially ironwares, increased the flow of furs and copper, which came from as far north as Hudson Bay. Holding Tadoussac enabled Anadabijou and the Montagnais to prosper. It also made them a target of attack from other tribes anxious to control that trade, notably the Mohawks. Anadabijou greeted Champlain with pomp and feasting; he needed an alliance with the French as much as they needed one with him.

Champlain understood that without the support of the Montagnais, the French could not survive a single winter, let alone insinuate their way into existing trading networks. At the same time, however, Champlain realized that allowing Anadabijou to control his access to trade reduced his profits. He had to leapfrog over the Montagnais and expand his contacts farther up the St. Lawrence River to move closer to beaver country. That is why he went on the warpath on Lake Champlain in 1609. He needed allies in the interior to guide him farther up country, and the surest way to secure them was to go with them to war. Trade would pay for the costs of his exploration, but war would earn him the trust on which trade depended. The Montagnais were the first of the "nations," as Champlain called them, with whom he built a ladder of alliances over his next thirty

years—though by 1608 he was ready to sidestep Anadabijou and re-
locate the French base farther upriver to the narrows at Québec. But
he still traded with the Montagnais and was careful to honor them by
traveling exclusively in their canoes when he went upriver to Lake
Champlain the following year.

That summer in Québec, Champlain forged an alliance with the
son of Iroquet, an Algonquin chief.[3] Iroquet was keen to improve his
access to European trade goods. He also wanted an alliance, for the
Algonquins were even more exposed to the summer raiding of the
Mohawks than the Montagnais. Champlain pledged to his son that
he would return in June the following year to join Iroquet's band of
warriors in a raid on the Mohawks. With the Algonquins and Montagnais came members of a third nation, the Hurons.[4] The four tribes
making up the Huron Confederacy lived in some two dozen large
settlements across the woodlands north of Lake Ontario, the first of
the Great Lakes. They spoke an Iroquoian rather than an Algonkian
dialect, but were allied to the Algonquins, not the Iroquois south of
Lake Ontario. Champlain had not yet managed to penetrate Huron
territory, but he was already known to them. Ochasteguin, one of the
Huron tribal chiefs, was allied with Iroquet and used him to gain an
introduction to Champlain in 1609. Like Iroquet, Ochasteguin wanted
to trade, but he also wanted an ally in his ongoing war with the Iroquois Confederacy.

The Mohawks were the easternmost of five nations that had formed
the Iroquois Confederacy in the sixteenth century and controlled the
entire woodland region south of Lake Ontario. The Mohawks were
known as the eastern gate of the Iroquois and were charged with protecting them on that flank—which exposed them to the arriving Europeans before any of their confederates. They were eager to gain
access to European trade goods, especially axes, and raided annually
into the St. Lawrence Valley to acquire them. Champlain called the
Mohawks the "bad Irocois," by way of contrasting them with the
Hurons, whom he termed the "good Irocois" (the Hurons spoke an Iroquoian dialect).[5] The Mohawk threat induced the Hurons, Algonquins,

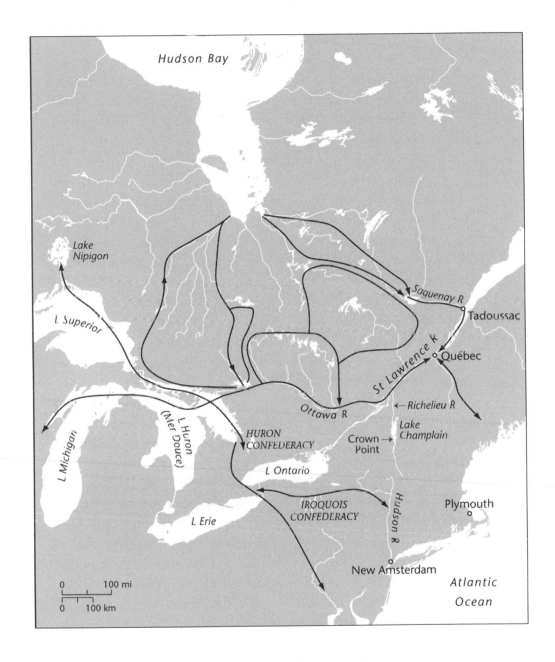

TRADE ROUTES IN THE GREAT LAKES REGION

and Montagnais to revitalize an alliance among themselves to deal with this threat. They were initially unsure how staunch their French allies would be, and suspected that, being traders, they might have no great enthusiasm for going to war. Iroquet and Ochasteguin both confided to Champlain that a rumor had been circulating during the hard winter of 1608 that the French were traders who had no interest in fighting.

Champlain challenged the rumor, assuring them it was untrue. "I have no other intention than to make war; for we have with us only arms and not merchandise for barter," he declared at their first meeting. "My only desire is to perform what I have promised you." He even returned the challenge. "Had I known what evil reports would be made to you, I should have held those making such reports far greater enemies than your own enemies." Iroquet and Ochasteguin graciously replied that they had never believed the rumor, indeed had not even listened to it. Everyone knew they were talking about the Montagnais, who were not happy to be losing their privileged access to French goods, but they shared a larger goal: attacking the Mohawks. The multinational alliance set off on 20 June.

After part of the group split off to take their wives and trade goods back to Huronia, the war party consisted of twenty-four canoes, each with three men. The French had brought along their own shallop, a two-masted riverboat that could seat ten rowers plus a man at the tiller. The French traveled in the shallop, though Champlain preferred to join the Montagnais in their canoes. That shallop soon became a problem. The party had to paddle up the Richelieu River toward Lake Champlain, but there were rapids to ascend. The French boat was too heavy to go up the rapids and too awkward to portage. In the memoirs he wrote for public consumption (and to gain financial support for his venture) in France, Champlain writes that he complained to the chiefs that "they had told us the contrary of what I had seen at the rapids, that is to say, that it was impossible to pass them with the shallop." The chiefs expressed their sympathy for Champlain's distress and promised to make up for it by showing him other "fine things." Ochasteguin and Iroquet had not been so ungracious as to tell him directly that bringing the shallop was a bad idea. Better that he learn by his own experience rather than confront him and create ill feelings.

As the party went forward, scouts were sent ahead to look for signs of the enemy. Each evening as the light fell, the scouts returned to the main party and the entire camp went to sleep. No one was put on watch. This laxity provoked Champlain, and he made plain his frustrations with his Native allies.

"You should have men posted to listen and see whether they might perceive anything," he told them, "and not live like *bestes* as you are doing." *Bestes*, the old French spelling for *bêtes*, or "beasts," might be better translated as "silly creatures," or worse, "dumb animals." A certain level of mutual linguistic incomprehension probably insulated both sides from each other's verbal barbs. In any case, the problem between them was not just language. A sensible precaution from Champlain's point of view was, from a Native point of view, nothing of the sort.

"We cannot stay awake," one of them patiently explained to this exasperated European. "We work enough during the day when hunting."

The French military perspective could not grasp the logic at work in this situation: that one did only what one had to do, not what one did not have to do. It was folly not to post guards when warriors from the Iroquois Confederacy were close, but it was worse folly to waste precious energy posting them when the enemy was not within striking distance. Champlain imagined warfare in other ways. He could not grasp that Natives organized warfare carefully, but differently from Europeans.

When they came within a day's journey of Lake Champlain, the war party had to decide whether to forge ahead or turn back. By then the Native warriors were devoting much attention to looking for signs not just of whether Iroquois were in the vicinity, but of whether luck would be with them on this venture. Telling and listening to each other's dreams was a means to detect the future, yet no one had had a decisive dream. It was time to consult the shaman.

The shaman set up his spirit-possession wigwam that evening to divine the wisest course. Having arranged his hut to his satisfaction, he took off his robe and laid it over the structure, entered it naked, and then went into a trance, sweating and convulsing so violently that the wigwam shook with the force of his possession. The warriors crouched in a circle around the enchanted wigwam, listening to his stream of unintelligible words that seemed be a conversation between the shaman's own clear voice and the croak of the spirit with whom he was speaking. They also watched for signs of spirit fire that might appear in the air above the wigwam.

The result of the divination was positive. The war party should proceed. That decision made, the chiefs gathered the warriors and laid out the order of battle. They placed sticks on a cleared piece of ground, one for each warrior, to show every man what position he should take when the time for battle came. The men then walked through these formations several times so that they could see how the plan worked and would know what to do when they met the enemy. Champlain liked the planning but not the divination. The shaman he called a "wizard," a "scoundrel," a "scamp" who faked the entire production. Those who attended the ceremony got the same contemptuous treatment. Champlain pictured them as "sitting on their buttocks like monkeys" and watching the divination with rapt attention. He calls them "poor people" who are being deceived and defrauded by "these gentlemen." As he confides to his French readers, "I often pointed out to them that what they did was pure folly and that they ought not to believe in such things." His allies must have thought him spiritually stunted for his failure to grasp the need for access to higher knowledge.

On one matter of divination, Champlain ended up compromising with local practices. His Native companions regularly asked him about his dreams, as they asked about each other's, and he was just as persistent in denying having any. But then he did. His dream came when the party was only two or three days away from the moment of contact. By this point they were paddling south on Lake Champlain, hugging its western shore and far enough south that the Adirondack Mountains were coming into view. They knew that they were getting close to Mohawk territory and now had to travel by night, spending the daylight hours silently hiding in the densest parts of the forest. No fire could be lit, no sound made. Champlain finally succumbed to dreaming.

"I dreamed that I saw in the lake near a mountain our enemies the Iroquois drowning before our eyes," he declared when he awoke and they asked, as they always did, whether he had had a dream. His allies were thrilled to receive this sign. When he tried to explain that he had desired to save the drowning men in his dream, he was laughed at. "We should let them all perish," they insisted, "for they are worthless men." Nonetheless, Champlain's dream did the trick. It gave his allies such confidence that they no longer doubted the outcome of their raid. Champlain may have been annoyed at "their usual superstitious ceremonies," as he puts it, but he was canny enough to cross the line of belief that separated him from them and give them what they wanted.

As 29 June dawned and they set up camp at the end of a night of paddling, the leaders met to revise tactics. They explained to Champlain that they would form up in good order to face the enemy, and that he should take a place in the front line. Champlain wanted to suggest an alternative that would make better use of the arquebuses the French were carrying. It annoyed him that he could not explain his battle tactic, which was intended not just to win this battle but to deliver a resounding defeat. Historian Georges Sioui, a Wendat descendant of the Hurons, suspects that Champlain's goal was to annihilate the Mohawks, not just beat them in one battle. European warfare was not content with just humiliating the enemy and letting them run away, which Native warfare could accept. Their purpose, phrased in our language, was to adjust the ecological boundaries among the tribes in the region. Champlain's goal, by contrast, was to establish an unassailable position for the French in the interior. He wanted to kill as many Mohawks as possible, not to gain glory as a warrior but to prevent the Mohawks from interfering with the French monopoly on trade. And he had the weapon to do this: an arquebus.

Champlain's arquebus would be the hinge on which this raid turned, the stone that shattered the precarious balance among the many Native nations and gave the French the power to rearrange the economy of the region. In 1609, the arquebus was a relatively recent innovation. It was a European invention, although Europeans did not invent firearms; the Chinese were the first to manufacture gunpowder and use it to shoot flames and fire projectiles. But European smiths proved adept at improving the technology and scaling down Chinese cannon into portable and reliable firearms. The arquebus, or "hook gun," got its name from a hook welded to the carriage. The weight and unwieldiness of the arquebus made it hard to hold steady and take aim with any accuracy. The hook allowed the gunner to suspend his weapon from a portable tripod, thereby steadying it before firing. The other way to stabilize the arquebus was to prop it on a crutch that stood as high as the marksman's eyes. By early in the seventeenth century, gunsmiths were producing ever lighter arquebuses that could dispense with such accessories. Dutch gunsmiths got the gun down to a marvelously light four and a half kilograms. The weapon Champlain carried was a gun of this lighter sort, French rather than Dutch made but capable of being aimed without the impediment of a hook or crutch.

However streamlined an arquebus might get, firing was still cumbersome. The trigger was in the process of being invented in 1609. As of that date, an arquebusier still had to make do with a matchlock—a metal clip that held a burning fuse known as a match to the gunpowder in the flashpan. When the arquebusier flipped the match down onto the flashpan, the gunpowder ignited and burned its way through a hole in the barrel, causing the gunpowder charge inside the barrel to explode. (By the middle of the seventeenth century, gunsmiths figured out how to build a trigger that was not prone to go off whenever the gun was dropped, at which point the musket replaced the arquebus.) Despite its cumbersome firing mechanism, the arquebus redrew the map of Europe. No longer did the size of an army determine victory. What mattered was how its soldiers were armed. Dutch gunsmiths put themselves at the forefront of arms technology, providing the armies of the new Dutch state with weapons that were more portable, more accurate, and capable of being mass-produced. Dutch arquebusiers ended Spain's continental hegemony in Europe and positioned the Netherlands to challenge Iberian dominance outside Europe as well. And French arquebusiers like Champlain gave France the power to penetrate the Great Lakes region, and later to trim Dutch power in Europe.

The development of the arquebus was impelled by the competition among European states, but it gave all Europeans an edge over peoples in other parts of the world. Without this weapon, the Spanish could not have conquered Mexico and Peru, at least not until epidemics kicked in and devastated local populations. This technological superiority allowed the Spanish to enslave the defeated and force them to work in the silver mines along the Andean backbone of the continent, mines that yielded huge quantities of precious metal to finance their purchases on the wholesale markets of India and China. South American bullion reorganized the world economy, connecting Europe and China in a way they had never been connected before, but it worked this magic at gunpoint.

The magic of firearms had a way of slipping from European control when they entered metalworking cultures. The Japanese were particularly quick to learn gunsmithing. The first arquebuses to enter Japan were brought by a pair of Portuguese adventurers who had taken passage there on a Chinese ship in 1543. The local feudal lord was so impressed that he paid them a king's ransom for their guns and then promptly turned them over to a local swordsmith, who was manufacturing passable imitations inside a year. Within a few decades, Japan was fully armed. When Japan invaded Korea in 1592, the invading army carried tens of thousands of arquebuses into battle against the defenders. Had the Dutch not arrived with superior firearms that the Japanese were keen to acquire, they would not have been allowed to open their first trading post in in Japan 1609—the very same year in which Champlain demonstrated the power of his arquebus to the dumbfounded Mohawks. (Once Japan had come under a unified command, its rulers chose in the 1630s to opt out of the vicious cycle of escalating firearms development by banning all further imports, effectively imposing disarmament on the country, which lasted until the middle of the nineteenth century.)

Native American cultures did not yet know how to work metal, but quickly learned to use firearms and acquired them through trade. Champlain tried to block guns from leaking into Native culture, realizing that it would undercut his military advantage. He was able to win his battle on Lake Champlain in 1609 because guns had not yet fallen into the hands of the Mohawks. Other European traders were not so careful. The English traded guns for fur pelts, but only with their allies. The Dutch trading out of New Amsterdam (now New York) were less discriminating. They sold arquebuses to anyone. Native traders soon learned the value of guns and made access to them the price of trade. As a result, guns poured into the interior and were soon being traded well beyond the reach of the Europeans. The Dutch eventually realized that the arquebuses they were selling to their allies were ending up in the hands of their enemies, so they declared that any European trading guns to the Natives would be executed. Unfortunately for them, that order was too late by at least a decade.

Champlain's arquebus played one more role in his campaign. It happened the day after the battle was over. One price of defeat was human sacrifice. The sacrifice could not be performed at the site of the battle. The Algonkians and Hurons were deep in Mohawk territory and feared the quick return of their enemies, and in greater numbers. The surprise of the first victory could not be repeated; they had to leave. But they would not give up the Mohawk warriors they had captured. Young males were too valuable to waste. Some would be taken home and, if possible, integrated into the tribes of those who had captured them. But one, at least, would be sacrificed. They hobbled the captives by cutting the sinews in their legs, bound their arms, trundled them into their canoes, and headed north as fast as they could paddle. By sunset that day they put close to forty kilometers behind them, enough distance to perform the business of sacrifice. It was serious business, and would take all night.

The sacrifice of one Mohawk warrior was performed to thank the spirits who had aided them in battle, honoring them for the dream signs they had given and avenging the spirits of warriors whom other Iroquois had killed in earlier raids. It was also a rite of the deepest seriousness for the victim, the ultimate test of courage that either would mark him as a great warrior or humiliate him as a coward. The rite started with an invitation to sing his war chant. As he sang, his captors drew glowing sticks from the fire and burned his torso. They did this slowly. The ordeal had to last until the sun rose. Whenever the Mohawk warrior passed out, they poured cooling water on his back to revive him. A night of torment ended at dawn with disembowelment and ritual cannibalism.

Champlain wanted to end the torture before it had run its course. The captured Mohawk had committed no crime, nor did he possess useful information, and that in European terms was supposed to rule out the use of torture.

"We do not commit such cruelties," Champlain declared. "We kill people outright. If you wish me to shoot him with the arquebus, I should be glad to do so." Then he stalked away, making a show of his displeasure. His Native allies were distressed, and invited him to return and shoot their victim, if that would please him. Champlain got his way—not because the Natives accepted that his course was right and theirs wrong, but because etiquette required them to defer to a guest's wishes. Perhaps they assumed that an arquebus shot was how Frenchmen conducted their victory sacrifices.

OCHASTEGUIN AND CHAMPLAIN LINKED UP again the following summer and inflicted a second crushing defeat on the Mohawks. At their third meeting, in the summer of 1611, Ochasteguin brought with him several other chiefs from the Huron Confederacy. Both sides wanted to negotiate an enlargement of direct trading. As a pledge of their good faith, the Huron chiefs gave four strings of shell beads to Champlain—what is known as wampum, a form of both currency and contract in Native culture. The four strings tied together signified that the chiefs of the four tribes of the Huron Confederacy committed themselves to an alliance with the French. The Huron Alliance Belt, as it is known, still survives.

Along with the wampum, the Huron chiefs presented Champlain with a gift of what he most wanted: fifty beaver pelts. The Hurons may not have understood why the French wanted an endless supply of beaver fur, other than knowing how valuable it was in their own culture. The French did not want the pelts for the lustrous outer fur, as Natives did, to line or trim garments. What they wanted was the underfur, which provided the raw material for manufacturing felt. Beaver fur is uniquely barbed and therefore prone to bind well when stewed in a toxic stew of copper acetate and mercury-laced Arabic glue. (Hatters had a reputation for being mad because of the toxic soup they inhaled during their work.) The result, once pounded and dried, is the very best felt for making the very best hats.

Before the fifteenth century, European hatters had made felt for hats from the indigenous European beaver, but overtrapping decimated the beaver population and the clearing of wilderness areas in northern Europe eradicated their natural habitats. The fur trade then moved north into Scandinavia until overtrapping drove Scandinavian beavers into extinction as well, and beaver hats along with them.

In the sixteenth century, hatters were forced to use sheep's wool to make felt. Wool felt is not ideal for hats, being coarse by comparison and lacking the natural ability of beaver hairs to thatch. Felt makers could mix in a dose of rabbit hair to help the thatching, but the result was still not as sturdy. Wool felt tended to absorb the rain rather than repel it, and to lose its shape as soon as it got wet. Wool was also unattractive because of its indifferent pale color. It could be dyed, but the natural dyes felt makers used did not fix well, especially in the rain. Wool felt also lacked the strength and pliability of beaver fur.

The standard headgear of the Dutch poor, the *klapmuts*, was made out of wool felt, which is why it slouched.

Toward the end of the sixteenth century, two new sources of beaver pelts opened up. The first was Siberia, into which Russian trappers were moving in search of better hunting. The overland shipping distances were great, however, and the Russian supply was unreliable, despite Dutch attempts to control the Baltic trade to guarantee the shipping of furs into Europe. The other source opening at about the same time was Canada. Europeans fishing along the eastern coast of North America where the St. Lawrence River opened into the Atlantic discovered that the eastern woodlands were full of beavers, and Native trappers were prepared to sell them for a good price.

When beaver pelts from Canada began to come onto the European market in small quantities in the 1580s, demand skyrocketed. Beaver hats made a huge comeback. The fashion first caught on among merchants, but within a few decades the style spread to courtly and military elites. Soon, anyone with any social pretension had to have a "beaver," as these hats were known. In the 1610s, the price of a beaver had risen to ten times the price of a wool felt hat, splitting the hat market into those who could afford beavers and those who couldn't. (One effect of the price split was the emergence of an active resale market for those who could not afford a new beaver but did not want to resort to wearing a klapmuts. European governments regulated the secondhand hat market closely, out of a reasonable fear of lice-borne diseases.)

Status competition among those who could afford beavers, and the struggle for market share among those who made them, drove hatters to concoct ever more outlandish creations in order to stay ahead of their competitors. Fine distinctions of color and nap fed into the fashion whirligig and kept the style conscious on their toes. Crowns went up and down, narrowed and widened, arched and sagged. Brims started widening in the 1610s, turning up or flopping down as fashion dictated, but always getting bigger. Colorful hatbands were added to distinguish the truly fashionable from the less so, and showy decorations were stuck into them. We can't tell what the soldier in *Officer and Laughing Girl* has stuck in his hatband, but his headwear was the very latest in Dutch male fashion—it was also coming to the end of its fashion life, and would be gone within a decade or so.

The opening of the Canadian supply of beaver pelts stimulated the demand for hats, which in turn pushed up prices for consumers and profits for pelt dealers. This surge was a huge boon for the French then trying to establish their first tiny colonies in the St. Lawrence Valley, for it furnished them with an unexpectedly profitable source of income to cover the costs of exploration and colonization. Trade goods valued at one livre when they left Paris bought beaver skins that were worth 200 livres when they arrived back there. The trade also bound Native people closer to the Europeans. In the early years, Native trappers thought they were getting the better of their trading partners. "The Beaver does everything perfectly well," chuckled a Montagnais trapper to a French missionary. "It makes kettles, hatchets, swords, knives, bread; and, in short, it makes everything." Europeans he thought gullible for the prices they paid for pelts, particularly the English in New England, to whom he sold his pelts. "The English have no sense; they give us twenty knives like this for one Beaver skin." The French paid at rates slightly below the English. What the Europeans gave was of far greater value than what the beaver skins were worth in the Native economy. Each side thought the other was overpaying, and both in a sense were right, which is why the trade was such a success.

The year 1609 was for Champlain a crucial moment in the fur trade. The ten-year monopoly that his business consortium enjoyed had been set to run out the previous year, and the Parisian hatters' corporation fought hard to end the monopoly so that prices might come down. Champlain fought back, fearing that, without the monopoly, his project would become financially unviable. Before the monopoly expired, he appealed to King Henri for an extension. His application succeeded, but only to the extent of gaining him one year. So as of 1609, the beaver market was open to all comers. Competitors moved in immediately, driving the price of beaver fur down by 60 percent. Champlain's sole hope was to use his personal alliances to position his operations farther upriver than his competitors. To keep the Huron market to himself, he exchanged a symbolic son (having married late, he had none of his own) with Ochasteguin as a pledge of mutual support. The loss of the royal monopoly thus had the effect of spurring Champlain to probe farther into the continent.

Champlain pushed west in search of furs, but he went in search of something else as well: China. When he explained to Henri why he needed the monopoly continued, he pointed out that he was not seeking simply to benefit his business partners. The furs he was buying were needed to pay for something more important: "the means of discovering the passage to China without the inconvenience of the northern icebergs, or the heat of the torrid zone through which our seamen, with incredible labours and perils, pass twice in going and twice in returning." Champlain needed to keep fur prices high in Paris so that they could pay for the costs of getting to China.

This was not a new idea. It is set out in the terms of the original commission he received from Henri in 1603: that he should "try to find a route easy to traverse through this country to the countries of China and the East Indies, or elsewhere, as far as possible, along the coasts and on the mainland." His charge then had been to search for "a passage that would facilitate commerce with the people of the East." That is what continued to inspire his westward penetration of the continent.

The two known routes from Europe to China, around the southern tips of Africa and South America, were notoriously long and difficult, and were in any case heavily patrolled and defended by the Portuguese and Spanish. Then there were the Northwest and Northeast passages, one around the Americas and the other above Russia. The Dutch and English had already shown the Arctic routes around Russia and Canada to be infeasible, though some still hoped that the passage Henry Hudson found into Hudson Bay might yield a connection to a route through to the Pacific. France's sole hope of getting to the fabled East without being knocked about by icebergs or the other European powers was to find a passage across the North American continent. Champlain needed Native knowledge to show him this hidden way, and he also needed Native trade to provide him with commodities profitable enough to pay for the costs. He was not interested in conquest or colonization for their own sakes. He had one dream only: to find a passage to China.

Jacques Cartier before him had explored the mouth of the St. Lawrence, and Jean Alfonse de Saintonge had sailed along the Labrador coast in the 1540s, though neither succeeded in finding a route to China. But that was the reason why they and others after them were exploring these waters. When the Englishman George Weymouth sailed into the Arctic during Champlain's first visit to the New World, he carried a letter from Elizabeth I addressed to the emperor of China, with translations in Latin, Spanish, and Italian just in case a Jesuit missionary who knew no English was handy to translate from one of these languages into Chinese. Weymouth never reached his destination or delivered Elizabeth's letter to her brother-monarch, but that had been his hope. Champlain was fired by the same hope. He, however, decided that the route to China lay not around the continent but through it. His hope was that the St. Lawrence River would lead to China. A memory of that dream still lingers at Sault St. Louis, a set of rapids near the top of the St. Lawrence where Champlain had to turn back in 1603. Fifteen years later he proposed this as the location for a riverside customs house that would tax the trade goods passing this point once the connection had been made. The place is now called Lachine—"China."[6]

THE DREAM OF GETTING TO China is the imaginative thread that runs through the history of early-modern Europe's struggle to escape from its isolation and enter the wider world. The thread begins where the fourteenth century ends, when a Venetian merchant returned from his travels in China and regaled anyone who would listen with stories of strange lands and fabulous wealth in the East. The

Venetians called him Il Milione, "the Man of a Million Stories," Marco Polo. His enthralling *Travels*, written down for him by a writer of popular romances while they were both whiling away their time in prison, became the bestseller of the fifteenth century. Polo's vision of China under the Mongol rule of Khubilai Khan—"the great Cham," as Europeans knew him—was compelling for the simple reason that there was no court as splendid, no realm as vast, no economy as large, and no cities as grand in fourteenth-century Europe. The place called Cathay was the epitome of wealth and power at the far, unreachable end of the Eurasian world.

When Christopher Columbus launched his fleet of three tiny ships westward across the Atlantic a century later in 1492 (taking a copy of Marco Polo's *Travels* with him), he already understood that the world was round, and that sailing west would convey him to Asia. He knew enough to expect to reach Japan first, with China just beyond it. What he didn't know was how great a distance separated Asia from Europe. And what he didn't expect was that a continent lay between them. When he returned to Spain, he reported to King Ferdinand that, upon reaching the island of Hispaniola (now the Dominican Republic), "I thought it might be terra firma, the province of Cathay." It wasn't, so Columbus had to convince the king that the first voyage had almost reached its destination, and that the second could not fail to complete the journey. If the island wasn't China or Japan, then it must be an island off Japan's east coast. The fabled riches of China were therefore within reach. In the meantime, he assured Ferdinand, the island he had discovered was sure to yield gold, once his sailors went looking for it. He thus turned his losing card—Hispaniola wasn't Japan or China—into a winning card. But he believed that the next island would be Japan, and beyond that would be China.

China's fabled wealth was Europe's obsession, which is why Ferdinand agreed to fund Columbus's second voyage. As Europeans developed a better sense of global geography, the passion for getting to China only grew stronger, and the possibility of actually doing so more within reason. Shakespeare echoes this fantasy when he has

Benedick scorn the company of Beatrice in *Much Ado About Nothing* by declaring that he would rather fetch "a hair of the Great Cham's beard" than speak to her. His London audience knew what he was talking about. They would have agreed that it might be about the most difficult vow a man could put on himself, but it could be done. At the turn of the seventeenth century, the idea of this fabled realm was very much alive, and the dream of riches that went with it only shone brighter. A Chinese proverb of the time held that Chinese have two eyes, Europeans have one, and the rest of the world is blind—a backhanded compliment for a people consumed with a single vision.

This is why Champlain was journeying up the St. Lawrence: to find a transcontinental water route to China. The idea was well-established, for the great Antwerp mapmaker Abraham Ortelius marks such a channel in red on a map he printed in 1570. Even after Champlain, the French cartographer Jean Guérard perpetuates the idea on the map of North America in his *Universal Hydrographical Chart* of 1634, noting in the blank space west of the Great Lakes that "it is believed there is a passage from there to Japan."[7]

Asking Natives what route to take to get to China elicited no response, so Champlain instead asked them about saltwater. One Native up the St. Lawrence River told him in the summer of 1603 that the water of the lake (today's Lake Huron) beyond the lake (Lake Erie) that flowed into the next lake (Lake Ontario) was salty. This was the news Champlain thirsted after, but other Algonquins in the area contradicted this report. Still he kept asking. An Algonquin youth claimed that the water at the far west end of the first lake he would come to (today's Lake Ontario) was brackish. This was all the encouragement Champlain needed. He vowed that he would return and taste it for himself, though it would be years before he could go that far into the interior. In 1613, Étienne Brûlé, the symbolic son Champlain had exchanged with Ochasteguin, reported to him that Lake Huron was after all not salty. It was two more summers before Champlain himself visited the lake. He tasted the water and found it *douce*, "sweet." This confirmed the sad fact that Lake Huron was not linked to the Pacific Ocean.

Champlain was a cartographer—it was his mapmaking skills that first brought him to the attention of his superiors on his first voyage—and through his life he drew a series of detailed maps of what was then called New France. His third map, produced in 1616, is the first to show Lake Huron. He labels it Mer Douce, the Sweetwater Sea, acknowledging the new truth while perhaps reminding himself that the search was still underway. Champlain introduces one ambiguity into this map, and one exaggeration. The ambiguity is where the Sweetwater Sea ends—he has allowed it to extend mysteriously off the left-hand side of the map, for who knows where it might lead? The exaggeration lies to the north. He has drawn the shoreline of the Arctic Ocean, the Mer du Coté du Nord, such that it sweeps south and comes very close to Lake Huron—a link to saltwater was surely out there somewhere. His message? The French need only to persevere with their explorations and they (he) will find the hidden transcontinental passage connecting France to China.

Sixteen years later, Champlain published his final map of New France. This version provides a much fuller portrait of the Great Lakes, though Erie and Michigan have still not appeared. Champlain has learned that Mer Douce, the Sweetwater Sea, does not stretch on forever westward to the Pacific but comes to an end (this name would soon fade away in favor of Lac des Hurons, or Lake Huron). Beyond this freshwater lake and connected by a series of rapids, however, there appears yet another body of water, a Grand Lac of unknown size and extent (today's Lake Superior): another lake in a chain that might one day prove to be the route to China.

Champlain never got to Lake Superior, but Jean Nicollet did. Nicollet was one of Champlain's *coureurs de bois*, or "woodland runners," who were infiltrating the interior and operating extensive networks of trade. A year or two before Champlain published his map of 1632, Nicollet reached a tribe that no European had yet encountered, whom he, or someone, called the Puants, the Stinkers. Champlain includes them on his final map, on which he indicates a "Nation des Puants," or Nation of Stinkers, living beside a lake that drains into

the Sweetwater Sea. "Stinkers" is an unfortunate translation of an Algonquin word meaning dirty water—which is the term Algonquins
used to describe brackish water, that is, water that tasted of salt. The
Stinkers did not call themselves Puants. They were Ouinipigous, a
name we spell today as Winnebagoes.[8] But the word got attached to
them by a convoluted logic that was always insisting that the next
body of water over the horizon must be salty, must be "stinky"—
must be the Pacific Ocean.[9]

The chief of the Winnebagoes invited Jean Nicollet to be his guest
at a great feast of welcome. Nicollet understood the importance of
protocol. When he presented himself before the thousands who came
great distances to attend the feast hosted in his honor, he wore the
finest item he had in his baggage: a Chinese robe embroidered with
flowers and birds.

There was no way that an up-country agent such as Nicollet acquired this garment on his own. He would not have had access to
such a thing, let alone the money to buy it. The robe must have been
Champlain's. But how did Champlain acquire it? Only in the early
years of the seventeenth century were curiosities of this sort starting
to make their way from China to northern Europe. As this garment
no longer exists, we have no way to trace it. The likely origin was a
Jesuit missionary in China, who brought or sent it back to Europe as
a testimonial of the cultured civilization to which he had devoted his
life. The English traveler John Evelyn saw a set of Chinese robes in
Paris, and marveled at them. They were "glorious Vests, wrought &
embroidered on cloth of Gold, but with such lively colours, as for
splendor and vividnesse we have nothing in Europe approaches."
Nothing like Nicollet's robe could have been obtained in Paris during Champlain's early years in Canada, so he must have bought it on
his two-year furlough in 1624–26—and paid an exorbitant price—
because he believed the thing had value for his enterprise in Canada.
He knew that Jesuits dressed themselves in the Chinese manner when
they appeared at court, and if he himself did not have a chance to
wear the Chinese robe, then his envoy might. When you show up at

court, you have to be correctly dressed. As things turned out, it was the Winnebagoes, not the Chinese, who got to enjoy the sight.

Nicollet's robe is simply another sign that Champlain's dream was to reach China. The dream had been with him right from the beginning of his adventures in North America. As a poet friend who composed a dedicatory verse for his first memoirs in 1603 wrote, Champlain had dedicated himself "to travel still further, convert the peoples, and discover the East, whether by North or South, so as to get to China." All his exploring, alliance building, and fighting was for this purpose alone. China was the reason why Champlain risked his life to shoot and kill the three Mohawk chiefs on the shore of Lake Champlain. He needed to control the trade that supplied the felt makers of Europe, but far more than that, he needed to find a route to China. Nicollet's robe was a prop for this vision, Vermeer's hat a by-product of the search.

CHAMPLAIN'S GREAT VENTURE DID NOT succeed, of course. The French would never get to China by canoeing across Canada. Whether they failed or succeeded, their effort imposed terrible losses on the inhabitants of the eastern woodlands. Worst hit were the Hurons. Waves of infectious diseases spread from the Europeans into the Huron Confederacy in the 1630s, climaxing in 1640 with a virulent smallpox epidemic that slashed the population to a third of its original number of 25,000. Desperate to save their communities from annihilation, some Hurons turned to the teachings of the French Jesuit missionaries, who started infiltrating Huronia in the 1620s. Some may have gained comfort from Jesuit lessons in Christian humility, but that benefit did little to offset the more tangible effect of a collapse in their capacity to resist the Iroquois. The French decision to reverse the ban on firearms sales to the Hurons in 1641—though only to Christian converts—came too late for this nation to arm itself effectively against its enemies.

In the summer and fall of 1649, several thousand Hurons withdrew to Gahoendoe, an island in the southeastern corner of the Sweetwater

Sea. Some four dozen French missionaries, artisans, and soldiers joined them. The Hurons preferred to set up camp by the edge of an inland lake, whereas the French decided to construct a visible palisade by the shore, preparing for a last stand against the Iroquois. This last stand is commemorated in today's name for Gahoendoe, Christian Island.

That last stand turned out to be a battle not against Iroquois warriors but against hunger. The island was too small to support enough game to feed so many refugees, and the corn they planted went in the ground too late to ripen. As fall lengthened into winter, the fish they could catch and the six hundred bushels of acorns they bought from tribes further north proved insufficient to feed everyone, and famine struck. Hardest hit were the children. A Jesuit missionary who visited the village describes a slack-breasted mother who watched her children "die in her arms, one after another, and had not even the strength to cast them into the grave." The melodrama of his account communicates the severity of the suffering that winter, though he was wrong about that last detail. When a team of archaeologists and Native assistants excavated the site some three decades ago, they uncovered in the sandy soil next to the village the skeletal remains of children who died of malnutrition, and those remains had been buried with care. After the dig was completed, the bones were just as carefully relaid, and the young deciduous forest allowed to reclaim the site so that no one would know where the graves lay, and none could come again to disturb them.

Toward the end of the winter, several hundred Hurons decided to take their chances crossing the ice and surrendering to the Iroquois parties patrolling the mainland, but the ice underneath their feet gave way and many drowned. The rest waited for the thaw, then set out on different courses. One group disappeared northward into the interior, and another escorted the French back to Québec. Their descendants, the Wendat, still live there today.

An airy grove of beech and birch trees has grown over the site of the last Huron village on Christian Island. Unless you happen to know where the village was, you will never find it. I spend my summers on Christian Island, which is now an Ojibwe reserve, and I cannot walk the dappled path that angles past the place where the children are buried without thinking back to the starvation winter of 1649–50, marveling at the vast web of history that ties this hidden spot to global networks of trade and conquest that came into being in the seventeenth century. The children are lost links in that history, forgotten victims of the desperate European desire to find a way to China and a way to pay for it, tiny actors in the drama that placed Vermeer's hat on the officer's head.

A DISH OF FRUIT

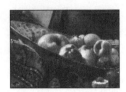

VERMEER PAINTED *Young Woman Reading a Letter at an Open Window* (see plate 3) around the same time he painted *Officer and Laughing Girl*. We see the same upstairs room, the same table and chair, the same woman wearing even the same dress, again his wife Catharina Bolnes, or so I believe. Although the action in the two paintings is different, both narrate much the same story: the story of courtship between a man and a woman. The story is overt in *Officer and Laughing Girl*, where we see courting in action. In *Young Woman Reading a Letter*, on the other hand, we see only the woman. The man has a presence in the picture, but only in absentia: the letter the woman is reading. He is away, possibly half a world away. She reads by the window for the light, but the window is not just ajar this time. It is wide open. The man is out there somewhere, able to speak to her only through letters. His physical absence induces Vermeer to construct a different mood. The brilliance of light conversation has been replaced by an internalized tension, as the young woman concentrates on words that we, the viewers, are not allowed to read.

If the two paintings share space and theme, they differ in the objects they display. *Young Woman Reading a Letter at an Open Window* is uncluttered, but there are more objects in the painting, and they are doing more of the work of creating visual activity. To balance the busyness of these objects, Vermeer has left the wall empty. Empty but far from blank, this is surely one of the most richly textured empty walls in Western art. X-ray analysis reveals that Vermeer originally had hung a cupid painting on that wall (he used it later in *Lady Standing at the Virginals*) to let the reader know that she is reading a love letter, but he later decided against such obvious symbolic hints and painted it out. To lend a sense of depth and volume to the room, he has used the conventional technique of hanging curtains, one draped over the open window, the other pulled to one side in the foreground as though drawn back to reveal the painting (it was common practice to hang curtains across pictures to protect them from light and other damage). The table is covered, this time with a richly colored Turkish carpet—such carpets were too valuable to throw on floors, as we do today—which has been bunched to one side to lend vitality to the scene. And there, askew on the carpet in the middle of the table, is an object that, like the officer's hat, points toward the wider world in which perhaps her lover or husband has gone: a china dish under a heap of fruit.

Our eyes go first to the young woman, but the dish would have competed for the attention of Vermeer's contemporaries. Dishes like this were a delight to behold, but they were still uncommon and expensive enough that not everyone could buy one. Go back a decade or two and Chinese dishes rarely make appearances in Dutch paintings—but go forward a decade or two and they are everywhere. The decade of the 1650s is just the moment when Chinese porcelains were taking their place in Dutch art as in Dutch life. In fact, these dishes became part of the emergence of a newly popular painting genre, still lifes, which seventeenth-century Dutch artists turned into an art form. The artist selected objects of a similar type (fruit) or plausibly sharing in a common theme (decay, the sign of vanity) and arranged them on a table in a visually pleasing way. A large Chinese dish was just the sort of thing that could serve to unify smaller objects, like fruits, and jumble them together in a dynamic heap. The challenge of the still life was to make the scene so real that it would fool the eye into believing that this was not a picture—and the clever artist might paint a fly into the scene, as though the fly too had been fooled. Creating trompe l'oeil reality was just the challenge that Vermeer played with throughout his painter's life.

The dish of fruit on the table in front of Catharina is there to de-light the eye, but Vermeer is using the still life of tumbled fruit to convey the tumble of emotions in her mind as she reads the letter from her lover far away—perhaps as far away as the Dutch East Indies—and struggles to control her thoughts. Her posture and man-ner suggest a person of calm, but even she cannot hold her thoughts steady. So too the fruit topples out of the dish before her. It is all ar-ranging and playacting, of course. The lover is fictional, the sheet of paper the model holds may well have no words written on it, and the carpet and dish and curtain have all been artfully positioned. But the world is real, and that is what we are in pursuit of. This dish, appro-priately for a picture painted in the town that created delftware, will be the door through which we head out of Vermeer's studio and down a corridor of trade routes leading from Delft to China.

SIXTEEN DEGREES BELOW THE EQUATOR and two hundred kilometers from the coast of Africa, a volcanic island breaks the surface of an otherwise empty South Atlantic. The British East India Company in-corporated St. Helena into the British Empire in the eighteenth cen-tury. They built Jamestown at what had been known as Church Bay (now Jamestown Bay) on the leeward side of the island. The island's main claim to fame lies in being the place to which the British ban-ished Napoleon after defeating him at the Battle of Waterloo in 1815—the closing scene in the long drama that led to Britain's ascen-dancy as the leading world power in the nineteenth century.

Before the English occupied St. Helena, the island served as a way station for ships of any nation making the long journey from Asia back to Europe. Lying directly in the path of the southeast trade winds carrying ships northward from the Cape of Good Hope, it was a place of refuge where vessels and crews could recover from the storms and diseases that dogged marine travel; a haven for rest, repair, and the taking on of fresh water before the final leg home. Modern shipping has no need of such islands and now passes St. Helena by, leaving it, in its oceanic remoteness, for none but tourists to visit.

The only ship in Church Bay at midmorning of the first day of June in 1613 was an English ship, a small East India Company vessel called the *Pearle*. The *Pearle* had arrived in Church Bay two weeks earlier as part of a convoy of six ships coming back from Asia to London. There was one other English ship in the convoy, the *Solomon*, but the other four sailed for the Dutch East India Company. Even though the Dutch and the English were often at war in the seventeenth century, the captains on both sides were content to put aside their differences and sail together for protection against their real competitors, the Spanish and Portuguese. The six ships passed two weeks at St. Helena resting and refitting for the final leg of the journey back to Europe. But when the convoy departed at dawn on first of June, they left the *Pearle* behind. Half the *Pearle*'s crew of fifty-two had been on the sick list when the ship arrived at St. Helena, and most were as yet too weak to work. The *Pearle*'s water casks were still being filled and loaded that morning. Captain John Tatton had no choice but to delay departure until the following morning and hope to catch up with the rest of the fleet.

Tatton and his crew were busy preparing the *Pearle* after the others departed when later that morning two great Portuguese ships came into sight around the southern point of the bay. These were carracks, the great armed transport ships that the Portuguese built to ferry merchandise across the oceans. They had made their maiden voyage to Goa, Portugal's little colony on the west coast of India, and were on their way back to Lisbon with a great cargo of pepper. Tatton understood that the *Pearle* was no match for these two great vessels, the largest wooden ships Europeans ever made. The better part of valor was to scurry out of range of their guns, so he hoisted his sails and fled. The hasty exit meant abandoning his water casks and the sick half of his crew on the island. But he was not cutting and running. Tatton had another plan. He went off in hot pursuit of the rest of the Anglo-Dutch convoy, hoping to convince the Dutch admiral, Jan Derickzson Lam, to turn the fleet around and return to capture the two carracks in Church Bay.

The *Pearle* caught up to Lam's flagship, the *Wapen van Amsterdam*, past nightfall. Lam "was very glad and made signs to his Fleet to follow," Tatton afterward reported. Not all the Dutch ships heeded his order to turn around, however. The *Bantam* and the *Witte Leeuw* (*White Lion*) turned about and came alongside, but the *Vlissingen* failed to acknowledge the signal, as did the other English ship, the *Solomon*. Lam was undeterred. Four against two might not be as overpowering as six against two, but his fleet had the advantage of surprise.

After a day and a half of hard tacking against the wind, the Anglo-Dutch quartet arrived back at St. Helena. Lam and Tatton were right to bank on surprise. Jeronymo de Almeida, the admiral of the Portuguese fleet, must have seen the *Pearle* flee but had then put the English ship out of his mind and made no preparations for its return. *Nossa Senhora da Nazaré* (*Our Lady of Nazareth*), his flagship, lay at anchor with its full length exposed to the open ocean. *Nossa Senhora do Monte da Carmo* (*Our Lady of Mount Carmel*) was anchored alongside it, effectively boxed in by the bigger vessel.

Lam attacked before the Portuguese could reposition their carracks for a better defense. He launched the *Bantam* and the *White Lion* toward the bow and stern of the *Nazareth* at angles that made it almost impossible for the Portuguese to fire its cannon at them, then sailed the *Wapen* straight toward it. Tatton later wrote that Lam should have tried to negotiate a Portuguese surrender, but it seems that Lam would settle for nothing less than capture. "Too covetous" was Tatton's judgment.

The *Bantam*'s attack on the *Nazareth*'s bow "much cooled the Portugals courage," according to Tatton. Then the captain of the *White Lion*, Roeloff Sijmonz Blom, fired on the stern of the *Nazareth*, puncturing it above the waterline. Blom brought the *White Lion* in close enough to cut the carrack's anchor cables, hoping to force it to drift to shore. The crew of the *Carmel*, caught powerless behind the *Nazareth*, was nonetheless able to pass a replacement cable to the other ship and resecure it. Preparing to board the flagship, Blom moved the *White Lion* alongside the *Nazareth* and the *Carmel*. As he did so, his starboard gunners exchanged fire with the *Carmel*.

Opinions are divided as to what exactly happened next. Some said that the Portuguese scored a direct hit on the *White Lion*'s powder magazine. Others insisted that a faulty gun on the *White Lion*'s lower deck exploded. Whatever the cause, the explosion blew off the back end of the ship. The *White Lion* sank to the bottom in moments. Tatton believed that Blom, his crew of forty-nine, along with two English passengers on board died in the blast or were drowned in the bay, though some in fact were rescued and taken back to Lisbon for repatriation.

Having lost an entire ship along with crew and cargo, Admiral Lam could not afford to gamble anything more. He ordered the other ships to withdraw. Tatton was able to take the *Pearle* in close enough to the shore north of the bay to pick up eleven of his abandoned crew, who had gathered there in the hope of rescue, before retreating. The misfortunes of this voyage would be played out only at the very end. As the *Bantam* passed through the channel at Texel on its way into the Zuider Zee (now the IJsselmeer), Amsterdam's inland sea, it went aground and broke apart. It was atrocious luck for Lam. The number of VOC ships that sank in this channel can be counted on the fingers of one hand, but this was one of the fingers. (The Portuguese fleet fared only slightly better. Admiral Almeida was able to get both ships back to Lisbon, but the *Carmel* had been so badly damaged that it had to be removed from service.)

When the *White Lion* sank in thirty-three meters of water, a large cargo went with it to the bottom. The ship's manifest survives in a Dutch archive, from which it is possible to find out exactly what was lost. The manifest lists 15,000 bags of pepper,[1] 312 kilograms of cloves, 77 kilograms of nutmeg, plus 1,317 diamonds having a combined weight of 480.5 carats. The manifest was drawn up on the docks at Bantam, the VOC trading port at the westernmost tip of Java. Given the VOC mania for accuracy of detail and thoroughness of accounting, there is no reason to suspect that anything got into the cargo hold that wasn't first recorded in the company ledgers. This is why the marine archaeologists who went down to excavate the wreck of the *White Lion* in 1976 were surprised by what they found. They knew that the spices would long ago have rotted and the diamonds been lost in the harbor's shifting sands. They did not expect to find cargo. They were intent instead on recovering the ship's metalwork, especially its cannon. And yet there in the mud under the vessel's shattered hull were strewn thousands of pieces of the very thing that, in 1613, was synonymous with China itself—china.

Could the porcelain have been dropped on top of the wreck by later ships lightening their load while at anchor? It is possible, but there was too much porcelain in one place, and when pieces were brought to the surface, their styles and dates indicated that they were produced during the reign of the Wanli emperor, which came to an end in 1620. All the evidence—other than the ship's manifest—points to this being cargo from the *White Lion*. What the explosion destroyed, it paradoxically saved. Had the carefully packed bales of porcelain made it to the docks of Amsterdam as they were supposed to, they would have been sold and resold, chipped and cracked, and finally thrown away. This is the ordinary fate of almost all the porcelain that made it back to the Netherlands in the seventeenth century. There are pieces scattered about the world in museums and private collections, but they survive as individual remnants cut loose from the circumstances that got them to Europe and separated from the shipments of which they were a part. The explosion of the *White Lion* inadvertently saved this particular shipment from this fate. True, most of the pieces recovered are broken, but ironically enough, more have survived than would have made it through the four centuries between 1613 and the present. They may be damaged, but they are still together (now in the Rijksmuseum in Amsterdam), and that means that they can show us what a shipment of porcelain in the early seventeenth century looked like.

THE FIRST CHINESE PORCELAIN TO reach Europe amazed all who saw or handled it. Europeans could think only of crystal when pressed to describe the stuff. The glazed surfaces were hard and lustrous, the underglaze designs sharply defined, the colors brilliantly vivid. The walls of the finest pieces were so thin that you could see the shadow of your hand on the other side when you lifted a plate or cup to the light.

The style that most caught the attention of Europeans was blue-and-white: thin white porcelain painted with cobalt blue and coated in a perfectly transparent glaze. This style was actually a late development in the history of Chinese ceramics. The potters of Jingdezhen, the kiln city in the inland province of Jiangxi where imperial orders were regularly filled, developed the technology to fire true porcelain only in the fourteenth century. Porcelain production requires driving kiln temperatures up to 1,300 degrees Celsius, high enough to turn the glazing mixture to a glassy transparency and fuse it with the body. Trapped permanently between the two were the blue pictures and patterns that so captured the eye. The closest European approximation was faïence, earthenware fired at a temperature of 900 degrees Celsius and coated with a tin oxide glaze. Faïence has the superficial appearance of porcelain, but lacks its thinness and translucence. Europeans learned the technique from Islamic potters in the fifteenth century, who had developed it to make cheap import substitutes that could compete with Chinese wares. It was not until 1708 that a German alchemist was able to reproduce the technique for making true porcelain in a town outside Dresden called Meissen, which soon was also synonymous with fine porcelain.

European buyers were delighted by the effect of blue on white. Although we think of deep cobalt blue lines and figures on a pure white background as quintessentially Chinese, it is a borrowed, or at least an adapted, aesthetic. At the time Chinese potters began firing true porcelain, China was under Mongol rule. The Mongols also controlled Central Asia, enabling goods to move overland from one end of their continental empire to the other. Persian taste had long favored Chinese ceramics, which had been available there since the eighth century. Unable to match the whiteness of Chinese ceramics, their potters developed a technique of masking their gray clay with an opaque white glaze that looked Chinese. Onto this white base they painted blue decorative figures, using local cobalt for the color. The effect was striking. Once Persia and China were more directly linked by Mongol rule in the thirteenth century, Chinese potters had much better access to the Persian market. Ever sensitive to the demands of that market, they adjusted the look of their products to appeal to Persian taste. Part of this adaptation was to incorporate cobalt decoration into their designs. As Chinese cobalt is paler than Persian, the potters of Jingdezhen began importing Persian cobalt to produce a color they thought would appeal to Persian buyers.

Blue-and-white porcelain emerged from this long process of innovation. It sold well in Persia, in part because of the Koran's ban on eating from gold or silver plates. The wealthy wanted to be able to serve guests on expensive tableware, and if they were blocked from presenting food on precious metals, they needed something as lovely and as expensive but that wasn't available in the time of the Koran. Porcelain from Jingdezhen fit the bill. Mongol and Chinese buyers were also charmed by the look of this porcelain. What we recognize as "china" today was born from this chance intercultural crossover of material and aesthetic factors, which transformed ceramic production worldwide. Syrian potters in the court of Tamerlane, for instance, started making their products look Chinese early in the fifteenth century. As the global trade in ceramics expanded in the sixteenth century to Mexico, the Middle East, and Iberia, and to England and the Netherlands in the seventeenth, potters in all of these places followed suit. Everyone tried—though for a long while they also failed—to imitate the look and feel of Chinese blue-and-white. The ceramic stalls of seventeenth-century bazaars outside of China were cluttered with second-rate imitations that fell far short of the real thing.

Dutch readers first learned about Chinese porcelain in 1596 from Jan Huygen van Linschoten, a Dutchman who went to India in Portuguese employ. Van Linschoten's best-selling *Itinerario* inspired the coming generation of Dutch world traders. Van Linschoten saw Chinese porcelains in the markets of Goa. Though he never went to

China, he managed to pick up reasonably sound information about the commodity. "To tell of the porcelains made there"—he is speaking of China on the basis of what he learned in Goa—"is not to be believed, and those that are exported yearly to India, Portugal and New Spain and elsewhere!" Van Linschoten learned that the porcelain was produced "inland"—as Jingdezhen was—and that only the second-rate stuff was exported. The best pieces, "so exquisite that no crystalline glass is to be compared with them," were kept at home for the court.

Indian traders had been bringing Chinese porcelain to the subcontinent since at least the fifteenth century. They acquired it from Chinese merchants in Southeast Asia, who brought it from ports along the southeast coast of China, to which ceramics dealers had in turn shipped it out from the interior. The development of a maritime trade route around Africa suddenly opened up a market in Europe. The Portuguese were the first Europeans to acquire Chinese porcelain in Goa, though soon enough they would extend their trade routes to south China where they could deal directly with Chinese wholesalers. This was the route that the Dutch wanted to get in on, and soon enough they did. But the first major shipment of Chinese porcelain to Amsterdam was not a Dutch enterprise. It was the result of the Dutch-Portuguese rivalry on the high seas, off St. Helena no less. Eleven years before the sinking of the *White Lion*, a fleet of Dutch ships seized the Portuguese *San Iago* there in 1602. The *San Iago* was captured without difficulty and taken to Amsterdam with all its cargo. Onto the docks of that city emerged the first great trove of china to reach Holland, and buyers from all over Europe fought for a piece. The Dutch called it *kraakporselein*, "carrack porcelain," in acknowledgment of the Portuguese carrack from which it had been taken.

The next great porcelain cargo to arrive in the Netherlands came the same way the following year. The *Santa Catarina* was captured off Johore in the Strait of Malacca, the sea-lane connecting the Indian Ocean to the South China Sea. This was the most famous seizure of the new century. The *Santa Catarina* was carrying a hundred thousand pieces of porcelain weighing a total of over fifty tons. (It also held twelve hundred bales of Chinese silk, which sold well because Italy's silk production had failed that year.) Buyers for the crowned heads of northern Europe flocked to Amsterdam with orders to pay whatever the going price might be.

The seizures of the *San Iago* and the *Santa Catarina*, and the sinking of the *White Lion*, were skirmishes in the larger war the Dutch were waging not so much against the Portuguese as against the Spanish. The Portuguese were the junior partners of the Spanish during the period 1580–1640, when their crowns were joined, and that in Dutch eyes made them legitimate targets of attack as well. But Spain was the arch-enemy: Spain was the state that had occupied the Low Countries in the sixteenth century and had used spectacular violence to suppress the Dutch independence movement. Even though the truce Spain and the United Provinces signed in 1609 ended direct hostilities in the Low Countries for a time, outside Europe the struggle between the Spanish kingdom and the Dutch republic continued to be waged.

The rivalry being played out on the high seas—the Spanish not unreasonably called it "piracy"—had to do with more than the Dutch struggle for independence at home, however. It had to do with re-defining the global order. Its roots have to be traced back to 1493, the year after Columbus's first voyage to the West Indies. In light of the new lands discovered across the Atlantic, the pope decreed that same year that Spain should enjoy exclusive jurisdiction over every newly discovered land lying to the west of a north-south meridian drawn 100 leagues west of the Cape Verde Islands off the coast of Morocco, and that Portugal could claim every land to the east of that line. All other European states were excluded from any right to trade into or possess the newly discovered regions. Spain and Portugal al-tered the terms of the papal bull of 1493 the following year by con-cluding the Treaty of Tordesillas. This agreement moved the line 270 leagues farther west, possibly because the Portuguese knew, or at least suspected, that a piece of South America might protrude east of that line (they were correct: it was Brazil).

The Treaty of Tordesillas said nothing about where the line of demarcation should fall on the far side of the globe, since neither of the treaty parties had yet gone there. So Portugal and Spain quickly set off in opposite directions on their race around the globe, Portugal via the Indian Ocean and Spain via the Pacific. They knew that China was there on the opposite side of the globe, and that whoever could establish a presence in that part of the world stood to gain the richest prize of all. The Chinese government was not enthusiastic about letting either state establish a foothold on Chinese soil. Foreigners were permitted to stay in China only as temporary visitors who came as members of visiting diplomatic embassies. The concept of diplomatic embassy was sufficiently elastic, and understood to be so on both sides, that embassies from neighboring states that came to submit "tribute" to the Chinese throne operated as de facto trade delegations. Ambassadors were allowed to engage in trade so long as the volume was kept within modest limits. Traders had to be ambassadors, and that is what the Portuguese wanted to be. They reached China before the Spanish did, and made strong efforts to open official channels of communication with the Chinese court. Consistently rebuffed, they had to make do with illegal trading in the lee of offshore islands. An unofficial agreement in the middle of the sixteenth century at last gave them a foothold on a slender peninsula on the south coast known as Macao, and there they dug in, establishing a tiny colonial base from which to handle trade with both China and Japan.

At the turn of the seventeenth century, VOC ships were also in the South China Sea, probing along the coast north of Macao as far as Fujian Province for a place where they could set up trade with China. As the Chinese government already had a trading arrangement with one set of "Franks," as they then called Europeans (they picked up the term from the Arabs), in Macao, it was not interested in making concessions to another set. But private Chinese merchants were eager to trade with any Franks, and some officials were willing to come to an understanding if the price was right. Most notorious of the Chinese officials was Gao Cai, an imperial eunuch in charge of collecting maritime customs duties. As customs receipts went directly into the accounts of the imperial household rather than the ministry of finance, Eunuch Gao bent the rules of the bureaucracy for the benefit of his master. In 1604, he set up a private trading entrepôt in the lee of an offshore island where his agents could trade with the Dutch in return for handsome gifts for himself and the emperor. The provincial governor soon got wind of the scheme and sent in the navy to curtail the eunuch's smuggling.[2]

The absence of strong states in Southeast Asia, compared to China, made that region a more promising region for the Dutch to find a foothold. The Spanish (based at Manila in the Philippines) and the Portuguese were too few to dominate the thousands of islands in that zone, so the Dutch moved in swiftly, seizing what were called the Spice Islands from the Portuguese in 1605. Four years later, the VOC set up its first permanent trading post at Bantam on the far west end of the island of Java. After capturing Jakarta to the east, the company moved its headquarters to this location, renaming the town Batavia. Holland now had a base on the other side of the globe from which to challenge the Iberian monopoly on Asian trade. The new arrangement worked well for the company. The value of Dutch imports from the region grew by almost 3 percent annually.

The *White Lion* became one of the Netherlands' earliest and more spectacular casualties in the war to dominate the trade with Asia. The ship had sailed on its maiden voyage from Amsterdam to Asia— a distance of some fourteen thousand nautical miles (twenty-five thousand kilometers)—as early as 1601, a year before the VOC was formed.[3] It reached home in July of the following year. Mounting tension with Portuguese vessels in Asian waters justified its being refitted with six new bronze cannon fore and aft. When it embarked on its second journey to Asia in 1605, the *White Lion* sailed as a VOC ship. The new business arrangement is recorded on the backs of the copper cannon, which the salvage archaeologists fished out of the bay in 1976. Foundry master Hendrick Muers inscribed them with his name and the date—*Henricus Muers me fecit 1604*—above which he overlaid the interlocking company initials, *VOC*, plus an *A*, the insignia of the Amsterdam Chamber of the VOC.

The *White Lion* successfully completed a second voyage and then set off on its fateful third in 1610. It was unloaded at Bantam, then reassigned to a naval squadron charged with suppressing an uprising for nutmeg traders in the Spice Islands. The *White Lion* spent that winter as part of a fleet preying on Spanish ships sailing out of Manila. Five were captured. It was put into interisland shipping for the spring and summer, then ordered back to Bantam to load up for its third return journey to Amsterdam. On 5 December 1612, it departed as one of four ships under the command of Admiral Lam. On the first of June the following summer, it left St. Helena on the final leg of its voyage to Amsterdam. We know the rest of the story.

Dutch piracy provoked diplomatic protests from other European nations, and not just Portugal.[4] When the Dutch seized the *Santa Catarina* in 1603, Portugal demanded the return of the ship with all its cargo, insisting that it had been an unlawful seizure. The directors of the VOC felt they had to make a case for themselves that did more than glorify their capacity to get away with such theft. They needed principles of international law to prove they were justified in their actions, so they commissioned a bright young lawyer from Delft, Huig de Groot (better known in English by the Latin version of his name, Grotius) to write a brief justifying their claim that the seizure was not piracy but an act taken in defense of the company's legitimate interests.

In 1608, Grotius delivered what the VOC directors wanted. *De jure praedae*, translated into English as *The Spoils of War*, argued that the Spanish naval blockade of the Netherlands, then in force, was an act of war. Such provocation gave the Dutch the right to treat Portuguese and Spanish ships as belligerent vessels. One of their ships captured in war was legitimate booty, not illegal seizure. The following year, Grotius expanded *The Spoils of War* into his masterwork, *Mare Liberum*, or in its full English title, *The Freedom of the Seas or the Right Which Belongs to the Dutch to Take Part in the East Indian Trade*.

In *The Freedom of the Seas,* Grotius makes several bold and novel arguments. The boldest of all is one that no one had thus far thought to make: all people have the right to trade. For the first time, the freedom of trade is declared a principle of international law, as it has been of the international order ever since. From this fundamental principle, it follows that no state has the right to prevent the nationals of another state from using sea-lanes for the pursuit of trade. If trade was free, then the seas on which they traded also were free. Portugal and Spain had no basis for abrogating that right by monopolizing the maritime trade to Asia. Grotius would not accept their argument that they had earned the monopoly by dint of the work they did to carry Christianity to the natives in those parts of the world where they traded. The duty of converting the heathen not only did not trump freedom to trade; for Grotius, it was offensive to the principle that all should be treated equally. "Religious belief does not do away with either natural or human law from which sovereignty is derived," he stated. That people should refuse to accept Christianity is "not sufficient cause to justify war upon them, or to despoil them of their goods." Nor is the expense to convert them to be redeemed by preventing other nations from trading with them. Armed with a hugely self-interested interpretation of Grotius's argument, the VOC allowed its captains to use force wherever they were blocked from trading.

The VOC directors also recognized that the best way to dominate the trade in porcelain was to acquire it through regular trade channels, not steal it from other ships. They started informing their captains departing for Bantam that they should not think of coming back without some Chinese porcelain. In 1608, they sent a shopping list: 50,000 butter dishes, 10,000 plates, 2,000 fruit dishes, and 1,000 each of salt cellars, mustard pots, and various wide bowls and large dishes, plus an unspecified number of jugs and cups. This order represented a spike in demand that Chinese merchants at first failed to meet. Instead, demand drove up prices. "The porcelain here comes generally so expensive," noted the dismayed head of operations in Bantam in a letter to the VOC directors in 1610. Worse, whenever a fleet of Dutch ships arrives in port, the Chinese merchants "immediately run up the prices so much, that I cannot calculate a profit on them." The only way to control this price volatility was to stop all further purchases and negotiate improved supply with the Chinese. "We shall henceforth look out for porcelain and try to contract with the Chinese that they bring a lot," he wrote, "for what they have brought until now does not amount to much and is mostly inferior." He decided not to buy any of what was on offer that year. "Only very curious goods will serve," he decided.

By the time the *White Lion* was loading at the docks of Bantam in the winter of 1612, Chinese suppliers were meeting the higher standard that the VOC expected. The *Wapen van Amsterdam*, the flagship of Lam's decimated fleet, brought back only five barrels of porcelain, each of which contained five large dishes. These were special purchases brought as gifts to VOC officials. It was the other Dutch ship that made it to port, the *Vlissingen*, that carried the main china cargo. It disgorged 38,641 pieces, ranging from large, expensive serving dishes and brandy decanters to modest but attractive oil and vinegar jars and little cups for holding candles. The load was worth 6,791 guilders—not an unimaginably vast sum when you consider that a skilled artisan at the time could earn 200 guilders in a year, but substantial nonetheless. This was the start of a long and growing trade in porcelain. By 1640, to choose a date and ship at random, the *Nassau* alone carried back to Amsterdam 126,391 pieces of porcelain. Porcelain was not the most profitable cargo on the ship—that was pepper, of which the *Nassau* carried 9,164 sacks—but it was the commodity that created the greatest presence in Dutch society. Over the first half of the seventeenth century, VOC ships delivered to Europe a total of well over three million pieces.

CHINESE POTTERS PRODUCED FOR EXPORT markets all over the world. They also produced for the home market, in quantity and quality far beyond the stuff they shipped abroad. Chinese of the Ming dynasty were as keen to own beautiful blue-and-white porcelain as were

Dutch householders, but they acquired it guided by much more complex standards of taste.

Wen Zhenheng was a leading connoisseur and arbiter of taste of his generation (he died in 1645). He was living in the cultural metropolis of Suzhou when the *White Lion* exploded and sank. His home city produced and consumed the very finest works of art and cultural objects to be found in China, as well as the most commercial. Wen was perfectly placed to produce his famous handbook of cultural consumption and good taste, *A Treatise on Superfluous Things*. The great-grandson of the greatest artist of the sixteenth century, an essayist in his own right, and a member of one of the richest and most exclusive families in Suzhou, Wen had all the credentials needed to pass the judgments of his class on what was done and not done in polite society, and on what should be owned and what avoided—which is what *A Treatise on Superfluous Things* is all about. A guide to the dos and don'ts of acquiring and using nice things, it was an answer to the prayers of readers who, unlike a gentleman such as Wen, were not sufficiently educated or well bred to know these things by upbringing. It was for the nouveaux riches who yearned to be accepted by their social superiors. On Wen's part, it was also a clever way to profit from their ignorance, for the book sold well.

In the section on decorative objects, Wen Zhenheng sets the bar for good quality porcelain very high. He allows that porcelain is something a gentleman should collect and put on display, but doubts that anything produced after the second quarter of the fifteenth century has any value, at least as something you would want to let your friends know you owned. The perfect piece of porcelain, he declares, should be "as blue as the sky, as lustrous as a mirror, as thin as paper, and as resonant as a chime"—though he has the sense to wonder whether such perfection has ever been achieved, even in the fifteenth century. He does let a few sixteenth-century pieces pass his scrutiny—but only so long as they were only for everyday use. A host might serve tea to his guests in cups produced by Potter Cui, for instance. (Cui's private kiln at Jingdezhen turned out fine porcelain, both blue-and-white and multicolored, during the third quarter of the sixteenth century.) But really, Wen complains, the cups are a little too large to be elegant. They should be used only if nothing else is on hand.

Owning objects of high cultural value was a treacherous business among those struggling up the ladder of status. Even if you possessed a piece of porcelain that Wen considered fine enough to own, care still had to be taken not to use it in the wrong way or at the wrong time. For instance, to set out a vase for people to see, the only piece of furniture on which it was acceptable to put it was "a table in the Japanese style," as he describes it. The size of this table depends on the size and style of the vase, and that in turn depends on the size of the room in which the vase is displayed. "In the spring and winter, bronze vessels are appropriate to use; in the autumn and summer, ceramic vases," he insists. Nothing else is acceptable. "Value bronze and ceramic, and hold gold and silver cheap," he instructs. Objects made of precious metals should be avoided not to cool the sin of pride, as the Koran warned, but to keep those who were merely wealthy and without education or taste in their places. "Avoid vases with rings," he also advises, "and never arrange them in pairs." It was all very complicated.

Among his many rules, Wen included some for the flowers you were allowed to put in your vase. These admonitions end with the severe caution that "any more than two stems and your room will end up looking like a tavern." The exuberance of the floral displays that Europeans gaily stuffed into their newly acquired Chinese porcelains, and that Dutch artists loved to paint when they weren't painting tavern scenes (and sometimes when they were) would have struck Wen as utterly tasteless and hopelessly lower class. Just imagine the dismay he would have felt over how Europeans used their teacups. Wen allowed that it was all right to put out fruit and nuts when drinking tea from one of Potter Cui's cups, for instance, but never oranges. Oranges were too fragrant to be served alongside tea, as was jasmine and cassia. In the war that Wen waged against bad taste, Europeans would have lost hands down.

Europeans could know nothing of these status games. They were too new to the art of owning porcelain to worry about anything except getting their hands on some. They had their rules too, but their cultural terrain of luxury ownership, at least in ceramic matters, was not so heavily mined. The precious pieces of porcelain that came out of the hold of the *Vlissingen* and were put on auction at VOC warehouses in 1613 were highly desired, regardless of their style or even their quality. The only cultural values they carried was that they were rare, exclusive, and expensive. Having no experience with porcelain, Europeans could let their new acquisitions migrate into whatever niches their buyers fancied. Chinese dishes started to appear on tables at meal times, since porcelain was marvelously easy to clean and did not pass on the flavor of yesterday's food to today's dinner. They were also put on display as costly curiosities from the far side of the globe. They decorated tables, display cabinets, mantles, even the lintels over doors. (Careful attention paid to doorframes in mid- to late-seventeenth-century paintings of Dutch interiors will reveal dishes or vases perched on them.) It would have been pointless to restrict the placing of fine vases to low Japanese-style tables, since Europeans had no idea what those were. They put them anywhere they liked.

These things mattered deeply to Wen Zhenheng. In his world of complex status distinctions, the superiority of the refined over the vulgar was always threatening to get lost whenever the uncultured rich asserted their power over the merely well educated. Wealth was no guard against vulgarity. On the contrary, as the ever-growing ranks of the nouveaux riches in the commercial age in which Wen found himself rushed to live ostentatiously without learning to live well, wealth was more likely to produce vulgarity than assist someone to buy his way out of it. The untutored ate off gold and silver plates without the least awareness that they were engaging in boorish display. They washed their calligraphy brushes in recently fired porcelain cups, when they really shouldn't have used porcelain at all, but jade or bronze—Wen allowed the use of a porcelain water pot only if it had been produced before 1435. These were tough rules. They favored the cultural insider with knowledge that the merely wealthy could not hope to gain—except, ironically, by buying a copy of *A Treatise on Superfluous Things*. In the war of status, the recently arrived were always at risk, since they did not get to the write the rules. On the other hand, at least they could play the game. The poor, after all, never got the chance.

Had Wen Zhenheng gone to the wharves along the Grand Canal, which ran through his city, to inspect the ceramic cargoes being shipped out to the Dutch, he would have ridiculed what he found. Most of it was carrack porcelain, made for export. Seen through Wen's eyes, carrack porcelain was too thick and clumsily painted, and the motifs with which it had been decorated lacked all delicacy. It was just the sort of junk that you could pawn off on foreigners who didn't know any better. A Suzhou gentleman would never have dreamed of passing around snacks in shoddily painted bowls with "high-quality item" written on the bottom (a mark a lot of the export pieces bore), or serving candied fruit on footed dishes with milky glazes pricked with perforations and bases bearing fake fifteenth-century dates, or pouring fine tea into cups that had been made only the year before. A snooty Beijing guidebook of 1635 allows that Jingdezhen potters are still able to turn out the occasional "fine piece" that would not embarrass its owner, but observes that the true connoisseur would do best to stay away from anything contemporary. When in doubt, old porcelain was usually the safer choice.

If Europeans were, by Chinese standards, poor judges of what was being unloaded from VOC ships, they were excellent judges by their own. For what could they compare the Chinese porcelain with but the rough, brittle earthenware plates and jugs that Italian and Flemish potters produced? These the Chinese wares surpassed in fineness, durability, style, color, and just about every other ceramic quality. They were beyond the capacity of any European craftsman to reproduce, which is why, as soon as a VOC ship reached Holland, people came from all over to buy these wares.

At the start of the seventeenth century, when porcelain first began to arrive in northern Europe, the prices it fetched were high enough to be out of reach of most people. In 1604, when Shakespeare has the comic Pompey in *Measure for Measure* regale Escalus and Angelo with a long-winded account of the last pregnancy of his employer, Mistress Overdone, he tells them that she called for prunes. "We had but two in the house, which at that very distant time stood, as it were, in a fruit-dish, a dish of some three-pence;—your honours have seen such dishes; they are not Chinese dishes, but very good dishes." Mistress Overdone did well enough as a procuress to be able to afford good dishes, but not Chinese porcelain. The line would not have worked even just a decade later, when Chinese porcelain starting flooding the European market and prices began to come down. As the author of a history of Amsterdam observed exactly ten years later, "the abundance of porcelain grows daily" such that Chinese dishes have "come to be with us in nearly daily use with the common people." By 1640, an Englishman visiting Amsterdam could testify that "any house of indifferent quality" was well supplied with Chinese porcelain.

The supply of porcelain was all because of what the Amsterdam author called "these navigations," which were changing the material lives of Europeans in ways and at a rate that often surprised them. This is why René Descartes was moved in 1631 to call Amsterdam an "inventory of the possible." The English traveler John Evelyn was equally impressed by Amsterdam when he visited the city a decade later. He marveled at the "innumerable Assemblys of Shipps, & Vessels which continualy ride before this Citty, which is certainely the most busie concourse of mortall men, now upon the face of the whole Earth & the most addicted to commerce." Amsterdam, however remarkable, was no great exception compared to other urban centers in Europe. When Evelyn visited Paris three years later, he was struck by "all the Curiosities naturall or artificial imaginable, Indian or European, for luxury or Use" that "are to be had for mony." In a market area along the Seine, he was particularly amazed by a shop called Noah's Ark in which he found a wonderful assortment of

"Cabinets, Shells, Ivorys, Purselan, Dried fishes, rare Insects, Birds, Pictures, and a thousand exotic extravagances." Purselan—porcelain—was one of the extravagances one could now easily buy.

The explosive growth of the market for Oriental manufactures soon began to affect their production. Chinese potters had for centuries been keenly aware of the importance of shaping their wares to foreign tastes, flattening the usual gourdlike shape of a vase to look like a Turkish flask, or building up dividers on plates to suit Japanese eating habits. As European demand grew, Chinese porcelain dealers in Southeast Asian ports learned what Europeans liked, then took that knowledge with them back to their suppliers on the mainland to redesign their products accordingly. When it came to supplying the foreign market, the potters of Jingdezhen were unconcerned about Wen Zhenheng's standards of Chinese taste. They wanted to know what would sell and were ready to change production by the next season to accommodate European taste. When Turkish tulips became all the rage in northern Europe in the 1620s, for example, Jingdezhen potters painted tulips on their dishes. Never having seen a real tulip, the porcelain painters produced blooms that are almost unrecognizable as tulips, but that didn't matter. The point was that they responded immediately to changes in the market. When the tulip market famously collapsed in 1637, the VOC rushed to cancel all orders for dishes decorated with tulips, for fear of being stuck with stock no one would buy.

One of the more striking hybrids to emerge from the potteries of Jingdezhen specifically designed to appeal to European taste is a large soup dish the Dutch called a klapmuts. The shape of this dish was reminiscent of the cheap wool felt hats worn by the lower classes in Holland, hence the name. Judging from the great number of klapmutsen in the *White Lion*'s hold, this was a popular item, and the name, though it gestured to something unsophisticated, stuck.

The Chinese had no use for such a dish. The problem was soup. Unlike European soup, Chinese soup is closer to broth than stew; it is a drink, not an entrée. Etiquette, therefore, permits lifting your bowl to your lips to drink it. This is why Chinese soup bowls have steep vertical sides: to make it easier to drink from the brim. European etiquette forbids lifting the bowl, hence the need for a big spoon specially designed for the purpose. But try to place a European spoon in a Chinese soup bowl and over it goes: the sides are too high and the center of gravity not low enough to balance the weight of the handle. Hence the flattened shape of the klapmuts, with the broad rim on which a European could rest his spoon without accident.

Chinese consumers were not much interested in the export ware made for the Europeans. If the odd piece circulated within China, it did so purely as a curiosity. The few carrack porcelains that have surfaced in two early-seventeenth-century Chinese graves probably came into their owners' possession for this reason. One serving plate decorated in the European style was found in the grave of a Ming prince who died in 1603, and two pairs of plates in the klapmuts style were found entombed with a provincial official. Both grave sites are in the province of Jiangxi, where the porcelain manufacturing center Jingdezhen was located, which helps to explain how these men got hold of these pieces. Why they wanted them is something we can only guess. They may have regarded the carrack style as a bit of tasty foreign exotica that happened to be locally available. There is an intriguing convergence here: the upper classes at the opposite ends of the Eurasian continent were both acquiring carrack porcelain, Chinese because they thought it embodied an exotic Western style, and Europeans because it seemed to them quintessentially Chinese.

Once VOC ships started delivering their ceramic loads more regularly in the 1610s, Chinese dishes did more than decorate tables, fill sideboards, and perch atop wardrobes: they appeared on Dutch canvases. The earliest Dutch painting showing a Chinese plate, by Pieter Isaacsz, was painted in 1599, several years before the first big auctions of captured Portuguese cargo were making these objects available to Dutch buyers. The first painting to display a klapmuts is a still life by Nicolaes Gillis painted two years later. Gillis has arranged a litter of fruits, nuts, jugs, and bowls on a table. To us it looks like any other

Dutch still life, but to a viewer in 1601, it featured a Chinese porcelain of the sort that only the wealthiest could afford, and that most Dutch people had never seen in real life, let alone touched. Gillis could not have afforded to own the piece he painted. It would be another two years before the cargo of the *San Iago* arrived in Amsterdam, and another decade before Chinese wares were priced within the reach of ordinary buyers. It is therefore likely that he was painting it on commission for the owner: not just a still life, then, but the portrait of a prized possession.

By the middle of the seventeenth century, a Dutch house was a house decorated with china. Art followed life, and painters put Chinese dishes into domestic scenes to lend a touch of class as well as a patina of reality. In Delft, Chinese porcelain started to become available before Vermeer's lifetime. The flagship of the Delft Chamber of the VOC, the *Wapen van Delft*, sailed twice to Asia, returning in 1627 and 1629 with a combined load of fifteen thousand pieces of porcelain, some of which would have remained locally. The largest personal collection in the city belonged to Niclaes Verburg, the director of the Delft Chamber. Verburg could afford whatever his ships brought to Rotterdam and his barges floated up to Delft, for when he died in 1670, he was the richest man in Delft.

Though not quite in Verburg's league, Maria Thins aspired that her house should meet current standards of elegant taste. If Vermeer's canvases are anything to go by, the Thins-Vermeer household owned several pieces. The klapmuts in *Young Woman Reading a Letter at an Open Window* also appears in *A Woman Asleep*, so that was probably a family possession. The household may also have owned a blue-and-white Chinese ewer, or pitcher, for one appears behind a lute on a table in *Girl Interrupted at Her Music*. This could not have come directly from the VOC, however, as a European craftsman has gilded the lily by adding a silver lid. There is also a carrack-style ginger jar sitting on the table at the left-hand side of *Woman with a Pearl Necklace*. The curving reflection of an unseen window to the left on the surface of the jar shows why Vermeer, who was so captivated by light, must have enjoyed painting something as lustrous as a Chinese pot. On the same table, directly in front of the woman with the necklace, there is a small bowl with steep curving sides—evidence of yet a fourth Chinese piece in the Thins-Vermeer collection?

THE PORCELAINS THAT VOC SHIPS brought back to Europe were expensive items of conspicuous consumption that fell into the hands only of those who could afford them. For everyone else, European ceramics producers came up with import substitutes to cash in on the taste for things Chinese. Among the most successful were the potters and tile makers of Delft. They were descendants of sixteenth-century Italians from Faenza (which gave its name to the polychrome earthenware known as faïence) who had migrated north to Antwerp in the sixteenth century looking for work, and continued farther north to escape the Spanish military efforts to suppress Dutch independence. They brought their knowledge of ceramics production with them and were able to set up kilns in Delft's renowned breweries, many of which had been forced to close down as working-class taste shifted from beer to gin. In these newly converted potteries, they began to experiment with imitations of the new ceramic aesthetic coming from China, and buyers liked what they produced.

Delft potters were unable to match the quality of Chinese blue-and-white, but they did manage to produce passable imitations at a low price. Delftware became the affordable substitute for ordinary people who wanted Chinese porcelain but in the early years of the VOC trade could not dream of acquiring more than a few pieces. Delft potters did not just imitate; they also innovated. Their biggest success at the low end of the market was blue-and-white wall tiles for the new houses that the Delft bourgeoisie were building. The blue of these tiles exuded an enticing whiff of Chineseness, and the sketching style in which the figures were painted onto their surfaces vaguely replicated what people might have thought of as Chinese. Anthony Bailey puts it nicely in his biography of Vermeer. "Seldom has long-distance plagiarism produced such an original result—the creation of a type of folk art." The industry boomed. By the time Vermeer was painting, a quarter of the city's labor force was engaged in one way or another with the ceramics trade. Delft porcelain sold well and widely among those who could not afford the Chinese product, and the city's name traveled with the product. Dishes in England became known as "china," but in Ireland they were called "delph."

Delft tiles appear in five of Vermeer's paintings. As painters and ceramic tile makers were members of the same artisans' guild, St. Luke's, of which Vermeer was a headman, he certainly knew the men who owned the kilns. He would even have known some of the ceramic painters, who enjoyed a status above ordinary tile makers. Vermeer seems to have enjoyed the whimsical sketches that decorate the tiles—buildings and ships, cupids and soldiers, men peeing and angels smoking—since he reproduces some of these in his own paintings. He seems to have loved the cobalt blue they used, as it became one of his trademarks as a colorist. Perhaps in his use of cobalt blue and his detailed re-creations of light on shining surfaces we begin to see the first hints of a decorative style known as chinoiserie that would overwhelm European taste in the eighteenth century.

Absent concrete evidence, we can still imagine that as a working artist living in one of the VOC chamber towns, Vermeer saw examples of Chinese painting. We know that several Chinese paintings made it into the collection of Niclaes Verburg, the Delft VOC director, but these are unlikely to have been shown outside his home. Still, some images of what the Chinese regarded as beautiful must have been brought back by curious sailors and circulated in the public realm. John Evelyn reports that he saw unusual foreign pictures in Noah's Ark in Paris. Were there Chinese paintings among them? When a satirist in Amsterdam amused his readers by imagining "a painting in which twelve mandarins were sketched with a single stroke of the brush," he expected his readers to be familiar with the bold, flowing brushstrokes of Chinese artists. If Chinese paintings were circulating in the Netherlands, surely Vermeer would have managed to see them.

The circulation of decorative objects did not go only from China to Europe. European objects and pictures circulated in China too. On 5 March 1610, while the *White Lion* was on its third voyage from Amsterdam to Asia, and a few years before Wen Zhenheng started writing his *Treatise on Superfluous Things*, an art dealer called Merchant Xia paid a call on a favored customer. Li Rihua was a renowned amateur painter and a wealthy art collector living in Jiaxing, a small city on the Yangtze Delta southwest of Shanghai. Li moved in the same social circles as the Wen family and probably knew the author of *Superfluous Things*. He was one of Merchant Xia's regular customers, having bought paintings and antiquities from him over a long stretch of years. Xia was just back from Nanjing, the center of the antiques and curiosities trade at the opposite end of the Yangtze Delta. He brought a selection of rarities for Li to view: a porcelain wine cup from the 1470s; an old bronze water dripper of the sort calligraphers used to thin their ink, which was fashioned in the shape of a crouching tiger; and two greenish earrings the size of a thumb. Xia assured Li that the earrings were a rare type of crystal from a kiln that produced such things only in the 950s, implying that he expected them to fetch a high price.

Li liked most of the things on offer, but he quickly realized that Merchant Xia was wrong about the earrings. He decided to have fun with Xia by pretending to examine them with due care, and then pointing out that they were made of glass. Not only were the earrings not tenth-century antiques; they were not even Chinese. As Li wrote in his diary later that day, "These items were brought here on foreign ships coming from the south—items of foreign manufacture, in fact. The glass objects you find these days are all the work of the foreigners from the Western [Atlantic] Ocean, who make them by melting stone, and not naturally produced treasures." Li enjoyed getting the better of Merchant Xia, but not out of malice. He knew that forgery was all part of the game of buying and selling antiques, and quite enjoyed the fact that this time it was the dealer who had been fooled, not the customer. Merchant Xia left suitably chastened, and

probably embarrassed more for having paid a high price for the earrings in Nanjing than for trying to sell them to someone as alert as
Li Rihua.

Does this anecdote demonstrate that the Chinese were not curious
about foreign objects? Not at all. We have to realize what Li was doing when he collected. For him, the point of collecting was to discover objects that confirmed the cultural authority of the ancients; this
was why authenticity was so important to him. He wanted things that
connected him to better times, which were always in the past. What
the anecdote does show is that foreign articles circulated in China in
the seventeenth century. If they were reaching Nanjing and then circulating out in the hands of traveling dealers to the surrounding cities,
there must have been some sort of market for them. They did not circulate on the scale that foreign manufactures did in Europe, but then
they reached China in much smaller volume. Also, unlike in Europe,
where roughly a century of plunder and trade around the world had
trained Europeans into becoming connoisseurs of foreign curiosities,
demand for such objects in China was not well developed. Foreign
things were not out of bounds for Chinese collectors. Wen Zhenheng
encourages the readers of *Superfluous Things* to acquire certain foreign
objects. He recommends brushes and writing paper from Korea, and
he advocates owning a wide range of Japanese objects from folding
fans, bronze rulers, and steel scissors to lacquered boxes and fine furniture. Foreign origin was not a barrier to appreciation.

If foreign objects were a "problem" in China, it was not due to
some deeply embedded Chinese disdain for foreign things. It had to
do with the pliable nature of things themselves. Objects of beauty
were valued to the extent that they could carry cultural meanings; in
the case of antiques, meanings having to do with balance and decorum and a veneration of the past. Antiques were valued because they
brought their owners into physical contact with a golden past from
which the present had fallen away. Given the burden of meaning that
objects had to carry, it was difficult to discern what value to attribute
to objects coming from abroad. Rarity was a quality to be prized, and

curiosity about things marvelous or strange was a laudable impulse for the collector, but the essential impulse for collecting was to bring oneself into contact with the core values of civilization. This is why Wen could recommend Korean and Japanese objects to his readers. China had a long history of cultural interaction with Korea and Japan, so Korean and Japanese things could be seen as sharing in the same civilizational ethos as Chinese things. They were different, but the difference was tame. It did not slide from the odd to the bizarre.

The same could not be said for European things. Li Rihua was not indifferent to knowing about what lay beyond China's shores; indeed, his diary includes numerous remarks about what he heard concerning foreign ships and sailors who wandered into Chinese coastal waters. But the objects coming from foreign lands had no place in his symbolic system. They embodied no values. They were merely curious. In Europe, by contrast, Chinese things had a greater impact. There, difference became an invitation to acquire. Europeans felt inclined to incorporate them into their living spaces, and even beyond that, to revise their aesthetic standards. The dish that Vermeer set in the foreground of *Young Woman Reading a Letter at an Open Window* is a foreign thing, nestled in turn within the Turkish carpet, another foreign thing. These objects stirred no contempt or anxiety. They were beautiful, and they came from places where beautiful things were made and could be bought. That was all, and enough to make them worth buying.

If there was a place for such foreign objects in European rooms, there wasn't in Chinese rooms. This issue was not ultimately one of aesthetics or culture. It was the relationship with the wider world that each could afford to have. Dutch merchants with the full backing of the Dutch state were traveling the globe and bringing back to the wharves of the Kolk marvelous evidence of what the other side of the world might be like. The people of Delft looked on Chinese dishes as totems of their good fortune and happily displayed them in their homes. Of course they were beautiful, and taking pleasure in that beauty was what Dutch householders liked to do. But the dishes were also symbolic of a positive relationship to the world.

What did Li Rihua see, as he looked beyond the wharves of his native Jiaxing, other than a coast beset by pirates? From where he stood, that wider world was a source of threat, not of promise or wealth, and still less of delight or inspiration. He had no reason to own symbols of that threat and place them around his studio. For Europeans, on the other hand, it was worth no little danger and expense to get their hands on Chinese goods. Which is why, four years after the sinking of the *White Lion*, Admiral Lam was back in the South China Sea looting Iberian ships and seizing Chinese vessels in the hope of acquiring more.

Geography Lessons

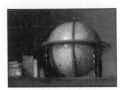

THERE IS ONE painting by Vermeer, *The Geographer* (see plate 4), that requires little effort to locate signs of the wider world that was enveloping and invading Delft. The painting opens conventionally on the artist's studio, the same closed space we expect to find in a Vermeer painting where bright windows again have been painted at an angle so oblique that their panes transmit no image of what lies in the street outside. This time, however, the room is cluttered with objects that gesture exuberantly to a broader world. The drama that Vermeer sets on his stage is not about the engagements of love, the theme in the two preceding paintings, or about the drive for moral perfection, which will animate another painting that we will soon examine. It is about a different drive altogether, the desire to understand the world: not the world of domestic interiors, or even of Delft, but the expansive lands into which traders and travelers were going and from which they were bringing back wondrous things and amazing new information. The things engaged the eye, but the information engaged the mind, and the great minds of Vermeer's generation were absorbing it all and learning to see the world in fresh ways. They were making new measurements, proposing new theories, and building new models on scales that stretched macroscopically as far as the entire globe and microscopically into the mysterious depths that were beginning to be revealed in a drop of rain or a mite of dust.

This is what *The Geographer* is about. It is no surprise, then, that it evokes in the viewer a mood different from those of Vermeer's other paintings. He has characteristically constructed the canvas around a figure who is absorbed in his own doings and is not posing for the viewer. Still, the sense of intimacy of the other paintings isn't there. We are drawn to the geographer as he pauses to cogitate, just as we are drawn to the young woman who reads her letter, but we don't really enter onto a deeper plane of reflection. Perhaps with *The Geographer* (and its companion painting, *The Astronomer*) Vermeer intended to move into new subject matter but hadn't quite figured out how to make the intellectual drama an emotional experience for the viewer. The passion to know the world by mapping it was not quite as compelling for viewers, or the artist, as the passion to know another person through love. Perhaps the paintings were commissioned by a buyer who fancied owning images of the new thirst for scientific knowledge, which left Vermeer feeling undermotiviated. Indeed, perhaps they were commissioned by the man who posed for them, by best guess the Delft draper, surveyor, and polymath, Antonie van Leeuwenhoek.

Leeuwenhoek's surname was his address: "at the corner by Lion's Gate," which was the next gate to the right of the pair of gates shown in *View of Delft*. He is best known for the experiments he conducted with lenses, for which he is credited today as the father of microbiology. No documentary evidence directly links Vermeer and Leeuwenhoek, yet the circumstantial evidence that they were friends is strong. The fact that the two men were born in the same month, lived in the same part of town, and had friends in common might not be enough to convince the skeptical. But Leeuwenhoek played a key role after Vermeer's death. Vermeer died when his business as a painter and art dealer was at a low ebb. His widow, Catharina, had to file for bankruptcy two months later, and when she did, the town aldermen appointed Leeuwenhoek to administer the estate. Judging from a later portrait, the man who has pushed back the Turkish carpet on the table and bends over a map with a set of surveyor's dividers in his hand is Leeuwenhoek. Even if he weren't, Leeuwenhoek was just the sort of person the painting lionizes.

The signs of the wider world are everywhere. The document that the geographer has spread out before him is indecipherable, but it is clearly a map. A sea chart on vellum is loosely rolled to his right under the window. Two rolled-up charts lie on the floor behind him. A sea chart of the coasts of Europe—the subject becomes apparent when you realize that the top of the map points west, not north—hangs on the back wall. The original of this sea chart has not been found, but it is similar to one produced by Willem Blaeu, the commercial map publisher in Amsterdam who printed the map on the back wall of *Officer and Laughing Girl*, among many others. A terrestrial globe literally caps the entire painting. This is the 1618 edition of a globe published by Hendrick Hondius in 1600.

Vermeer includes just enough detail on the Hondius globe to show that it is turned to expose what Hondius calls the Orientalus Oceanus, the Eastern Ocean, which we know today as the Indian Ocean. Navigating this ocean was a great challenge for Dutch navigators in the opening years of the seventeenth century. The Portuguese route to Southeast Asia ran around the Cape of Good Hope and up past Madagascar, following the arc of the coastline. This route had the advantage of many landfalls, but it was hampered by unfavorable currents and winds and was under Portuguese control, however unevenly defended. In 1610, a Dutch mariner discovered another route. This involved dropping down from the cape to 40 degrees southern latitude and picking up the prevailing westerlies, which, combined with the West Wind Current, could speed a ship across the bottom of the Indian Ocean, then veering north to Java on the southeast trades, bypassing India entirely. The route to the Spice Islands was thereby shortened by several months.

The cartouche (the ornamental scroll with an inscription that many a cartographer of the time used to fill in the empty areas of a map) on the lower part of the globe is illegible in the painting, but can be read on a surviving copy of this globe. In it Hondius has printed in his defense a brief explanation as to why this globe differs from the version he published in 1600. "Since very frequent expeditions are started every day to all parts of the world, by which their positions are clearly seen and reported, I trust that it will not appear strange to anyone if this description differs very much from others previously published by us." Hondius then appeals to the enthusiastic amateurs who played a significant role in compiling this knowledge. "We ask the benevolent reader that, if he should have a more complete knowledge of some place, he willingly communicate the same to us for the sake of increasing the public good." An increase in the public good was also an increase in sales, of course, but no one at the time minded the one overlapping the other if that made the product more reliable. There was a new world out there, and knowledge of it was worth paying for, especially as one of the tangible costs of ignorance was shipwreck.

THE SPANISH JESUIT Adriano de las Cortes experienced the consequence of having less than "complete knowledge" of the South China Sea on the morning of 16 February 1625, when *Nossa Senhora da Guía* was driven onto the rocks of the Chinese coast. The *Guía* was a Portuguese vessel on its way from the Spanish colony of Manila in the Philippines to the Portuguese colony of Macao at the mouth of the Pearl River. The ship had departed from Manila three weeks earlier, tacking up the west side of the island of Luzon and then heading west across the South China Sea to China. On the third day crossing the open water, a cold fog becalmed the ship. The navigator should have carried the charts he needed to make the well-traveled crossing from Manila to Macao, but charts were only as good as the bearings he could take from the sun and stars. The combination of fog, slowdown, and drift defeated him. Approximating his distance from the equator was not too difficult, but estimating where the ship was between east and west was impossible. (The instrumentation needed to determine longitude at sea was not developed for another century and a half.) The wind came back up two days later, but then it whipped into a gale so fierce that it blew the ship even farther off

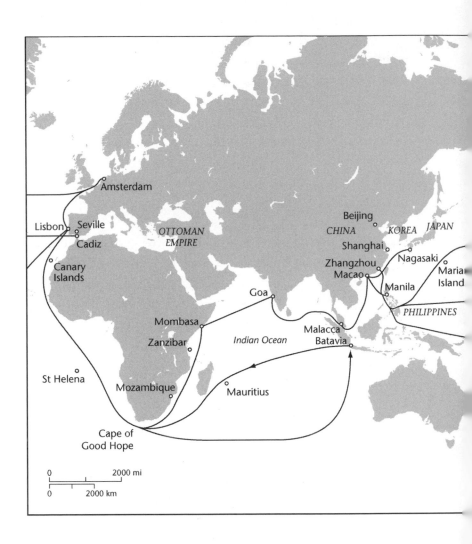

Amsterdam

Lisbon
Seville
Cadiz

OTTOMAN
EMPIRE

Beijing
CHINA
KOREA
JAPAN
Shanghai
Zhangzhou
Nagasaki
Macao
Maria
Island
Manila

Canary
Islands

Goa

PHILIPPINES

Mombasa
Zanzibar

Indian Ocean

Malacca
Batavia

St Helena

Mozambique

Mauritius

Cape of
Good Hope

0   2000 mi

0   2000 km

GLOBAL TRADE ROUTES IN

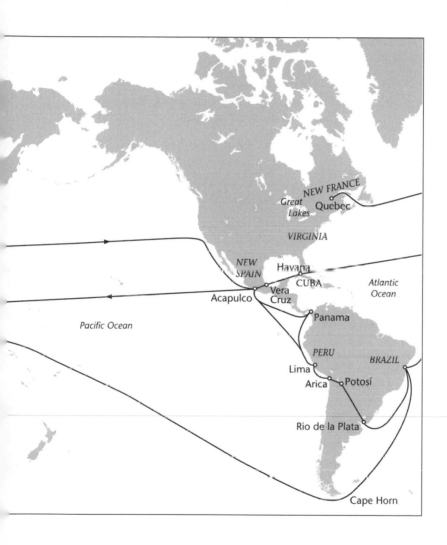

NEW FRANCE

Great Lakes

Quebec

VIRGINIA

NEW SPAIN

Havana

CUBA

Vera Cruz

Acapulco

Panama

Atlantic Ocean

Pacific Ocean

PERU

BRAZIL

Lima

Arica

Potosí

Rio de la Plata

Cape Horn

THE SEVENTEENTH CENTURY

its course. The *Guía*'s pilot had no way to reckon their position and could do nothing but wait until land came into sight and try to figure out their location from the profile of the shoreline.

Two hours before dawn on 16 February, the gale unexpectedly drove the ship onto the China coast. The place was uncharted and unknown to those on board. Only later would the survivors learn that they had run aground three hundred and fifty kilometers northeast of their destination, Macao. The water where the ship broke up was shallow enough that most of the over two hundred people taking passage on the *Guía* were able to get to shore. Only fifteen failed to make it: several sailors, several slaves (one of whom was female), a few Tagals from Manila, two Spaniards, and a young Japanese boy.

The inhabitants of a nearby fishing village came down to the shore to stare at the host of foreign people coming ashore, giving them a wide berth as they scrambled out of the waves. Most may never have seen foreigners at close range before, as this spot on this coast was off the two main sea-lanes handling foreign trade, one from Macao to Japan, and the other to the Philippines from Moon Harbor (now Amoy), which lay two hundred kilometers in the opposite direction from Macao. The fishing people living along this coast were aware that foreigners were sailing in these waters. They would have heard about the Portuguese in Macao (official Chinese discourse called them the Aoyi, the Macanese Foreigners) and known that they were unlikely to be attacked by these people. Those they feared were the Wokou, or Dwarf Pirates (the colloquial term for Japanese), and the terrible Hongmao, or Red Hairs (a recently coined name for the Dutch). Dwarf Pirates had been raiding the coast for a century in reaction to the Chinese government's 1525 ban on maritime trade with Japan. They were feared for their skill as swordsmen. Local people still told the story of a dozen sword-wielding Japanese who managed to kill three hundred Chinese militiamen sent against them. The Red Hairs excited an even greater fear. The Dutch had been preying along this coast only in the last two or three years but they had quickly established a reputation for being violent and dangerous. The Chinese name for these people tells us what most struck Chinese when they saw Dutchmen. Among Chinese, black is the normal color for hair. As Portuguese tended also to be dark haired, they were considered simply ugly rather than bizarre. The same could not be said for the Dutch, whose blond and reddish hair was a shock to Chinese eyes. Anyone with hair this color was a Red Hair, and therefore Dutch, and therefore dangerous.

Red Hairs, Dwarf Pirates, and Macanese Foreigners were not all that came ashore. Scattered among them were another category altogether: Heigui, or Black Ghosts. These were the African slaves who worked as servants of the Portuguese and who were ubiquitous in the European colonies in East Asia. Truly unlike any person the Chinese had ever seen, they were feared above the rest.

The sight of these foreigners stalled the villagers only briefly. Their eyes quickly turned to the chests and barrels floating ashore with the survivors. They began hauling the flotsam up the beach and scavenging through the cargo. Soon enough the local militia arrived carrying swords and arquebuses. Their duty was to keep the survivors at the site where they came ashore until a military commander showed up to take charge. They too were interested in picking up whatever might have washed ashore from the shipwreck. As the scavengers had beaten them to the cargo, the militiamen turned on the sodden survivors, frisking some and strip-searching others for the silver and jewels they suspected must be hidden on them. The survivors were at first too exhausted and frightened to do anything but comply, though a few quietly resisted. Before the militiamen had a chance to find much, the survivors gathered together and began to walk inland.

Fearing they would be punished for failing to control the crowd, the militiamen began to throw stones and jab their spears to make them understand that they should remain on the beach. Still the crowd of two hundred foreigners pressed forward. The Chinese arquebusiers opened fire. One hit his target, a Dwarf Pirate, though the gunpowder charge was so weak that the ball simply buried itself in the man's clothing without doing any damage. The militia's swords were more effective. A Portuguese sailor named Francesco was stabbed and then beheaded. He was the first of the survivors to die at the hands of their captors. Then a Macanese by the name of Miguel Xuarez was speared. A priest took Xuarez in his arms, but militiamen hauled him away and decapitated him.

A military officer finally arrived on horseback with a small retinue. Benito Barbosa, captain of the *Guía*, hurried toward the officer to appeal for mercy for his passengers and crew, but the officer brandished his sword in a show of intimidation and ordered his attendants to slice a piece off Barbosa's ear, marking him as a prisoner. There would be no negotiation; only surrender.

Then the shakedown began in earnest. Militiamen freely moved among the shipwrecked survivors, searching them and grabbing whatever they could find. Some had managed to come ashore with a little of their wealth, and most surrendered it when accosted—but not everyone. Ismaël, an Indian Muslim merchant from Goa, had already removed an outer garment and folded it into a parcel. The parcel attracted the suspicious notice of a militiaman. Ismaël refused to hand it over, and in the tug of war that ensued, the bundle slipped from his grip. Out fell six or seven silver pesos. Furious at being resisted, the militiaman ended the tussle by cutting off Ismaël's head. Budo, another Indian merchant from Goa, got caught in a similar struggle. One of the militiamen guessed correctly that Budo had hidden something in his mouth. When the militiamen tried to force his mouth open, Budo spat two rings on the ground and then kicked them into the sand to make them disappear. The disappointed militiaman feigned indifference, but ten minutes later, slipped up behind Budo and lopped off his head, carrying it aloft as a trophy.

Others perished for reasons besides holding back their wealth. A man named Suconsaba and a Franciscan layman born near Goa had sustained injuries during the shipwreck and were near death by the time they made it ashore. According to Adriano de las Cortes, the Spanish Jesuit who wrote a memoir of the wreck of the *Guía*, "several of us suspected that they weren't yet dead when the Chinese sliced off both their heads." Masmamut Ganpti, who may have been a slave of the ship's owner, Gonçalo Ferreira, made it ashore without incident but got into trouble defending his master against militiamen who tried to take his clothes. The Chinese responded by grabbing him, chopping off his hands and feet as punishment for attacking them, then cutting off his head. Ganpti, whom Las Cortes describes as "a Moorish sailor" and "a brave Black," died "for no reason and without having given the Chinese the least pretext." Another of Ferreira's attendants suffered the same fate, not for challenging the militiamen but for being too weak to keep up when the Chinese later force marched the survivors inland.

The list of those drowned and murdered that morning consists of people identified as Moors, Blacks, Goans, South Asian Muslims, Macanese, Portuguese, Spaniards, slaves, Tagals, and Japanese.[1] The casualty list is in effect a short summary of the *Guía*'s remarkably diverse passenger list. Ninety-one on board were Portuguese. Some of them were born in Macao or lived and worked there, while others hailed from Portuguese colonies scattered around the globe, from the Canary Islands to Goa and Macao. The only other Europeans on board were six Spaniards. A mutual agreement between Spain and Portugal restricted the ships of one from carrying the nationals of the other, but this agreement was ignored as the need arose, especially when the people involved were priests or Catholic laymen on mission business, as all six were. One of the six had come from as far away as Mexico.

The Europeans made up slightly less than half the passenger list. The next largest group on the ship were sixty-nine Japanese—the Dwarf Pirates. The Portuguese in Macao hired Japanese in significant numbers to handle their business dealings with the Chinese. They could write Chinese characters and therefore do a better job of communicating the details of a business arrangement than the Portuguese. Their physical features also meant that Japanese were able to move more freely among Chinese than Europeans were. They even sometimes slipped into the interior, avoiding detection as Portuguese never

could. Las Cortes knew one of the Japanese, a Catholic priest named
Miguel Matsuda. It was he who was miraculously saved when his
clothing stopped an arquebus ball. Banished by the Japanese government to the Philippines in 1614 for converting to Christianity, Matsuda trained with Jesuit missionaries in Manila to become a priest.
Now he was on his way to Macao with the plan of returning to Nagasaki on a Portuguese ship and infiltrating his way back into Japan
to spread Christian teachings. It was a dangerous mission, and would
end in Japan with Matsuda's capture and execution.

Next most numerous, after the Japanese and the Europeans, were
the group to which Ismaël and Budo belonged: thirty-four Muslim
merchants from the Portuguese colony of Goa in India, two of
whom were traveling with their wives. Finally, Las Cortes mentions
in passing "Indians from around Manila" (Tagals), Moors, Blacks, and
Jews, without giving numbers for these people.

The extraordinary cross section of humanity on the *Guía*'s passenger list reveals who was moving through the network of trade that
Portuguese shipping sustained. Had Las Cortes not taken the trouble
to write an account of the shipwreck, and had his manuscript not
been preserved in the British Library, we would not know of the extraordinary mix of people traveling on the *Guía*. The ship's owner
and captain were Portuguese, but their passengers were a remarkably
international crowd, from as far east as Mexico to as far west as the
Canary Islands. Las Cortes's memoir thus reveals that the majority of
people on what we would identify as a "Portuguese ship" weren't
Portuguese at all, but people from literally everywhere on the globe.
The *Guía* was not exceptional, for other records reveal the same thing.
The last successful Portuguese trade vessel to Japan, which sailed in
1638, consisted of ninety Portuguese and a hundred and fifty "half-
castes, Negroes, and colored people," to quote from another such
record. European ships may have dominated the sea-lanes of the seventeenth century, but Europeans were only ever in a minority on
board.

The villagers on shore were amazed by the microcosm of people from all over the globe, who gathered out of the waves. From the villagers' reactions, Las Cortes supposed that they "had never before seen foreigners or people from other nations." He guessed that "none of them had ever gone to other countries, and most had never even left their homes." The two worlds that encountered each other on the beach that February morning existed at opposite ends of the range of global experience available in the seventeenth century: at one pole, those who had lived their lives entirely within their own cultural boundaries; at the other, those who crossed those boundaries on a daily basis and mixed constantly with peoples of different origins, skin colors, languages, and habits.

As we have no record of how these villagers reacted to the sight of Europeans, we can only fill in the gap with descriptions from other contexts. This is one Chinese writer's impression of Spanish merchants visiting Macao: "They have long bodies and high noses, with cat's eyes and beaked mouths, curly hair and red whiskers. They love doing business. When making a trade they just hold up several fingers [to show the price], and even if the deal runs to thousands of ounces of silver they do not bother with a contract. In every undertaking they point to heaven as their surety, and they never renege. Their clothes are elegant and clean." This author then does his best to assimilate these Europeans to a history with which he is familiar. As these men were from what Chinese called the Great West (Europe), which lay beyond the Little West (India), they must be linked to India in some way. The writer may have picked up some snippets of Christian beliefs, for he goes on to suggest that the Spaniards must originally have been Buddhists, but that they had lost their identity and in religious matters now had access only to corrupt doctrines.

If the white men were a curiosity, black men were a shock. "Our Blacks especially intrigued them," writes Las Cortes. "They never stopped being amazed to see that when they washed themselves, they did not become whiter." (Las Cortes traveled with a black servant.

Are his own prejudices showing through?) Chinese at the time had
several terms to name such people. As all foreigners could be called
"ghost" (*gui*), they were simply Black Ghosts. They were also called
Kunlun Slaves, using a term coined a thousand years earlier for dark-
skinned foreigners from India, which was a land that lay beyond the
Kunlun Mountains at the southwestern limit of China. Li Rihua, the
collector from Jiaxing who recognized the glass earrings his dealer
was trying to pass off as ancient Chinese wares, lived on the Yangtze
Delta well to the north and had never seen a black, but he notes in his
diary that they were called *luting* (a term for which the etymology is
lost), and that they swam so well that fishermen used them to lure real
fish into their nets. Every fishing family in south China owns one, Li
was told.

The Chinese geographer Wang Shixing provides a slightly more
reliable description. He pictures black men in Macao as having "bodies like lacquer. The only parts left white are their eyes." He gives
them a fearsome reputation. "If a slave's master ordered him to cut
his own throat, then he would do it without thinking whether he
should or not. It is in their nature to be deadly with knives. If the
master goes out and orders his slave to protect his door, then even if
flood or fire should overwhelm him, he will not budge. Should someone give the door the merest push, the slave will kill him, regardless of
whether or not theft is involved." Wang also mentions their underwater prowess, echoing Li Rihua. "They are good at diving," he writes,
"and can retrieve things from the water when a rope is tied around
their waists." The final thing he records about them is their high
price. "It takes fifty or sixty ounces of silver to buy one," a price calculated to amaze his readers, since that sum could buy fifteen head
of oxen.

Wang includes this information in his encyclopedic survey of Chinese geography to document the variety of places and people that can
be found within China's borders, which includes Macao. Li Rihua
includes his data for a different purpose: to illustrate his conviction

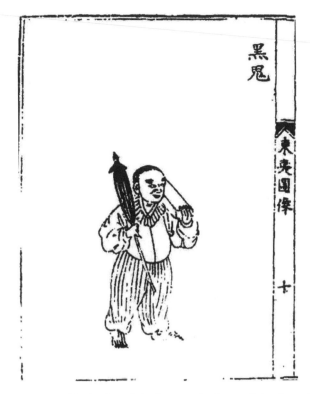

An engraving of a "black ghost," in the terminology of the time, dressed as a Portuguese servant in Macao, from Cai Ruxian's *Illustrated Account of the Eastern Foreigners* of 1586. Cai enjoyed the high post of provincial administration commissioner of Guangdong. This may be the earliest Chinese representation of an African.

that "within heaven and earth strange things appear from time to time; that the number of things in creation is not fixed from the start." Li grasped that he lived in a time when traditional categories of knowledge did not exhaust everything that existed in the world and new categories might be needed to make sense of the novelties coming into the ken of seventeenth-century Chinese. Unfortunately, even comically, much of this knowledge was hearsay. Li's description of Dutchmen—"they have red hair and black faces, and the soles of their feet are over two feet long"—presents an omnibus stereotype of a foreigner rather than information that could be called useful knowledge.

THE FIRST DAYS OF CAPTIVITY were grueling. The military officer was in no mood to be lenient. He was also unwilling to keep them in his own custody any longer than he had to in case his superiors found fault with his procedures, so he marched them off to Jinghai Garrison, one of a series of walled military posts along this stretch of the coast. The garrison commander examined them, but having no interpreter he learned very little. He too judged that it was safer to assume the worst than to later be found to have been carelessly lenient, so he dismissed their claim that they were innocent traders and treated them as the pirates he assumed they were. He in turn sent them up the ladder of command to the officials in the Chaozhou prefectural seat, who put them, and the Jinghai commander, through several days of close questioning. Again there was no interpreter, though after several days officials in Chaozhou were able to locate a Chinese who had worked in Macao and knew enough Portuguese to do basic translation. To everyone's surprise, the man recognized one of the Macao merchants, the Portuguese-born António Viegas, who had sold him cloves several years earlier. Then an officer came forward who had worked as a cobbler in Manila and knew enough Spanish to translate for the Spaniards. (Las Cortes was surprised that he wasn't too embarrassed to admit his profession, as Spaniards regarded shoe repair as a demeaning trade and would deny having such a disreputable past if they could.) The cobbler-turned-officer was a sympathetic soul, who intervened discreetly on the foreigners' behalf to better their situation. Chaozhou officials also found a man who had worked among the Chinese merchants in Nagasaki and had married a Japanese woman, who was able to translate for the *Guía*'s Japanese passengers.

The Jinghai commander laid out his charge of piracy before his superiors in Chaozhou. He claimed that the foreigners had started the fighting, attacking the militia like pirates and resisting arrest for an entire day. They had also carried silver ashore and buried it for future use. Being of so many different nationalities, they could not be on legitimate business but had to be a gang of desperadoes who had banded together to plunder. Two or three of them were blond, indisputable evidence that there were Red Hairs among them. Finally, no one could deny that the band included a large number of Japanese, who were absolutely forbidden to come ashore. The circumstantial evidence was that these were pirates, and that the commander had brilliantly apprehended them before they could do any damage.

The prefectural officials then wanted to hear from the survivors, particularly on the matter of the hidden silver. When asked whether any Chinese had taken any silver from him, a Portuguese priest named Luis de Ángulo stated that the militiaman who captured him had taken the fifty pesos he was carrying in his clothes. As soon as this came out and was translated, all the Jinghai soldiers present threw themselves on their knees and violently protested that none of them had done any such thing, as stealing a captive's property in the line of duty was a serious offense. At this point, all the interpreters asked to withdraw. They knew what the Jinghai soldiers would do to them if any more of the truth were to come out. It was enough to make the officials suspicious of the commander's story, and as other stories of theft surfaced in subsequent questioning, their suspicions grew. Now the investigation was turned in the other direction, and it was the Jinghai commander who was under scrutiny.

In any matter concerning foreigners, no final judgment could be reached at the prefectural level. The case had to be referred to the provincial authorities in Canton before any decision was made about releasing Las Cortes and the others to Macao. The process would end up taking a year.

ANXIETY ABOUT SEABORNE FOREIGNERS WAS not restricted to fishermen or officials charged with protecting that coast against smugglers and pirates. Lu Zhaolong, a native of Xiangshan, the county in which Macao was located, was a highly educated member of the Cantonese gentry who rose through the ranks of the bureaucracy during the

1620s to a secretarial posting in the central government. There is no reason to suppose that the story of the wreck of the *Guía* reached him, though this being an international incident, a report would have had to be sent to the court. Regardless, Lu kept abreast of what was going on in his home county, if only to keep an eye on the interests of his family and friends.

The presence of so many foreigners along the coast troubled Lu. So too did the far greater number of Chinese who were more than content to truck and barter with these pirates, especially with the Red Hairs. The Chinese in fact knew little about these people. The first account of a country called "Helan" (Holland) to appear in the Veritable Records, the daily court diary, appears in an entry from the summer of 1623. Although the report concedes that "their intention does not go beyond desiring Chinese commodities," court officials were anxiously aware of the Red Hairs as yet another uncontrollable presence along the coast. Some, such as Lu Zhaolong, wanted all the foreigners gone, not just the Red Hairs.

In June 1630, five years after the wreck of the *Guía*, Lu Zhaolong sent up the first of a series of four memorials, or policy recommendations, to Emperor Chongzhen. At this time the court was embroiled in a foreign policy controversy over where the real danger lay: south or north. Who was the greater threat to the regime: the European and Japanese traders on the south coast, or the Mongolian and Tungusic warriors on the northern border? This was a recurring conundrum for Chinese policy makers, and the answer determined the direction in which military resources should flow. Recent developments on both borders were forcing the question. The northern foreigners, who would soon adopt the ethnic name of Manchu, had taken most of the land beyond the Great Wall and were even now raiding across it at will. The Red Hairs, Macanese Foreigners, and Dwarf Pirates were disturbing the southeast coast. There was no Great Wall of China along the shore, behind which the military forces of the Ming dynasty could hunker down and hold a defensive position. There was only the open coast. Much of that coast was inhospitable to large ships, yet there were island anchorages enough where ships from the Great Western Ocean could make deals with Chinese merchants and thumb their noses at foreign trade regulations.

Lu Zhaolong was sure that the greater threat to China lay in the south rather than in the north. As a supervising censor assigned to oversee the operations of the Ministry of Rites, the arm of the Ming government charged with handling relations with foreigners, he was in a position to know what was going on there. And this ministry, over the 1620s, had regularly shown itself willing to find accommodation with the Portuguese in Macao and their Jesuit missionaries. Lu was alarmed. In the first of his four memorials to Emperor Chongzhen, Lu warned him against having anything to do with the foreigners in Macao.

"Your official was born and grew up in Xiangshan county and knows the real intentions of the Macanese Foreigners," Lu told his emperor. "By nature they are aggressive and violent, and their minds are inscrutable." He recalls that the first contacts were limited to trading in the lee of offshore islands, then notes that the Portuguese were able to get a toehold at Macao. "Initially they only put up tents and camped there, but over time they constructed buildings and walled Green Island, and after that they erected gun towers and stout ramparts so that they could defend themselves inside." With them came a motley collection of foreigners. As far as Lu was concerned, this was proof that the Portuguese were utterly indifferent to China's strict laws about who was allowed to enter China, on what terms, and how they should conduct themselves when they did. In particular, by allowing Japanese onto Chinese soil without first obtaining Chinese permission, the Portuguese demonstrated their utter indifference to Chinese laws.

"There are times when they embark on their foreign ships and force their way into the interior," Lu reminded the emperor. "To sustain their immoral intentions, they resist government troops, pillage our people, kidnap our children, and buy up saltpetre, lead, and iron," all of which were proscribed for export as military materiel. Even worse was the behavior this provoked among ordinary Chinese.

"Criminal types from Fujian Province go in large numbers to feed on Macao. Those who are induced to make a living there cannot be fewer than twenty or thirty thousand. The bandits of Guangdong Province rely on them to cause trouble, in numbers beyond counting." The key issue was not culture but criminality, especially on the Chinese side.

Two years before Lu Zhaolong addressed his emperor on this matter, the newly enthroned emperor had sided with the faction that feared the Manchus more than the Europeans, and had agreed to invite a team of Portuguese gunners to travel from Macao to Beijing to improve artillery defenses on China's northern border. But the other faction had been strong enough to stall the delegation in Nanjing. Even if a northern invasion was imminent, they argued, was hiring foreign mercenaries the solution to strengthening the underdefended border? Had Chinese not originally invented cannon? Why were Chinese munitions not adequate to the purpose? (Las Cortes in his memoir is scathing about the quality of Chinese firearms.) "How could it be that only after foreigners teach us are we able to display our military might?" Lu later asked. More to the point, did danger on one border justify exposing China to danger on another?

Many officials at court supported the idea of taking advantage of European ballistics to help China defend its borders. The most spectacular evidence of the superiority of European gunnery occurred in Macao in 1622. In June of that year, a fleet of VOC ships descended on Macao in the hope of grabbing this lucrative trading station from the hands of the Portuguese and taking over the China trade. The assault might well have succeeded, had the Jesuit mathematician Giacomo Rho not been doing the geometry calculations for one of the gunners defending the town. The gunner Rho was working with managed to score a direct hit on the cache of gunpowder kegs that the Dutch attackers had brought ashore with them. Perhaps Rho's shot had as much luck as aim in it, but that didn't matter. Rho was honored ever after for his mathematical prowess for saving Portuguese Macao from the Dutch.

Some Chinese officials took from this victory the complacent lesson that foreigners fought each other and China had only to manipulate them against each other, in this case by allowing the Portuguese to trade but barring the Dutch from doing so. "We don't spend a penny," declared Governor General Dai Zhuo in Canton, "and yet by employing the strategy of using foreigners to attack foreigners, our power extends even beyond the seas."

Lu Zhaolong did not agree that China should look to foreigners for a solution. Employing Portuguese gunners signified weakness, not strength. Others at court took a more aggressive view. For them, Rho's victory proved that China had to acquire better technology to defend itself. The Chongzhen emperor thought so too, and had already sent an edict giving the go-ahead to the Portuguese artillery team even before Lu sent in his first memorial.[2]

Gonçalo Teixeira Correa led the delegation of four gunners, two interpreters, plus two dozen Indian and African servants. One of the translators was Chinese, and the other was the senior Jesuit priest João Rodrigues, who had for years headed the mission to Japan. Rodrigues was already known to Chinese officials in the south, and not trusted. In Canton, Judge Yan Junyan, a friend of Lu Zhaolong, regarded Rodrigues as a meddler in China's internal affairs. He suspected that the old Jesuit was more than just an interpreter, but he had to respect orders from Beijing and allow him to pass through Canton.

Despite the imperial authorization that the delegation should approach Beijing, officials who shared Lu Zhaolong's opinion put up resistance at every turn. The team got stalled at Nanjing, just as the previous delegation had. Officials would not permit them to proceed farther without explicit confirmation from the emperor that they should do so. Rodrigues claimed in a report home that they were waiting for a favorable wind to carry them up the Grand Canal, but he was trying to save face all round. At long last, on 14 February 1630, the imperial edict arrived: proceed to the capital with all haste. Manchu raiding parties had been spotted moving in the vicinity of the capital. The services of the foreigners were needed.

Sixty-five kilometers south of the capital, a band of Manchu raiders crossed the Portuguese gunners' path. It was a chance encounter, but a piece of incredible good luck for the faction that advocated the use of European technology. The gunners retreated to the city of Zhuozhou nearby and mounted eight of their cannon on the city wall. The cannon fire did no real damage, but the effect was enough to persuade the Manchus to depart. No real battle ensued, and no real victory was earned. Still, it was all the supporters of the expedition at court needed to sweep aside the objections of opponents such as Lu Zhaolong.

Once Teixeira and Rodrigues were in the capital, they realized that their party was too small to make much difference in a full campaign against the Manchus. Four gunners stood little chance of turning the military tide against the Manchus, who were superbly commanded and had rapid deployment capacity, to say nothing of capable Chinese gunners working on their side. The Portuguese decided to capitalize on the sudden boost to their reputation by proposing that another three hundred mounted soldiers be recruited from Macao. Perhaps, and this seems very likely, they were put up to it by the vice-minister of war. The vice-minister was Xu Guangqi, who happened to be the very official who spearheaded the first request for military support back in 1620. He wrote to the throne on 2 March 1630 explaining that European cannon were cast more adeptly and from better metal than Chinese cannon. They used more volatile gunpowder, and better sighting gave them greater accuracy. After much deliberation, the emperor asked the ministry of rites to submit a concrete proposal concerning these arrangements. In the intervening time, the vice-minister of war was transferred to the post of vice-minister of rites. From that position, Xu submitted a formal proposal to the emperor on 5 June to send Rodrigues back to Macao to place an order for more cannon, recruit more gunners, and bring the lot up to Beijing to stiffen the Ming border forces. The same month, no less a figure than Giacomo Rho, the Jesuit mathematician who saved Macao, arrived in the capital at the invitation of the same vice-minister.

The Jesuits knew Xu Guangqi better by his baptismal name. Xu

Guangqi was Paolo Xu, the highest-ranking court official ever to convert to Christianity. Like Lu Zhaolong, Paolo Xu was from a coastal family, but from much farther up the coast—Shanghai, where seaborne threats came from Japan rather than Europe. The peace of Shanghai had not been disturbed by either Macanese Foreigners or Red Hairs. It was too far north of the coastal zone in which they traded. Still, through a series of encounters orchestrated by chance— yet spurred by Xu's powerful curiosity—this Shanghai native came to know many Europeans in the course of his life. The Europeans he knew, however, were neither Macanese merchants nor Dutch pirates. They were Jesuit missionaries from all over Europe, and they brought with them knowledge that Xu recognized could have enormous value for China.

Jesuits had been entering China from Macao for less than a decade when Xu, struggling to make his way up the examination ladder, met one of them in a southern provincial town in 1595. He had a second encounter five years later with Matteo Ricci, the brilliant Italian Jesuit who led the Jesuit mission in China until his death in 1610. In the course of his third encounter in 1603, Xu received baptism and took the Christian name of Paolo. Xu became a close associate of the Jesuits, particularly of the scholarly Ricci, with whom he collaborated on a range of religious and scholarly projects designed to show the value of the new knowledge that the missionaries brought from Europe. Few Chinese converted to Christianity; their traditions of ritual and belief taught them to be dubious about adopting a faith that required them to renounce prior rites and beliefs. Xu was not troubled by the commitment this new religious knowledge demanded. He figured that Christianity was just as much a part of the larger European system of knowledge as metallurgy, ballistics, hydraulics, and geometry, and these were the subjects he was eager to learn and adapt to China's use. He saw no reason to accept some branches of what came to be called Western Learning and reject others.

Lu Zhaolong regarded Paolo Xu, correctly enough, as his chief adversary in the debate over the use of European technology in China.

The only way to bring the emperor around to his view was to erode Xu's considerable authority. The minor Portuguese victory at Zhuozhou made his task that much harder. He had to proceed carefully. Lu's main argument was national security. "Inviting the distant foreigners will not only pose a risk to the interior, but it will give them a chance to detect our weaknesses and become familiar with our conditions, and so laugh at our Heavenly dynasty for lacking defenders." The only way China could keep foreigners in proper awe of China was to hold them at a distance. The sight of three hundred mercenaries—"people of a different sort, galloping their horses, brandishing their swords, and letting arrows fly from their bows inside the imperial capital"—was too disturbing to allow. Putting China's sovereignty in their hands was a crazy gamble. Besides, the cost of transporting and feeding such a horde was too high. For the same price, the government could afford to cast hundreds of cannon.

In the end, Lu Zhaolong rested his appeal on ad hominem attacks on Paolo Xu by targeting the point where Xu was most vulnerable, his Christianity. "The Macanese Foreigners all practice the teachings of the Lord of Heaven," he complained in the final section of his first communication with the emperor on this matter. "Its doctrines are so abstruse that they easily delude the age and confuse the people," and he gave instances of Christian cults that had appeared in several places in China. The charge went beyond concerns about how badly three hundred Portuguese soldiers might act. There lay a much deeper anxiety about foreigners infecting the core beliefs of Chinese culture. Lu even quietly suggested that a foreign religion might sway Chinese minds against the dynasty's authority. Millenarian Buddhist sects had recently been active in the capital region, on one occasion inciting an uprising inside the city. Might not secret Christian congregations get up to the same thing? Even worse, Chinese Christians would have secret connections to the foreigners, which meant secret connections to Macao, and who knew what such connections might bring? "I know nothing about there being such a thing in the world as the teachings of the Lord of Heaven," Lu declared, wanting to know why the emperor would listen to someone such as Xu who preferred them over the writings of Confucius. "How is it that he is so resourceful and keen in doing everything he can to guarantee the preservation of the Macanese Foreigners and plan for their long-term prospects?"

Xu's Christianity was not his only weak spot. His tie with Macao was another. Anxiety about what the foreigners got up to in Macao runs like a red thread through all Chinese complaints about Europeans in this period. This was the anxiety that lay behind the persecution of Christianity in Nanjing in 1616, when a very different vice-minister of rites, Shen Que, expelled two missionaries. Alfonso Vagnone and Álvaro Semedo were transported back to Macao in—to quote an English rendering of Semedo's later account—"very narrow cages of wood (such as are used in that Country to transport persons condemned to death, from one place to another) with Iron Chaines about their necks, and Manacles on their Wrists, with their haire hanging down long, and their Gownes accoutred in an odde fashion, as a signe of a strange and Barbarous people." Says Semedo, writing about himself and Vagnone in the third person, "In this manner were the fathers carried with an inexpressible noise, which the Ministers made with their ratling of Fetters and Chaines. Before them were carried three tablets, written on with great letters, declaring the Kings Sentence, and forbidding all men to have any commerce or conversation with them. In this equipage they went out of Nankim." For thirty days they were transported in these cages southward to Canton and from there dispatched to Macao with severe warnings to return to Europe and never come back.

Paolo Xu had been the lone voice defending these two Jesuits back in 1616, though even then he had warned another missionary that the Jesuits should take care to hide their contacts with Macao. "All of China is scared of the Portuguese," he stressed, and Macao was the place on which they focused their anxieties. Hostile officials regarded it not as an innocent trading post, but as a base from which the Portuguese were running a network of agents inside China to foment religious disturbances, smuggling, and espionage. The missionaries were seen as its spies. This is why Shen Que charged Semedo and Vagnone with being "the cat's paw of the Franks." A report from the Nanjing Ministry of Rites concurred. Macao was the base from and to which the Jesuits traveled, the port that provided them with passage anywhere in the world, and the funnel through which the ministry understood Vagnone received the 600 ounces of silver annually to distribute among the missions in China (the ministry later revised that number down to 120 ounces). Macao was not just a base for foreign trade, notes a report by the Nanjing Censorate three months later, but the base for Portuguese infringements on Chinese sovereignty: "their religion makes Macao its nest." The Jesuits eventually grasped the liability of their relationship with Macao, though they could never do without the colony. It was essential to their entire operation in China, and to give it up was to forego the organizational and financial support that kept the mission going.

Paolo Xu insisted on drawing a distinction between the Red Hairs and the Macanese Foreigners, exactly as his Jesuit friends would have instructed him to do. The Macanese Foreigners supported their mission and provided them with the base from which it was possible to send missionaries into China. If the Dutch took Macao from the Portuguese, the Jesuit mission in China would come to an end. Their friends and enemies had to be Paolo Xu's friends and enemies. Lu Zhaolong was not persuaded that any foreigners could be trusted, Portuguese or Dutch. "Rites official Xu has collected arguments he has heard and turned them into a memorial that chatters on for hundreds of words," Lu complained, "the gist of which is to argue that the Red Hairs and the Macanese Foreigners be distinguished, the one as obedient and the others as refractory." Xu needed to make this distinction in order to protect his connections with the Jesuits against the charge that there was no difference between Portuguese priests and Dutch pirates. Lu would have none of it.

The Jesuits well understood how vital their connection to Macao was to the success of their mission. In 1633, a year after João Rodrigues returned to Macao from his stint with the gunners, he sent a letter to the head of his Society in Europe.[3] In the letter he underlines the need to protect the colony and its reputation, "for on this depends the trade so vital for His Majesty's Two Indies [the East Indies and the West Indies– the latter meaning the Portuguese possessions in what is now Brazil] and also the mission to convert China, Japan, Cochinchina, Tonkin, and other countries to our holy religion." Macao was the financial and strategic heart of the Jesuit enterprise in the East. Rodrigues's language uncannily echoes the language of a statement issued by the Nanjing Ministry of Rites. "This city of Macao is the narrow entrance through which subjects and all the necessary supplies for Masses and temporal upkeep enter these countries." Had Rodrigues's letter fallen into Lu Zhaolong's hands, it would have bolstered his suspicions about Macao being a beachhead of foreign penetration into China. So too, had he learned that both the priests transported out of China in a cage in 1617 were back inside in the 1630s, defying Chinese laws and converting people to their suspect creed, his worst fears about Macao's threat to the authority of the dynasty would have been confirmed.

Macao's position as the financial clearinghouse for the Jesuit mission into China was the very reason why Las Cortes, the Jesuit chronicler of the wreck of the *Guía*, was on his way from Manila to Macao when the ship went down. In his memoir, he says only that he had business to transact in Macao and reveals nothing further. When he finally got to Macao, he transacted it with none other than João Rodrigues. What their business involved, Las Cortes does not say, but within two months he was on the next ship back to Manila.

On his return voyage, Las Cortes had the misfortune once again to sail through a storm. In a convoy of five ships that crossed the South China Sea together, only four reached Manila. In his memoir, Las Cortes expresses great concern for the loss of that ship's cargo, which he notes included Chinese silks purchased in Macao for three hundred thousand pesos. Sumptuous brocades and feather-light gauzes in a dazzling array of colors, these fabrics were of a sort that no European could weave or buy anywhere else, but Las Cortes was not interested in the beauty of the silks. He was interested in what they were worth. "If one took account of what it would have fetched once it was sold in Manila," he writes of the lost cargo, "one would without doubt have to add two hundred thousand pesos, which drives the loss up to half a million pesos." Being the last substantive entry in his account of his yearlong adventure in China, the calculation draws attention to itself. The lost cargo may reveal Las Cortes's own purpose in going to Macao: to buy Chinese silks that the Jesuits could then sell for a profit in Manila, generating proceeds that would fund their mission in the Philippines. Perhaps this also tells us that he was bringing a load of silver to buy such silks when he crossed to Macao on the *Guía*. If the missing silk was Jesuit property, Las Cortes's mission to Macao was a severe loss in both directions.

THE CONSEQUENCES OF SAILING OFF course and getting stranded on the China coast were just as huge for the people on board the *Guía* as for the owners of the cargo in the hold. An entire year passed before passengers and crew received a final judgment at Canton. The deliberation was handled by the provincial surveillance commissioner, whose position combined the responsibilities of chief prosecutor and provincial governor. Las Cortes does not record the commissioner's name, but it was probably Pan Runmin.

Pan Runmin had just stepped into the post of surveillance commissioner in 1625. Within a few months he would leave for a promotion elsewhere, but he was likely still in Canton when the case of the *Guía* came up. Little is known of Pan, other than that he was from Guizhou Province, deep in China's southwest interior, a tribal region where few ever got the education needed to become an official and the only foreigners were the tribespeople living in the mountains. Las Cortes may have been the first European Pan ever dealt with. The Jesuit sensed that Pan was intrigued by the foreigners and observant of details. Indeed, he seemed more interested in learning about the foreigners than in prosecuting the case.

Pan began his examination by scrutinizing the shipwrecked, even to the point of examining the soles of the barefooted to check whether they had been force marched. It was soon abundantly clear to him that the foreigners had suffered at the hands of his officers. He called the commander from Jinghai and put him through questioning. The commander stuck to the story he had told in Chaozhou: these were Red Hairs and Dwarf Pirates, not the innocent merchants from Manila and Macao they claimed to be, and his men had apprehended them accordingly. Some may have suffered injuries, but their injuries occurred on the day they were shipwrecked, before they came into his custody. He was not responsible for their condition. The commander urged the commissioner to focus on the main issue, which was that the shipwrecked were foreigners, including Japanese, who had entered the country illegally.

According to Las Cortes's account of their day in court, Commissioner Pan wanted to know whether any cargo came ashore with the foreigners. If so, that property would be treated as contraband, and any Chinese who handled such goods would be guilty of smuggling. (As Lu Zhaolong's friend, Judge Yan noted in a case involving illegal trade between Cantonese soldiers and Dutch traders, "Those on board [foreign ships] are not permitted to bring goods ashore and those on shore are not permitted to go on the boats and receive goods.") The Jinghai commander insisted that the survivors came ashore with nothing but what they were wearing. The *Guía* carried no silver, he insisted, and no one under his charge had taken a thing from the foreigners. Pan had enough judicial experience to know this was probably nonsense, but he lacked evidence to the contrary and had to give up trying to extract the truth from his subordinates.

Commissioner Pan then turned to Las Cortes. He posed a series of carefully phrased questions designed to pry out the truth. Trusting Las Cortes over his own officers, Pan soon determined that these people had indeed been maltreated, that the ship was carrying a cargo of silver, that its owners had been prevented from recovering it, and that some of it had been salvaged later. Pan expected as much, but knowing that the commander would not present any evidence that silver had been taken, he could do nothing. He then turned to the decapitations, the evidence for which—the severed heads of Ganpti and the others—was sitting in a row of baskets in the courtroom.

"Did you see anyone from Jinghai kill the people whose heads have been presented before this court?"

"In truth," declared Las Cortes, "we saw them decapitate seven of our people, but cannot say whether they cut off their heads while they were still living or after they had already died, whether from drowning or exposure or the injuries they suffered during the shipwreck."

Commissioner Pan was trying to get at the issue of whether any of the foreigners had died at Chinese hands, but Las Cortes chose to prevaricate. He suspected that nothing would be achieved by filing accusations of murder—other than delaying their departure. Pan seems to have understood Las Cortes's testimony for what it was: an agreement to compromise in order to close the case and allow everyone to go home. Having only the mute evidence of the heads, he dismissed the charge of murder with the platitude, "The dead cannot be brought back to life by us."

The problem of the missing silver had to be handled in the same way. Foreign ships were known to carry as much as ten thousand ounces (taels) of silver, as Judge Yan notes in another case, yet not a single ounce was reported lost or gained by either side. Pan had to dismiss the matter. "As for the silver the ship was carrying," he declares in his final judgment, "let it be deemed lost at sea, as nothing about its recovery can be determined." Pan also declined to order compensation be paid for the foreigners' losses, adding the observation that "it does not seem likely that so small a number of Europeans could have been in possession of any great quantity of silver." The observation assumed that the silver used in trade was in the possession of individuals, not of corporations. This was either an odd prevarication, an excuse for doing nothing, or a sign of Pan's lack of knowledge regarding foreign commerce.

Was Commissioner Pan duped? I think not. From Las Cortes's

account, he seemed to know exactly what was going on, and even more clearly to understand the limits of his powers to prosecute when no evidence had been brought forward from a crime scene three hundred and fifty kilometers away. He had to close the proceedings with the finding that the shipwrecked had arrived in China by misadventure, not by intention, that they were not engaged in piracy, and that they should be allowed to return to Macao. All charges were dismissed.

VERMEER'S CALM GEOGRAPHER IS A world away, physically and intellectually, from the arguments in Pan's courtroom. He is not a coastal villager threatened by pirates; nor need he fear the ocean, as his compatriots controlled it anyway; nor does he have an interest in the profits VOC merchants are making by traveling overseas. What interests him is the information they are bringing back: information he will collect, analyze, and synthesize into sea charts and maps, which the merchants can then take back into the wider world that is now better understood. And if that useful knowledge fails, then new knowledge will be collected and incorporated. The geographer's task in the seventeenth century was to engage actively in this endless loop of feedback and correction. This is exactly what Hondius had requested in the cartouche on the curve of the globe we see over the geographer's head. Would those embarking on the "very frequent expeditions" going "every day to all parts of the world" please report their positions back to him, so that he can produce a new edition that will improve upon the one that stands before them?

Through this sort of feedback mechanism (which involved a lot of heavy borrowing if not outright plagiarism from the work of others), European cartographers were constantly revising their maps during the seventeenth century. New knowledge replaced old, and then was replaced in turn by newer, and hopefully better, information. The process was not always perfect: many maps of North America showed a transcontinental channel well after the time when there was any hope that one would be found. Still, the cumulative effect was correction and elaboration, so that gradually the map of the world was filled in.

A few blank spaces tenaciously resisted this knowledge-gathering process—the African interior, the middle of the Pacific Ocean, the northern end of North America, the two poles—and explorers duly rose to the challenge of filling them in, often simply for the sake of doing it and not because anyone needed this knowledge. What merchants needed was precise information about the routes on which their ships traveled so as to lower the chance of shipwreck and increase the speed at which ships could go and return—and thereby increase the rate at which their capital turned over. This is not the story that Vermeer's *Geographer* tells, however. Leeuwenhoek poses as a man of science, not a man of business. Yet without scholars like him who devoted their energies to the accumulation of useful knowledge, the merchants would not have had their maps. The two impulses—knowledge and acquisition—worked together.

Chinese geographers were in a different situation. There was no feedback mechanism in operation and little impetus to alter what was already laid down. Even if knowledge of regions beyond their borders could have been acquired from coastal mariners, Chinese scholars tended not to take a great interest in it. An exception was the geographer Zhang Xie, who made a point of talking to mariners who had sailed into the waters of Southeast Asia when compiling his *Investigations of the Eastern and Western Oceans*. As he states in his introductory notes, "all the places recorded in this book are places merchant ships have gone." Zhang was scathing toward authors who write history by simply repeating ancient facts and dismissing recent developments. Such people perpetuate ignorance rather than produce knowledge. His goal was instead to record information on recent developments, including the Red Foreigners, because of the effect they were currently having on maritime commerce.

The book had no appreciable impact among those who actually traveled, however; but nor, to be fair, would any of Zhang's readers have thought it should. The material in the book, as the invited contributor of a preface writes, "was selected to provide material for historians of another day," not for mariners and merchants in Zhang's day, the very folk from whom Zhang gathered his materials. His book was not for this readership, but for other curious scholars such as himself who had no expectation of ever going abroad and simply wanted to know more about the lands beyond their shores. Zhang Xie knew that Chinese should now expect ships like the *Guía* to show up at China's edges, but it was not an idea that more traditionally minded readers would have known how to deal with.

Matteo Ricci, Paolo Xu's Jesuit collaborator and the senior missionary in China until his death in 1610, eagerly shared European knowledge of the natural world, as he assumed this would impress the Chinese and help him prove the truth of Christianity. What clearer form had he to present new geographical knowledge than maps? European world maps by this time came in several forms, and Ricci copied and revised examples of them, adding place names and explanations in Chinese in the hope of engaging the intellectual attention of the scholars he met. Chinese viewers in the late Ming liked maps. Commercial wall maps were not as popular as they were in Holland, but they existed and were hung. Seeing these European maps, Chinese viewers were unsure of what to do with the information they provided, for the simple reason that most lacked an experiential basis from which to interact with Ricci's images.

Paolo Xu delighted in Ricci's maps, as he was persuaded by the theory of a round earth and believed that maps could communicate this idea more forcefully than a written explanation. Ricci's European world maps were taken up by other scholars as well, for they made it into the two great encyclopedias of the era, the *Compendium of Pictures and Writings* and the *Assembled Pictures of the Three Realms* (the three realms being heaven, earth, and humanity). The compiler of the first was delighted to note that these new maps meant "you don't have to leave your house and yet you can have complete knowledge of the world." Yet the step from inside the house to outside the house did not happen. The publication of these maps in popular encyclopedias could have started a feedback loop, inspiring Chinese readers to go out, maps in hand, to test this knowledge. But it didn't. These maps were not subsequently refined and developed for other publications, as they were in Europe, nor did they dislodge the traditional cosmology. The problem was simply that almost no Chinese mariners had the opportunity to test and develop this knowledge. No Chinese merchant was circumnavigating the earth and finding it round. The only people bringing this information from the wider world were foreigners, who were not always to be trusted. Nor, accordingly, was there anyone like Vermeer's geographer who wanted, or was able, to incorporate endless data from the outside world, constantly revising the body of useful knowledge that someone actually needed.

For Europeans, the outside world was entering their lives in the forms of ideas and objects, some of which we see in the room Vermeer has painted. For most Chinese, the outside world remained outside. It may have infiltrated the mind of Paolo Xu; even Commissioner Pan sensed there was something to learn from the people whom the outside world had thrown into his custody. But if the Jinghai commander and Lu Zhaolong had their say, and they did, outside was where this world should stay.

SCHOOL FOR SMOKING

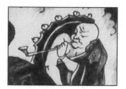

AMONG THE COLLECTORS of local exotica in nineteenth-century Delft, Lambert van Meerten was the most obsessed. The heir of a family that made its fortune in the liquor trade, Lambert devoted his life and fortune to amassing a vast collection of art objects, statues, ceramics, curios, and whatever architectural detritus he could pick up from buildings undergoing renovation. He acquired more objects than he could possibly afford to house, but had the good luck to have in Jan Schouten a wealthier and more sensible friend. Schouten came to his rescue and agreed to help pay for a massive three-story house, which now sits farther up the Oude Delft canal on the side on which the Delft Chamber of the VOC sits, where Van Meerten could store all his treasures. When Van Meerten died, Schouten converted the house into a museum, which it remains today.

When I visited the museum, I happened upon a large blue-and-white plate in a cabinet in a back room on the upstairs floor. The plate, forty-three centimeters in diameter, depicts a busy Chinese garden scene stocked with immortals, scholars, servants, and mythological creatures (see plate 5). The Portuguese were the first Europeans to try their hand at making dishes that looked Chinese, but Delft potters were the first to manage reasonable imitations. On this one, a faux-Chinese style of illustration has been accomplished with dramatic flair, but there is no chance of mistaking it for a real Chinese plate. Numerous little details betray its Dutch origins. The chips around the edge show the clay to be European, and the glaze lacks the hardness and evenness of Jingdezhen ware. The fatal giveaway is the three-character inscription on the tablet being carried by a Confucian official in the middle of the plate. A valiant attempt to make Chinese characters, it is entire nonsense. So the plate is a fake, though that sentence judges it too harshly. The decoration was never intended to fool a buyer. The Chineseness was simply there to please the eye and amuse the imagination. It is a happy, innocent fake.

The figures on the Van Meerten plate are busily doing the sorts of things Europeans expected Chinese to do in pictures, like floating in clouds, crossing bridges, and catching cranes. Among the quirks and inconsistencies you would never see on a "real" Chinese dish is a bald immortal riding a mythological tiger-dog and sucking fiercely on a long-stemmed pipe. No smoke issues from his mouth or pipe, but the swirling clouds of heaven through which he flies stand in for the fumes. No porcelain painter in China ever put a smoker on a dish, so far as I have seen. Not until much later in the eighteenth century would a Chinese artist even be willing to include someone smoking in his repertoire, and then only for sketches or woodcuts (we will see an early example later in this chapter). New practices take time to be culturally absorbed, and smoking was never absorbed well enough to be allowed into the realm of fine art before the twentieth century. Chinese painting is conservative on such cultural matters.

This is not the only piece of Dutch porcelain to depict a smoker. Delft tile painters had been putting smokers on their wares for some decades. Nor were porcelain painters the only artists to paint smoking. Delft painters had been doing this on canvas for just as long, using smoking to signal sociability and conviviality. The Delft "merry company" painter Jan Steen delighted in crowding his satirical scenes with smokers of all ages. The more genteel Pieter de Hooch and Hendrik van der Burch put pipes in the hands of male figures to give them something to do with their hands while they were engaged in conversation. Johannes Vermeer never painted anyone smoking, so no Vermeer painting gives us a ready door that we can open onto the global spread of tobacco. But this plate—which may be the earliest depiction of a Chinese smoker by a European artist—does.

Where did the painter get the idea that Chinese smoked? He was not copying a Chinese original, as no Chinese painter would have put a smoking scene on porcelain. If he was inventing his own image, it had to have been because he had heard that Chinese smoked. Some bit of global information had come his way. Europeans were used to smoking by this time, having become schooled in the pleasures of tobacco through the latter part of the sixteenth century. That Chinese, or all Asians for that matter, were joining them through the seventeenth, and doing so on their own without business or cultural elites telling them to do it—indeed, almost without anyone noticing it was happening—is one effect of global mobility in the seventeenth century that no one could have predicted. Tobacco smoking was not fated to go global, but it did. The smoking immortal on the Delft plate opens for us another door, and through it we will find our way back into the world as it was becoming in the seventeenth century.

BEIJING WAS THE CITY to which all educated young men in China went to make their reputation and fortune. Cold in winter, clogged with Mongolian dust in the spring, parched in the summer, pleasant only in the fall, it was nonetheless the emperor's home and the center of power. Its examination halls drew the ambitious few up through the exam system and into state service. The ladder of advancement was not to be scampered up quickly. Every candidate had to start on the same bottom rung down in his home county; a tiny few got to the ultimate degree of "presented scholar," and even fewer found themselves serving at court. To be from a presented scholar's family helped in preparing for the ordeal of scaling the ladder, but family made no difference once you went into your exam cubicle and wrote papers for three days, unless of course your family knew an examiner to bribe, but that was a capital offense and difficult to arrange. If you passed, being from a family of degree holders meant you had the social skills and political connections to get a decent appointment in the capital rather than being sent out to the provinces as a county magistrate and having to work your way back to the center. The ascent up the examination ladder to Beijing was forbiddingly steep. So too, the re-ascent from a posting as a county magistrate to an appointment in the capital was nearly as tough, and most magistrates never made it.

Yang Shicong came from a good family, but he did not pass the presented scholar exams until 1631, when he was already in his thirties. Family connections allowed him to make up for lost time. Yang was posted right into the Hanlin Academy, a policy think tank and secretarial agency in Beijing for Emperor Chongzhen, and he rose to the post of vice-minister of rites. He got the coveted post of instructor to the heir apparent when the prince came of age in 1637, which segued into the position of adviser to the prince in the 1640s. The emperor committed suicide when rebels captured Beijing in April 1644, a few short weeks before the Manchus invaded and took over. The heir apparent, who came under Jesuit influence, sent a desperate appeal to the pope to send an army to drive the Manchus out of China, but what could the pope do about an invasion half a world away?

Yang is not an exceptional figure in the history of the dynasty. One of many competent officials who rose to the vice-ministerial level and no higher, he makes no appearance in the standard histories of the period. But he has come to the attention of a few historians because of a collection of short anecdotes he compiled about life in the capital in the closing decade of the Ming. He finished the manuscript of *Collected Writings from Jade Hall* in 1643. It was not a great year to publish a book. A massive epidemic had just swept through north China the previous year, and a year later rebels would overrun the capital and topple the dynasty. This is why the book is now extremely rare. Yang did not know that the Ming would fall, but he knew the realm was troubled. His book, he tells us in his preface, was to remind people of what life in the capital was like when times were still good.

In an essay that appears in the first part of *Collected Writings from*

Jade Hall, Yang observes that Beijing people in the past decade had experienced two minor changes. They were changes you could see "on every street corner," as he puts it, and they were signs that all was not well. The first was that peddlers were selling wild sand grouse. This bird did not belong in the Beijing area. Their natural habitat was farther north along the southern edge of the Gobi Desert. According to local lore, these birds flew this far south only when military maneuvers on the northern border disturbed their habitat. Yang was told that sand grouse had started appearing in Beijing in 1632. Enterprising bird catchers were now catching them and selling them to cook for dinner. The arrival of sand grouse in Beijing could have been a sign of a change in the weather, for 1632 was a wet year and the rains might have had something to do with driving them south. But their presence was regarded locally as evidence of trouble on the northern border, where the Manchus were massing for an invasion. The sand grouse were the proverbial canaries in the coal mine. No one could actually say this, since even to mention the possibility of invasion was enough to be accused of treason as a fifth columnist. But everyone understood that that was what the availability of sand grouse really meant.

The second street-corner sign that the world was topsy-turvy was the appearance of tobacconists. In the year Yang was born, 1597, no one in his home province of Shandong, south of Beijing, had tasted tobacco. Few were the Chinese anywhere who had. There were smokers on the southeast coast, and the leaf had found its way to Beijing, where it appears in a list of county office purchases from 1596 (at a price twice what cinnamon or sulphur cost on the Beijing market, and seven times higher than jasmine tea). By the time Yang arrived in Beijing to take his exams in 1631, the taking of "smoke liquor," as some called it, was well established in the capital. Yang dates tobacco's arrival in Beijing to the reign of Emperor Tianqi, who was enthroned in 1621 and died six years later. Beijing farmers, he writes, have been cultivating tobacco for "the last twenty years."

Yang felt that he had to account for the strange plant being in Beijing. He starts his explanation by noting that smoking was unknown in ancient China, there being no references to it in the classics. It must have come from abroad. As the main smokers in the capital region were soldiers who had been moved north to defend the border against the Manchus, Yang suspected a southern origin. The soldiers' demand had induced local farmers to convert their fields to tobacco patches, and they were earning ten times what they could get by growing grain. With all that tobacco about, Beijing residents started picking up the habit. The shift eventually caught the attention of Emperor Chongzhen. He was unhappy that farmers were abandoning grain in favor of tobacco, fearing what this might do to food supplies in the capital region, so in 1639 he decreed that anyone caught selling tobacco in the capital would be decapitated. The official explanation was that tobacco was a waste of time, health, and money, but local people—and here Yang tells us something that official history would not record—thought the ban was an overreaction to a pun.

The standard expression at the time for smoking was *chi yan*, "eating smoke." (Today it is *chou yan*, "sucking smoke.") The trouble was, the phrase *chi yan* was homophonous with the phrase "eating the capital." *Yan* was smoke, but Yan, written with a different character, was the ancient name of the Beijing region. Eating Beijing was just what Manchu warriors and peasant rebels at that very moment were threatening to do. Merely to speak of smoking could thus be regarded as rumormongering by fifth columnists intent on destroying the dynasty. Had Yang known the Manchus were keen smokers before northern Chinese ever took up the habit, it would only have bolstered the case against smoking.

The first known case to test the new prohibition came to the Beijing courts the year after the ban was imposed, in 1640. A student from the southeastern coastal province of Fujian came that year to Beijing to take the national examinations with a servant in tow. The servant, presumably to help his master make ends meet while he was away from home, sold some of the tobacco they had brought north with them on the street, and was soon arrested. The sentence was automatically set at decapitation. The sentence went up for review to

Emperor Chongzhen, and he confirmed the judgment, making the poor man the first victim of the harsh new law. The penalty was hugely unpopular with the people of Beijing. It took the military governor general of the region two years to get the ban lifted in early 1642. When Yang returned to the capital that year after a brief absence, tobacco was selling in greater volume than ever, and what had been an exotic custom was considered strange no longer.

The governor general was only being sensible. Servants from Fujian were of no interest to him, but soldiers were, and soldiers liked to smoke. They believed smoking helped them ward off the cold and damp. Why damage their morale by taking this prophylactic away from them? The rumor still persisted that the court had imposed the ban for fear of sedition, but that was because residents of the capital had reason to feel threatened by the larger forces of rebellion, invasion, and epidemic. Being the newest new thing, tobacco was somehow implicated in changes with which most felt they could not cope. As indeed it was, though not quite in the way the people of Beijing thought. To see the bigger picture, we have to look at the globe.

THINK AGAIN OF THE SEVENTEENTH-CENTURY world as Indra's net, but one that, like a spiderweb, was growing larger all the time, sending out new threads at each knot, attaching itself to new points whenever these came into reach, connecting laterally left and right, each new stringing of a thread repeated over and over again. As the density of strands increased, the web became ever more extended, more tangled and complex, yet ever more connective. There were many spinners on this web, and many centers, and the web they made did not extend symmetrically to all places. Some places were favored more than others because of where they were and what was made there or brought to them. Other places tried to stay off the web by building fortifications and imposing regulations to isolate themselves. Still, the spiderweb grew and ramified wherever people moved, conquered, or traded—as they were doing during the first half of the seventeenth century at a faster pace and in greater numbers than ever before.

Along the threads ran all manner of people and goods, boats and
carts, warriors and weapons. So too ran a lot of other things: animals
and plants, pathogens and seeds, words and ideas. Movement along
the web was not ordered according to anyone's wishes, but it was
never random, for the only way things like plants or ideas could move
was by traveling in the company of those who moved, and those who
moved did so in relation to needs and fears that followed patterns—
even if where they ended up wasn't where they wanted to go. Many
things were swept along in the movements of people who traveled
across the globe without anyone intending that this should happen,
remaking the world in ways no one thought possible. American
members of the nightshade family—the tomato, the potato, the hot
pepper, tobacco—would all travel globally in just this way.

Christopher Columbus and his crew in 1492 were the first non-
Americans to see indigenous people of the Americas smoke, though
Amerigo Vespucci gets the credit for making the first reference to tobacco in print, in 1505. Jacques Cartier tasted tobacco in 1535 on his
second journey to the New World. The smoke felt hot in his mouth.
The only analogy he could create to describe the sensation to his readers, who had no idea what it was like, was to compare it to pepper—
which happens to belong to the same family. Champlain observed
tobacco when he made his first voyage to the Americas in 1599, describing it as "a kinde of hearbe, whereof they take the smoake."
When Montagnais chief Anadabijou fêted the French at Tadoussac in
1603, he did what a good Native host should do: he offered them tobacco. Champlain called the festive gathering a *tabagie*—the word that
today in Québec means tobacco shop.

Native Americans used tobacco to move between the natural and
the supernatural worlds and to communicate with the spirits. Smoking helped to get the spirits' attention, since the spirits loved the smell
of burning tobacco, and it helped to get the communicant in the
right frame of mind. Shamans used it to induce trances enabling
them to pass beyond the natural world to see what the spirits were up
to and to peer into the future. Cigarettes today are not particularly

hallucinogenic, but Native tobacco had a nicotine content many times higher than what is now smoked, inducing much stronger psychotropic effects. Champlain does not say whether the "wizard" who accompanied his war party to Lake Champlain in 1609 smoked himself into intoxication to prognosticate the outcome of their raid, but he probably did.

The analgesic properties of tobacco were thought to give smoking medicinal as well as religious properties, realms that overlapped in seventeenth-century pharmacology. In most premodern cultures, sickness signaled a rupture in the proper relationship between the human and spirit worlds, whether because a spirit was intruding into the human world or because the afflicted person's soul had become lost in the spirit world. Just as it was thought to ease a wide variety of complaints from toothache and snakebite to convulsions and hunger and even asthma, tobacco eased whatever problem arose between the natural and the supernatural worlds to cause the sickness. The healing property of tobacco was a direct application of its spiritual capacity.

In daily life, tobacco was an important medium of sociability that, like healing, was something that benefited from the spirits' kind support. Managing social relations on a personal or communal level required thoughtfulness and care, and could be best accomplished when the spirits were on one's side. Burning or smoking tobacco was a way of propitiating the spirits if they were in an ugly mood— as they so often were—and inducing them to bless your enterprise. Sharing a smoke at a *tabagie* was done in the presence of the spirits, and it helped the smokers find consensus when differences arose. The sociability of tobacco spread easily from such formal settings into all aspects of Native social life. You used tobacco with friends, you shared it with neighbors, you gave it as a gift to ask for a favor or return thanks. Native people are still great socializers, which is why many are still great smokers.

Tobacco moved along the webs of trade that Europe's desire for China was creating between the Americas and the rest of the globe, traveling to new sites and coming into the reach of people who had never taken smoke before, Europeans first of all. With smoking went religious, medical, social, and economic practices that had to find equivalent niches in the new culture. The Cuban historian Fernando Ortiz half a century ago called this process transculturation: the process by which habits and things move from one culture to another so thoroughly that they become part of it and in turn change the culture into which they have moved. Ortiz knew that the "intense, complex, unbroken process" of transculturation can be violently destructive of what is already there, but the outcomes of these globalizing processes cannot be controlled. One moment of culture can become another so quickly that it is difficult to remember how things were in the moment immediately preceding this one.

So it was with tobacco. Wherever tobacco showed up, a culture that did not smoke became a culture that did. Transculturation happened almost overnight, and was usually well advanced before elites bothered to notice that everyone was smoking and started thinking up reasons why this was not a good thing. Not all of the original meanings of Native smoking made the jump to other cultures, of course. But many did, including the notion that tobacco opened a door to the spiritual realm. Of course, smoking's religious significance had to change with every new environment it entered. In Tibet, it became the stuff that fierce protector deities consumed to make them even more fierce. The statue of the protector deity of Trandruk Temple in the Yarlung Valley, for instance, waves a human femur reworked into the shape of a pipe to show just how remorseless he can be when he turns his attention on the faithless.

So too in Europe, smoking drifted into the world of witchcraft. Tobacco was suspect as a medium for getting in touch with the devil. In 1609, the year Champlain went on the warpath, Henri IV commissioned an inquisitor to root sorcery out of rural France. One of the things the inquisitor discovered about witches was that they used tobacco. The inquisitor's investigations led him to conclude that every witch had "a plant in their garden, no matter how small, the smoke of which they use to clear their head, and to sustain themselves somewhat against hunger." Wasn't the simpler explanation that poor women kept a tobacco plant as a balm for hunger and misery? But the inquisitor was looking for witchcraft, not poverty. He was unsure quite what smoking had to do with the terrible things witches were accused of, "but," he insisted, "I well do know and it is certain that it makes their breath and bodies so stinking that no one who was not accustomed to it could stand it, and they use it three or four times a day."

The witch panic in Europe faded through the seventeenth century. With it went the idea that tobacco opened channels of communication with the devil. If suspicious women smoked, it was later reasoned, they did so simply because they liked to, not because they were intent on engaging in black magic. Once smoking was cleared of its association with witchcraft, even the clergy were free to take it up, and they did. The Jesuits remained hostile to the habit, and their Society forbade them from smoking, but they were a minority among the priests. The rest of the Christian clergy took to tobacco with gusto. Indeed, they became such avid smokers, inside churches as well as out, that the Vatican had to intervene. "Decent people" on their way into church, the pope noted in 1643, found the smell of smoking offensive and disliked having to step through the tobacco ash that tended to accumulate around church entrances. Lest their foul personal habits further damage the deteriorating public reputation of the clergy, the Vatican told priests that they could not smoke in church, nor even in the porches at church doors. Priests who wanted to smoke could do so, but not in church and well away from entrances.

The sight of other people blowing smoke out of their mouths excited both curiosity and suspicion among those seeing it done for the first time. What a strange and dangerous thing to do. The poor were already condemned to pass their winters in smoky hovels inhaling the noxious fumes from cooking fires. Why breathe in smoke when you didn't have to? Europeans accepted the idea of breathing incense when they went to church, but only as an environmental inhalant, not as a stream of concentrated smoke going directly to their lungs. Smoking is not a natural activity. It has to be learned. Reconstructing

that process of learning is what makes the early history of smoking
so intriguing.

Every culture learns to smoke in a slightly different way. How people smoke depends on where the practice comes from, who introduced it, and what local practices or ideas can be adapted to make
sense of this strange new habit. A particular challenge for European
elites was getting over the association between tobacco and whoever
was already smoking, such as Native Americans. The most famous
early European diatribe against the "vile barbarous custome" of
smoking, from the British monarch James I, struck this theme above
all others. Smoking was what "poor wilde barbarous men" did, James
pointed out. It belonged to "the barbarous and beastly maners of the
wild, godlesse, and slavish Indians" and was not something an Englishman should imitate. Natives were "slaves to the Spaniards, refuse
to the world, and as yet aliens from the holy Covenant of God"—
three strikes against any argument in favor of smoking, at least in the
king's eyes. The complaint had little purchase on the minds of his
contemporaries, however. The great Elizabethan historian William
Camden could complain all he liked that the English had "degener-
ated into the nature of Barbarians, since they are delighted, and think
they may be cured, with the same things which the Barbarians use,"
but by 1615 he had to admit that "in a short time many men everywhere, some for wantonness, some for health sake, with insatiable desire and greediness sucked in the stinking smoak thereof through an
earthen pipe." Unlike Camden or the king, ordinary people didn't
care who started the practice.

The history of tobacco's arrival in Europe has mostly been told
from the elite side. The account usually starts with the physician
Rembert Dodoens, who in 1553 published a popular Latin herbal in
Antwerp (a Dutch edition appeared the following year, and a German
edition the year after). Dodoens's herbal contains the first botanical
entry on tobacco to appear in a medical text. It is the first written evidence that knowledge of tobacco, possibly even the plant itself, had
arrived in the Low Countries. Dodoens didn't know what to call the

plant, so he borrowed the name of a plant with narcotic properties with which he was already familiar, henbane. This weed bears purple-streaked yellow flowers similar to those of the tobacco plant, so the name served provisionally. Shift the story to Portugal three years later, and we find Damião de Goes publishing the claim that his kinsman Luis was the first person to bring the plant from Brazil to Europe. Damião does not specify a date for this historic act, but as Luis later joined the Jesuits and went off to India in 1553, the year Dodoens published his herbology, he must have brought tobacco across the Atlantic before that date. So the distance between knowing about the plant, and experiencing it firsthand, closes. De Goes says he cultivated the plant in his garden in Lisbon, and if he was growing it, he was probably smoking it.

From Portugal, tobacco traveled to France thanks to the same person. Damião de Goes gave Jean Nicot seeds from his garden, and Nicot took them back to France to plant in his garden. This probably happened before 1559, when Nicot was appointed to be France's ambassador to Portugal. Nicot then boasted that he was the first to bring tobacco to France, though another Frenchman, André Thevet, was the first to present Brazilian tobacco to the French queen, Catherine de Medici, in 1556. Thevet called it *herbe de la royne* in her honor, a name that went over into English for a time as "the queen's weed." But that name soon faded in favor of others. Nicot did get to put his name on smoking in one sense, since the Linnaean term for tobacco is Nicotiane (the source of the word we use today for the addictive nitrogenous compound in tobacco, nicotine).

The history of tobacco's transculturation into Europe looks a bit different when told from the vantage point of ordinary people. If Dodoens included it in his herbal, that could only be because someone showed it to him—someone who had either brought it from the Americas or got it from someone who did. And since Antwerp in the 1550s was northern Europe's busiest port (Amsterdam would outclass it only in the next century), receiving as many as five hundred ships a day, that someone almost certainly stepped with it onto the Antwerp docks. The chain of knowledge ends in Dodoens's herbology, but it must have begun among those who actually smoked the plant: sailors. A sailor would not have called it "queen's weed" or "henbane." He would have used the common Native American term "petum"—which is still with us in the name of a relative of the tobacco plant, the petunia.[1] But why give Antwerp precedence when the first ships to cross the Atlantic were returning to Portuguese and Spanish ports? One source suggests that tobacco reached Portugal this way as early as 1548, two decades before Damião de Goes was writing about it, again probably in the pockets of sailors. So sailors, soldiers, and priests were the Europeans who started smoking first. Only later did aristocrats and other gentlemen adopt the taste and make it their own.

The Spanish herbologist Juan de Cárdenas interested himself in the medicinal properties of tobacco, and includes the plant in his study of native medical practices published in Mexico in 1591. Cárdenas acknowledges that he has categorized it pharmacologically on the basis of how Spanish soldiers in Mexico were using it: to stave off cold, hunger, and thirst—just as the governor general's soldiers on the northern Chinese border were doing in 1642. Europeans in the Americas acquired the idea that this is what tobacco did from Natives, who told them, as they told Jacques Cartier in the 1530s, that smoking kept them "healthy and warm." So tobacco was more than just a barbarous practice. It was good for you. An English commentator explains in 1593 that it was tobacco's medicinal properties that recommended it most strongly, especially to the damp and rheumatic English. Tobacco, he notes, was "gretlie taken-up and used in England, against Rewmes [colds] and some other diseases ingendered in the longes [lungs] and inward partes, and not without effect." It was not only smoked, but made into a topical cream to rub into the skin. Offering greater precision, the English herbologist John Gerard in his herbal of 1597 notes that the herb "prevaileth against all apostemes [abscesses], tumours, inveterate ulcers, botches and such like, being made into an unguent or salve." As of 1597, every English apothecary was prescribing the substance.

The demand for tobacco medicine proved to be a moneymaker for apothecaries. As John Gerard happily admits, he used tobacco to treat "all cuts and hurts in the head, wherewith I have gotten both crownes and credit." The profits elsewhere in the tobacco trade were even greater. When Virginian tobacco was still a novelty in England at the turn of the century, it was said that smokers would pay for its weight in silver. And when smokers pay huge sums to buy something, states like to collect huge duties when that something crosses the border. King James may have railed against smoking as a barbarian custom, but when the Virginia Company, which was importing tobacco from the English colony of that name, invited him to raise the import duty on tobacco to a level he found acceptable, he did. It seems, in fact, that his objection to tobacco was as much about revenue lost to smugglers as it was about its bad effect on his people.

High prices and high duties of course encouraged both smugglers and farmers to get in on the business—as we noted for Beijing. Dutch farmers started growing tobacco as an import substitute about 1610, quickly making the Netherlands the biggest tobacco producer in Europe. Farmers in England did the same, though neither could match the quality of Virginian tobacco. As homegrown tobacco was much cheaper than the imported product and free of duty, the commercial solution was adulteration: mix local and imported and tell your customer he was getting the pure stuff. Dutch traders used this technique in the 1630s to undercut the English tobacco trade in the Baltic. Another method was to stew imported Virginian tobacco and then soak local tobacco in this liquid to improve its quality, though the results were not great. Still, pleasure and profit were able to work out a variety of arrangements—from smuggling to false advertising— that kept Europeans in tobacco during those early years.

The profitable solution in the long run was to control both supply and quality at the source. This the Europeans accomplished by pushing aside Native producers in the Americas and setting up tobacco plantations. Tobacco would henceforth be grown by English planters, and the profits on the trade would remain within English hands. The

demand for tobacco was strong enough by the 1610s to make colonization no longer just a speculative venture but an affordable one. As
beaver pelts funded French exploration farther north, so tobacco gave
the English the means to transplant themselves to Virginia and dis-
possess Natives of their land.

Something else had to happen for tobacco to become a commercial crop. Tobacco farmers found that they needed more labor than
their own families could supply. Although the Jesuits had some success getting Indians in South America to work on tobacco plantations, most were unwilling to work on them. Even if forced, they
simply slipped away at night. The solution was to find people who
had no choice but to do the work—slaves. The Dutch, ever with an eye
to profitable business ventures, took the lead. Starting in the 1630s,
another state-mandated corporation, the Westindische Compagnie,
or West Indian Company—the WIC as distinct from the VOC—
secured strong positions on both sides of the south Atlantic, buying
slaves in Africa and selling them to tobacco plantation owners in the
Caribbean and Brazil. The WIC lost most of these colonies in the
1640s as other traders got into the business, yet during the last quarter of the seventeenth century, the WIC was running three to four
slave ships a year to the Caribbean, exclusive of its ships serving
South America.

From this new labor arrangement, a new system of trade emerged.
Tobacco (along with sugar) was a crop that could be used to make the
Americas profitable, while Africa supplied the labor to make plantation production in the Americas feasible and South American silver
paid for goods shipped from Europe and the Americas to Asia. Together the three prime commodities of the age—silver, tobacco, and
slaves to mine the first and harvest the second—set the foundation on
which the long-term colonization of the Americas rested. This sort
of transnational arrangement, which gradually incorporated other
commodities as well, became the pattern that enabled Europe to
dominate much of the globe for the next three centuries.

The global span of tobacco was not lost on contemporaries. In his satire on pretentious young men of fashion published in 1609, the English playwright Thomas Dekker addressed tobacco with this plea: "Make me thine adopted heire, that inheriting the vertues of thy whiffles, I may distribute them amongst all nations." The tobacco-loving English were content to see everyone smoke, so long as tobacco agreed to "make the phantastick Englishman (above the rest) more cunning in the distinction of thy Rowle Trinidado, Leafe and Pudding, than the whitest toothed Blackamoore in all Asia."[2] Let the world become a fellowship of smokers, but let the English rise to the status of being its cleverest connoisseurs and the unique beneficiaries of its inspirational qualities.

DEKKER WAS NOT WRONG IN supposing that tobacco would soon spread "amongst all nations," especially in Asia. He prophesied a little too early to know that China would become the foremost smoking nation, and the Chinese people even more enthusiastic to become tobacco's "adopted heire" than the English. It took little time for what appeared to the English to be a moderate virtue among themselves to appear, when it arrived among the Chinese, like an immoderate vice. An Englishwoman who visited China in the nineteenth century felt entirely justified to criticize the Chinese passion for smoking by declaring the Chinese to be "as fond of smoking as the Turks." This was not a compliment. She thought it was alright to smoke, just not to smoke to Turkish or Chinese excess.

Tobacco traveled to China by three routes: an eastward Portuguese route from Brazil to Macao, a westward Spanish route from Mexico to Manila, and a third route that consisted of a series of hops around East Asia to Beijing. The first and second routes developed about the same time, with tobacco converging on Macao and Manila, and from these trading ports proceeding into China: from Macao into Guangdong Province, and from Manila into Fujian Province farther up the coast. Certainly the habit was well entrenched by the first quarter of the seventeenth century, for when Adriano de las Cortes, the chronicler of the 1625 wreck of the *Guía*, came ashore near where these provinces meet, he discovered that the Chinese smoked. Las Cortes made the discovery at the end of his first day as a hostage. He was parched and made signs that he needed something to drink. His guards guessed correctly and gave him a bowl of hot water, which Chinese regard as more salubrious than cold water. Las Cortes was unused to drinking hot water and continued to mime, hoping for cold water. "They thought that I was actually asking for something else," he reports, "so they brought me some tobacco to smoke." Las Cortes wanted water, not tobacco, and in any case, being a Jesuit, was not permitted to smoke. He tried again to make himself understood and eventually, after much hilarity on the Chinese side, the charade was solved. They brought him a cup, not of cold water nor of hot, but of what he describes as "some hot water cooked with a herb called *cha*." This was Las Cortes's first encounter with tea. Tea had yet to transculturate its way into European society but by 1625, tobacco had become thoroughly entrenched along the China coast.

Between Guangdong and Fujian Provinces, it was Fujian that gained the reputation as the home of tobacco in China. It arrived on Chinese ships coming from Manila into several ports, the most important of which was Moon Harbor, serving the prefectural city of Zhangzhou at the south end of the Fujian coast. Fang Yizhi, a brilliant seventeenth-century scholar much intrigued by knowledge of the outside world, dates its arrival in Fujian to the 1610s—some three decades before he slipped into Fujian disguised as a drug peddler to evade the Manchu armies overrunning south China in 1645. Fang identifies the Ma family of Zhangzhou as the biggest tobacco processors. They clearly made a success of the new product which spread like wildfire. "It gradually spread within all our borders, so that everyone now carries a long pipe and swallows the smoke after lighting it with fire. Some have become drunken addicts."

The word Fang uses for tobacco is *danrouguo*, "the fleshy fruit of the *danbagu* plant." *Danbagu* was the name the Chinese in the Philippines used for tobacco. They coined it as a rough transliteration of the Spanish *tabaco*, which the Spanish had in turn transliterated from the Caribbean word for the hollow reed in which Caribbean Natives packed shredded tobacco leaves in order to smoke them. *Danbagu* was foreign sounding and awkward, so Chinese adapted their own word for "smoke" (*yan*) and came up with the expression *chi yan*, "eating smoke." One Chinese author, looking back from the end of the seventeenth century, suspected it was the Japanese who coined the term *yan* (pronounced *en* in Japanese) for smoking. This is plausible, Japan being one of the stepping stones on tobacco's third route into China. As *en* in Japanese is a loan word originally taken from Chinese, though, it is almost impossible to sort out how this word cycled between the two cultures—both of which continue to use it.[3]

Chinese intellectuals puzzled over the question of where tobacco originally came from. Some assumed it was native to the Philippines, since that is whence it arrived in Fujian. Others suspected that the people in the Philippines "got their seeds from the Great Western Ocean," a loose term for the distant region from which Europeans came. The thousands of Fujianese who traded with the Spanish in Manila knew the latter crossed the Pacific Ocean from a place called Yameilijia (America), and may have learned that this is where the seeds came from. But these were not the people who kept diaries or published essays. When it came to knowing about tobacco, the gap between the intelligentsia and ordinary people was as wide in seventeenth-century China as in Europe.

From Fujian, the habit of smoking worked its way into the interior and up the maritime coast. The plant reached Shanghai in the 1630s, according to Ye Mengzhu, a sharp-eyed memoirist writing at the end of the century. "Tobacco comes originally from Fujian," Ye begins, without bothering to guess where it came from before that. "When I was young, I heard my grandfathers say there was tobacco in Fujian, and that if you smoked it, it would make you drunk, so it was called 'dry wine.' There was none in this area." He then explains that sometime in the late 1630s, a man surnamed Peng planted some in Shanghai. "I don't know where he got the seeds from, but he planted them here, picked the leaves, dried them in the shade, and got workmen to cut them into threads. He then gave it to traveling merchants to sell elsewhere. Local people didn't dare taste it." The 1639 ban on cultivation in Beijing was enforced in Shanghai as well. Ye reports that the ban "stated that only bandits consume it to ward off the cold and damp, so people were not allowed to grow it and merchants were not allowed to sell it. Anyone breaking this law would be punished by analogy with the law against doing business with foreigners." This prohibition had its effect in Shanghai. Peng was the first to be denounced and everyone else was scared away from cultivating the plant, though not for long. Soldiers were all smoking tobacco within a few years, Ye reports, and in no time peddlers were selling it again throughout the realm. It became profitable for growers, and yet it did not supplant cotton as Shanghai's main commercial crop. "Very little is grown around here," Ye observes at the end of his note.

Macao-to-Guangdong and Manila-to-Fujian were the two first itineraries, but tobacco took a third route into China—a route that was effectively an extension of the first, but more complicated than either. Starting in Macao, it involved four steps. The first step was from Macao to the southernmost Japanese port of Nagasaki. Portuguese merchants sailing from Macao brought tobacco with them, and the Japanese were thrilled. Richard Cocks, who ran a short-lived English trading post there, was amazed at the new rage for tobacco. "It is strange," Cocks observes in his diary, "to see how these Japons, men, women, and children, are besotted in drinking that herb; and, not ten years since it was in use first." In his entry for 7 August 1615, he records that the local lord banned tobacco smoking and ordered all tobacco plants uprooted, to absolutely no effect. Tobacco had transferred effortlessly to Japanese culture. No official ban could stop it.

Cocks's comment that it was "not ten years since it was in use first" allows us to date the arrival of tobacco in Japan to about 1605. Once in Japan, tobacco took a second step, to Korea. The transfer was immediate, to judge from the comment of a Dutchman who was shipwrecked there in 1653. When he was surprised to see the locals smoking, his hosts told him that they had been smoking *nampankoy* or "the *namban* plant" (*namban*, "southern barbarian," was what the Japanese called the Portuguese) already for half a century. The third step was from Korea to Manchuria. The Manchus rapidly became keen smokers, so much so that a French missionary in the nineteenth century assumed that smoking was one of the "usages" that the Manchus imposed on the Chinese. Hongtaiji, the khan who ruled the Manchus in the decades before their conquest of China, was not so happy that this usage had rooted itself among his men. When in 1635 he discovered that his soldiers were selling their weapons to buy tobacco, he imposed a smoking ban.

Hongtaiji was not alone among rulers around the world who were concerned about the economic effects of smoking, nor was he uniquely ineffective. Two years earlier Sultan Murad IV outlawed the production, sale, and consumption of tobacco (as well as coffee) throughout the Ottoman Empire, stiffening earlier prohibitions by making these misdemeanors capital crimes—though this had no effect on his soldiers. A year before that, Christian IV of Denmark banned tobacco from being taken into Norway on the conviction that it was harmful to those of his subjects who lived there; eleven years later, Christian rescinded the ban as unenforceable. Hongtaiji had already done the same thing two years before that. Murad never rescinded his order, though his death in 1640 meant that the prohibition become defunct even before it was officially lifted in Norway and Manchuria.

The final step on this third route was from Manchuria into northeast China, especially Beijing. There tobacco was known as the "southern herb," though its arrival across the northeast border led some Chinese to suppose that tobacco was native to Korea. By 1637, the two types of tobacco fetching the best prices in Beijing were Fujianese and Manchurian. This is where Yang Shicong picks up the thread—and the association with sand grouse that leads him to suspect that smoking has to do with the Manchu threat on the border. The third route is thus a chain of links that no one could have predicted: the world empire of the Portuguese stretching from Brazil through Goa in India and up to Japan; the regional trading network of the Japanese into Korea; the circuit of exchange within the Korean peninsula that circulated goods up to Manchuria; and the cross-border trade between Manchuria and China that enabled the Manchus, thanks to their hugely profitable business in this and other commodities such as gold and ginseng, to finance their eventual conquest of China in 1644.

WE HAVE OBSERVED THAT sixteenth-century Europeans felt obliged to come up with ways of making sense of tobacco. Seventeenth-century writers in China worked at the same problem of understanding something so foreign and new.

Take Yao Lü, an obscure writer whose *Dew Book* is now extremely rare. In the front half of his book, Yao jots down his views on ancient matters; in the back, he muses on modern things, and that is where we find his thoughts on *danbagu*. Yao assumes his reader is ignorant of what smoking entails, so he explains that "you use fire to burn a bowlful, then bring the pipe to your mouth. The smoke goes through the stem and down your throat." The effect of inhaling the smoke he analogizes to drunkenness, referring to *danbagu*'s alternate name, "golden-shred inebriant." He gives Luzon as tobacco's place of origin and the Zhangzhou port of Moon Harbor as its point of entry. Indeed, he notes that the farmers of Zhangzhou adapted it so well that "now there is more here than in Luzon, so they ship it to that country to sell it." Serious smokers, however, felt that domestic tobacco was no match for Luzon tobacco—just as Filipinos regarded their tobacco as inferior to American, and as the English regarded their homegrown weed as weaker than Virginian. Within China, Fujian tobacco was considered the best. "People in the Yangzi Valley and the Hunan interior are planting it," another Chinese writer reports, "but theirs lacks the yellow hue and fineness of leaf of the tobacco grown in Fujian." Still, even this second-rate tobacco found a market.

Not all Chinese intellectuals were at ease with the idea that something so wonderful could be entirely foreign in origin. Some preferred to think that it had been in China all along, so they scanned the voluminous records of the past—the culture's repository of good sense—in the hope of discovering that tobacco was safely Chinese after all. The poet-painter Wu Weiye, for instance, could not rest easy with the common view that "the smoke plant was not heard of in ancient times." He eventually found a phrase in the official history of the Tang dynasty about "holy fire" and offered this reference as proof that Chinese were already smoking in the ninth century. Taking up smoking in the seventeenth century was simply reviving a precedent. This wasn't true, of course, but it was Wu's way of trying to come to terms with tobacco's foreign origin—trying, in effect, to negate the reality of transculturation by believing that the practice of smoking was already thoroughly and safely Chinese.

The more effective way of finding a legitimate cultural niche in China for tobacco was to argue, as many did early on, that tobacco could have a place in Chinese medicine. It was a herb capable of producing powerful effects within the body, after all, so why not graft it onto the existing system of medical botany? Yao Lü, for instance, believed that tobacco "can block malarial vapours." He also reported that pounding its leaves into a paste and rubbing that into the scalp got rid of head lice. Fang Yizhi accepted that tobacco had pharmacopoeic properties, though he worried that its drying capacity was too fierce for safe use. "It can be used to dispel dampness," he allows, "but long usage heats up the lungs. Other medicines mostly have no effect. Those afflicted with tobacco poisoning will suddenly vomit a yellowish liquid and die."

The best early medical assessment of tobacco comes from the influential Hangzhou physician and medical writer of the early seventeenth century, Zhang Jiebin. Zhang was puzzled as to how to classify this new plant. He decided, mistakenly, to put tobacco in his pharmacopoeia alongside plants that grow in marshy conditions, but it was a late addition. Zhang numbers the entries in his book, and the entry for tobacco appears between entries "77" and "78" under a heading that we might translate as "77+." Zhang starts the entry by describing tobacco's taste and properties. Then he outlines what ailments it can treat and under what conditions it should be avoided. He cross-references it to his entry on betel nut. There he notes that both plants inspire habitual use, especially among southerners, but that betel nut is milder and better suited for treating digestive ailments.

Zhang admits to having tried tobacco, as a good experimental scientist should. He did not become an enthusiast, however. He judged the taste acrid and the sensation that a few puffs produced, which he describes as a type of intoxication, not pleasurable. He found that the effect took a long time to wear off. For those who want to get rid of the sensation, Zhang advises taking cold water or refined sugar. These are strong yin substances that can counteract the near-pure yang of tobacco. In mild doses, Zhang allows that tobacco's yang can help the body to dispel phlegm, remove congestion, warm the internal organs, and speed circulation. Too much of the drug, however, will do more harm than good—though in that, tobacco was no different from any other medicinal plant.

Tobacco eventually shed the fanciful pharmacological and botanical explanations attached to it, and dire predictions about vomiting yellowish liquid dropped from sight. Especially after the ban became a dead letter, everyone in China started smoking. Dong Han, a Shanghai essayist writing late in the seventeenth century, wonders how this came about. Dong starts by noting that, outside Fujian Province, only 1 or 2 percent of people took up smoking before the 1640s. Thereafter, however, smoking spread throughout the Yangtze Delta, taking hold in the cities and then spreading into the villages, first among men and then with women. In his own time it had become standard etiquette when guests arrived to offer them a smoke. Dong has no answer as to why this happened, nor whether he became a smoker too. He can only shrug and say, "There's really no knowing why it is that people change their customs."

Other writers make much the same observations about smoking spreading rapidly to all classes, all ages, and both genders. As one pharmacologist put it, "Among those throughout the realm who enjoy smoking, there is no distinction of high and low, or of male and female." Even the very young, especially if they were from Fujian, took up the habit. European visitors to China in the nineteenth century were amazed to see girls of eight or nine years of age carrying pipes and tobacco in their pockets and purses. If they were not yet smoking, they were at least adopting the accessories they needed to appear grown up.

Upper-class women were especially enthusiastic about smoking. We catch a striking glimpse of unusual smoking practices among elegant women in a curious observation that an eighteenth-century writer records when writing about the customs of the elite of Suzhou, the busy commercial and cultural hub on the Yangtze Delta. It seems that the grand ladies of Suzhou smoked from the moment they got up to the moment they went to bed. Given their busy social schedules, the smoking habit put pressure on how they organized their days, more especially on how they organized their mornings. The writer says that elegant Suzhou women refused to get up until they had had several pipefuls of tobacco. Since this delayed the arduous but essential task of doing their hair and makeup before emerging, they ordered their maids to do their coiffures while they were still asleep. That way, they could afford the time to smoke before getting out of bed. The scene is a little hard to imagine.

Chinese women may have smoked just as fiercely as men, but their bodies were believed to be different. Smoking should have different effects based on the physiological differences between men and women. Being of the yang gender, men were better able to withstand the heat of smoking. The yang of their bodies counteracted the yang of the tobacco. Women were of the yin gender, and their damp constitutions might be damaged by the heating effect of so much yang. They needed to protect themselves from the natural excess of yang that came with smoking. The issue was not, strictly speaking, only one of gender, for doctors gave elderly men, whose natural yang was weak, the same advice. For both groups, the yang of tobacco smoke could be reduced by drawing it through pipes with longer stems. The Chinese pipe was an imitation of the Native American pipe, as were early pipes in Europe, but the stem of Chinese pipes grew longer and longer, and among women became almost unmanageable. A woman poet of the eighteenth century, remembered only as Master Lü's Wife, jokes about the inconvenience of smoking such a pipe in her dressing room:

> This long stick of a tobacco pipe
> Is too big to put on my dressing table;
> When I lift it, it tears the window paper—
> I hook the moonlight and drag it in.

Another way of mitigating the heat of tobacco was to cool the smoke by passing it through that most *yin* of substances, water—hence the appeal of the water pipe, or hookah. Unlike in the Ottoman world, where it was first developed, the water pipe in China was reserved exclusively for women. In fact, a finely crafted water pipe became the sign of an elegant female. By the nineteenth century, no woman of style would deign to puff on a plain-stemmed pipe. Pipes were strictly for men and the lower classes. The same fashion mechanism went into effect when factory-made cigarettes arrived at the beginning of the twentieth century and pursued their long-drawn-out battle against pipes. A man might take them up, but a woman who smoked a cigarette was being risqué. By the 1920s, however, a female urban sophisticate would not be caught dead smoking a pipe. That was for the old hags back in the villages.

Just as women fit tobacco into their lives in ways that suited their habits, so too did men. Gentlemen were particularly concerned to conform their smoking to the requirements of the socially elegant life. Addicted to tobacco, they wanted it to be seen as part of what made a gentleman a gentleman and not a commoner. Given that everyone already smoked, it was not immediately obvious how this should be done. But gradually a set of customs was developed to give smoking the patina of distinctive refinement. To start with, one had to buy the more expensive brands of tobacco, since price was assumed to discriminate the connoisseur from the mere consumer. Yet that was not enough of a barrier between elite and common, since anyone with enough money but no taste could still enter the charmed circle on this basis. There had to be rituals around these activities that distinguished the elegant gentleman from the rich boor. Gentlemen had to practice their indulgence of tobacco differently from ordinary people.

One way in which they construed their taste for tobacco differently was to treat the compulsion to smoke as a sign of the true gentlemen. Elegant men, declared one elite commentator, "cannot do without it however briefly, and to the end of their lives never tire of it." Addiction was not a physical shortcoming, as we like to interpret it, but the sign of a passionate mind. A gentleman did not smoke just because he liked to; everyone liked to smoke. He did so because his sensitive nature turned him into a *yanke*, "tobacco's guest" or "tobacco's bondservant." The refined gentleman experienced the desire to smoke as an estimable compulsion, something that his pure nature could not allow him to do without. It seems to us like an elevated way of explaining nicotine addiction before that concept was available; but for the Chinese elite it was more than that. It was a marker of social status deeply embedded in the particular cultural norms of late-imperial China.

Around this sense of compulsion grew up an elite culture of smoking, in praise of which the poets were enlisted. Hundreds of poems on the subject of tobacco survive from the seventeenth and eighteenth centuries. The noted poet Shen Deqian wrote an entire cycle of smoking poems, in which he presents smoking as the most refined of pleasures and the most elegant of pastimes, quite beyond the appreciation of ordinary folk. If they appear in the poems, it is only as servants, never as smokers. Here he describes his ivory pipe:

> Through my pipe I draw the fiery vapour,
> From out of my chest I spew white clouds.
> The attendant takes away the ash,
> Brings wine to amplify the intoxication.

I apply the flame to know the taste,
Letting it burn in the elephant's tusk.

Smoke in turns presents the poet with an image that allows him to align smoking to clouds and the heavenly realm of Daoist immortals and even the cosmos, all of which lie far beyond the reach of ordinary human experience. Another poet similarly associates tobacco smoke with the summoning of souls, like incense before an ancestral tablet:

Soul-summoning fragrance rises from the tobacco:
All over the country all the time the plant is being picked.
I laugh to think that in days of yore people had only
   ordinary leaves
As I watch a world of smoke and cloud pour out of you.

These poems appear in an anthology of poetry and prose devoted entirely to the theme of smoking. The collection was assembled in the eighteenth century by Chen Cong, a gentleman of leisure living just west of Shanghai. Chen had a local reputation as a poet, but *The Tobacco Manual* is the book for which he is best known. Smoking was the great passion of his life, and the only way he can explain this passion is to suppose an affinity with a past life. He muses that he must have been a Buddhist monk once, and that "my having burned incense in an earlier life" explains why he is compelled to inhale burning fumes in this life. In his book he anthologizes the work of prominent poets, like Shen Deqian, but he also includes poems he commissioned his friends to write specially for the volume. One friend responded to his invitation by describing Chen ("my arriving guest") coming to his home. Naturally, politeness demands that he receive his visitor by offering him a smoke:

The tobacco box is casually produced for my arriving guest,
A gentleman who has known all the matters of my heart for
   a decade.

Poetic blossoms have sprung from his brush since his childhood,
And now *The Tobacco Manual* emerges from our clouds of smoke.

If Chen Cong is smoking's literary chronicler, Lu Yao is its arbiter
of taste. His *Smoking Manual* of 1774 is a documentary of smoking
practices as well as a guide explaining how to smoke elegantly. "In recent times there has not been one gentleman who does not smoke,"
Lu declares. "Liquor and food they can dispense with, but tobacco
they absolutely cannot do without." Since everyone was smoking, it
was essential that the well-bred smoker learn not to do it like any
common rustic. Smoking was part of one's personality, and had to be
done in a way that expressed the smoker's social distinction. Lu's passion in his book is thus to align smoking with elegance. To this end,
he compiles several lists of good and bad smoking decorum: when it
is appropriate to smoke and when it is taboo, when the smoker should
restrain the urge to smoke and when it can be done without offense.
He notes that "even women and children all have a pipe in their
hands," but his instructions are not for them. They are for his social
peers.

Lu dictates certain occasions when it is appropriate to light up:
when you have just woken up, after a meal, and when you are enter-
taining a guest. He also advocates smoking as a stimulant for writing,
as many a contemporary did. "When you are moistening the ink and
licking the brush to compose poetry and just cannot loosen your
thoughts, hum in quiet meditation and inhale some fine tobacco: it
cannot help but be of some aid." There were, however, occasions
when it absolutely did not do to smoke: when listening to string music, for instance, or looking at plum blossoms, or performing a ritual
ceremony. He reminded his readers that smoking was definitely inap-
propriate when you appeared before the emperor. It was also not to
be indulged in while making love with a "beautiful woman," by which
he meant someone other than your wife.

Lu's book is also full of practical advice. Don't smoke while riding
a horse. You may stick your tobacco pouch and pipe in your belt so

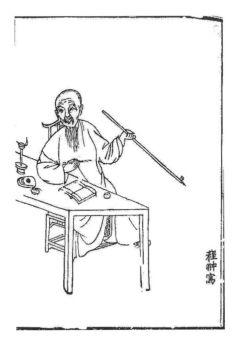

Tobacco enthusiast Chen Cong. From his *Tobacco Manual*, 1805.

that you can smoke once you get where you're going—to forget to bring your own tobacco could put you in an awkward situation later on—but don't light up until you dismount. Similarly, while walking on fallen leaves is not a good time to light up, nor while standing next to a pile of old paper. Lu also offers face-saving tips on decorum. Don't smoke while coughing up phlegm or when your breathing rasps. If you keep trying to light your pipe and it doesn't catch, just put it aside. In other words, don't let your smoking create a poor appearance. One final piece of strategic advice is offered for the socially overburdened. If you have a guest on your hands whom you would rather see depart, don't bring out the tobacco. He'll only linger.

THIS ELEGANT HABIT OF REFINED consumption morphed unexpectedly in the nineteenth century into something quite different, and quite unexpected: opium addiction. The poppy from which opium is refined was, like tobacco, of foreign origin, though it had long ago been indigenized in China as an expensive medicine used to relieve a range of ailments from constipation and abdominal cramps to toothache and general debility. It was not something you smoked, however; it was taken in pill or tonic form. By one report, a considerable amount of opium, under the pleasant name of "hibiscus medicine," went to the imperial palace in the later reigns of the Ming dynasty, where it was used for its pharmacopoeic properties and not as a recreational drug. Given the general understanding that all things ingested affected the well-being of the body, the line between the two was not sharply drawn.

At the turn of the seventeenth century, the Dutch started bringing opium from India into Southeast Asia, where they sold it as a mood enhancer, specifically with military applications. It was believed that if opium was given to soldiers, it made them fearless. In 1605, the VOC was able to use a gift of gunpowder and six pounds of opium to entice the king of Ternate, one of the smaller Spice Islands boasting a huge output of cloves, into a trading relationship. Both were to use in wars against his rivals. When Muslims in the southern Philippines were fighting the Spanish in the following decade, it was said that an assassin dispatched to kill the Spanish commander had rendered himself fearless by taking opium before carrying out his assignment.

The consumption of opium broadened only when it merged with an agent that could deliver the drug in a palatable form, and that agent was none other than tobacco. Soaking tobacco leaves in a solution derived from the sap of opium poppies produced a far more potent form of tobacco. This doctored product was called *madak*, and it seems to have been taken up as a more potent version of tobacco rather than as a different drug altogether. The practice started among Chinese trading with the Dutch on Taiwan, where they briefly maintained a base until 1662. From there it slipped into China. Chen Cong assumed that it arrived by the same route as tobacco, entering Moon Harbor from

Manila, but it is the Dutch rather than the Spanish who get the credit for the drug's introduction—yet another strand in Indra's seventeenth-century web.

Opium and tobacco had two things in common. They were smoked, and they had come to China from a distant place through foreign hands. Lu Yao and Chen Cong both decided that this was enough to justify including the subject of opium in their tobacco manuals, although opium was shifting away from madak form just at this time. By late in the eighteenth century, opium was not smoked as madak. It was consumed directly by igniting small lumps in a pipe bowl tilted over an oil lamp, then inhaling the smoke through the stem. The modern opium fix had found its form.

From what Chen Cong was able to learn about opium, the substance was not just a more potent form of tobacco. He makes this point after quoting at length this anonymous description of opium intoxication as "the realm of perfect happiness": "How shall I describe the beauties of opium? Its smell is fragrant, its taste lightly sweet, and it deals well with a dampened spirit and melancholy thoughts. As soon as I lie down and lean on an armrest to inhale, my spirit revives, my head clears, and my vision becomes sharper. Then my chest expands and my exaltation doubles. After some time my bones and sinews feel tired and my eyes want to close. At that moment I plump my pillow and lie in perfect peace without a care in the world"—to which Chen skeptically replies, "Oh, really?" Lu Yao likewise is suspicious of this potent form of "smoke." He even revives the specter of death by smoking, which Chinese tobacco wisdom had set aside a century earlier.

Opium's "realm of perfect happiness" was a space many Chinese chose to enter during the next great wave of globalization in the nineteenth century, when English traders brought opium from India to China to reverse the trade deficit that came from buying so much tea. (They also started building tea plantations in India to reduce the distance and therefore the cost of transport.) Chinese merchants proved willing to retail this profitable commodity, promoting its

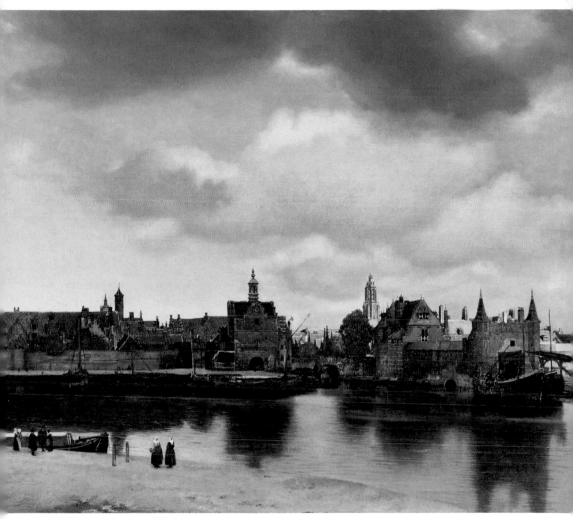

PLATE 1. JOHANNES VERMEER, *VIEW OF DELFT* (MAURITSHUIS, THE HAGUE). This painting, one of Vermeer's two outdoor scenes, depicts the skyline of Delft as seen from the southeast across the Kolk, Delft's river harbor. It was painted in 1660 or 1661.

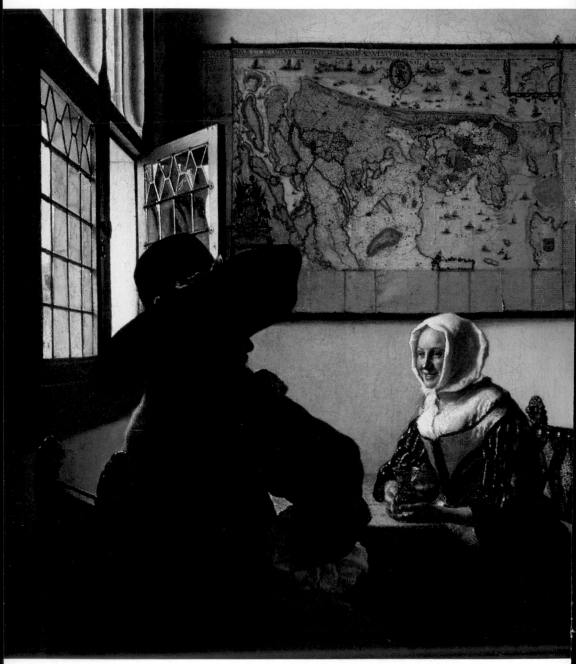

PLATE 2. JOHANNES VERMEER, *OFFICER AND LAUGHING GIRL* (FRICK COLLECTION, NEW YORK). Mild perspectival distortion imparts dynamism to this painting of what would otherwise be a static conversation. The map of Holland and West Friesland on the wall is a Willem Blaeu print from plates by Delft mapmaker Balthasar van Berckenrode. The painting dates from around 1658.

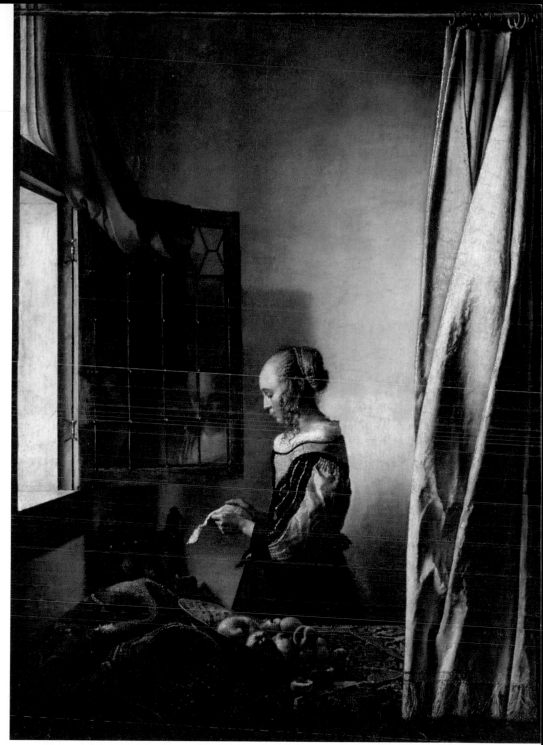

PLATE 3. JOHANNES VERMEER, *YOUNG WOMAN READING A LETTER AT AN OPEN WINDOW* (GEMÄLDEGALERIE, DRESDEN). This may be the earliest of the many works that Vermeer produced by the windows of his upstairs studio. The carpet and fruit in the foreground show his first use of the pointillist technique. It was painted about 1657.

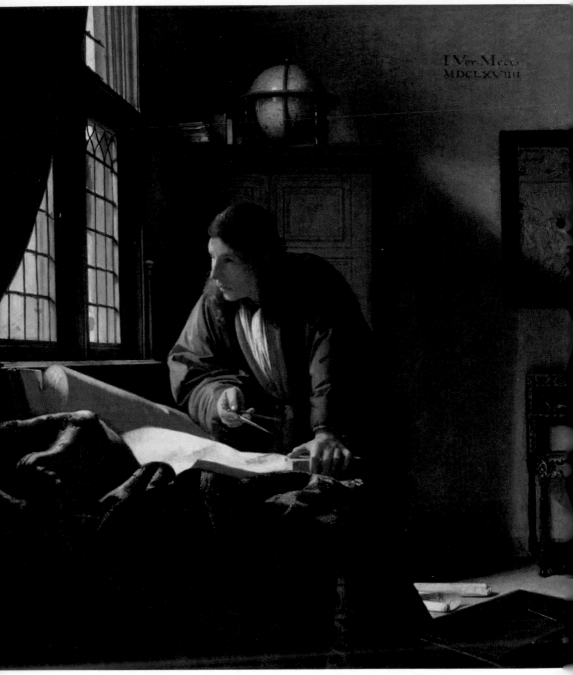

PLATE 4. JOHANNES VERMEER, *THE GEOGRAPHER* (STÄDELSCHES KUNSTINSTITUT, FRANKFURT-AM-MAIN). This is one of a pair of paintings (with *The Astronomer*), probably commissioned, of a man of learning who may be Antony van Leeuwenhoek. Although the date of 1669 that appears on the wall below Vermeer's signature is not original, it may correctly date the painting.

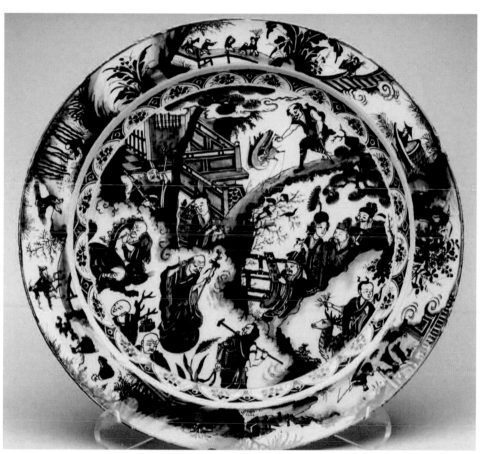

PLATE 5. A PLATE FROM THE LAMBERT VAN MEERTEN MUSEUM OF DELFT (GEMEENTE MUSEA DELFT). The plate was probably manufactured in Delft around the end of the seventeenth century. Its faux-Chinese decoration depicts five religious figures in the clouds in the foreground and a variety of male and female figures in a Chinese garden behind.

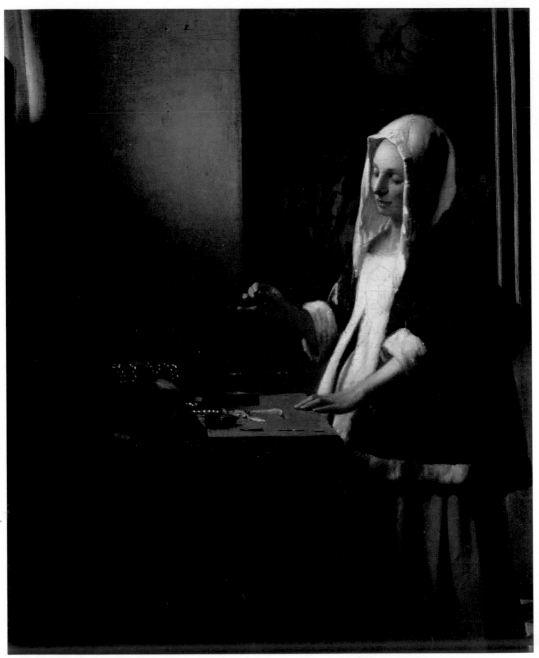

PLATE 6. JOHANNES VERMEER, *WOMAN HOLDING A BALANCE* (WIDENER COLLECTION, NATIONAL GALLERY OF ART, WASHINGTON, D.C.). Vermeer produced this work in about 1664. The model was probably his wife, Catharina Bolnes. The painting shows Vermeer at the height of his creative powers.

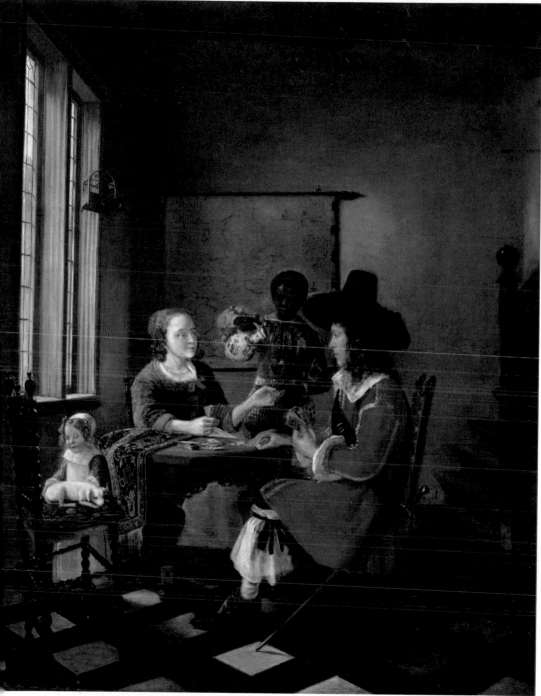

PLATE 7. HENDRIK VAN DER BURCH, *THE CARD PLAYERS* (DETROIT INSTITUTE OF ARTS, GIFT OF MR. AND MRS. JOHN S. NEWBERRY). Van der Burch handles the subject of a seated conversation between an officer and a young woman differently from Vermeer in *Officer and Laughing Girl*. The painting dates to about 1660, when Van der Burch was in either Leiden or Amsterdam, as he had left Delft by 1655.

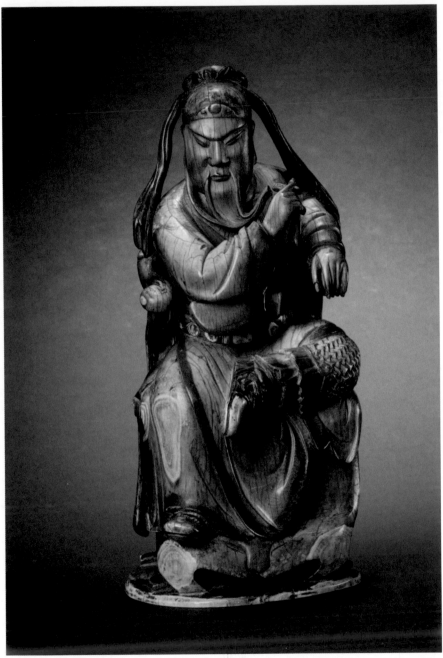

PLATE 8. EMPEROR GUAN, THE CHINESE GOD OF WAR, HERE DEPICTED IN IVORY. The statue that the Christian convert exhumed outside Manila in January 1640 would have been roughly contemporary with this figure.

distribution throughout the country. Opium would work its way into all levels of society, just as tobacco had done, forcing a far more troubling transculturation that still haunts Chinese memories of their past and serves as an enduring symbol of China's victimization by the West.

Just how successfully opium transculturated into China is illustrated by the following poem, which invokes all the standard Daoist tropes of tobacco poetry to domesticate the drug. This poem appears in a little booklet called *The Condolence Collection*. The booklet is a collection of verses suitable for sending on the death of a friend. Each verse is crafted to suit a particular occasion. The poems in the last section have been tagged according to cause of death. The following verse, marked as suitable for sending on the occasion of a death by opium overdose, shows how thoroughly the taste for opium was lodged in the culture that received it:

> Swallowing dawn mist and drinking sea vapors, he was
>   indifferent [to censure];
> Through opium pods and incense, he proved himself
>   immortal before his time.
> He may have sealed up his white bones with opium paste,
> Yet never he will be without a lamp to illuminate the Yellow
>   Springs [Hades].
> Relying on his opium pipe, he expended great effort to
>   comprehend his fate,
> In the midst of fire and smoke, he uttered his final thoughts.
> Mounting a crane and bestriding the wind, where has he
>   now gone?
> He has simply followed the tide of smoke, arriving at the
>   Western Heaven.

The romance of opium has long since disappeared. In its turn, the long era of global tobacco smoking is fitfully approaching an end. But we should remember that our rejection of smoking is quite recent. Back in 1924, tobacco was not something to deplore or give up.

When the German polymath Berthold Laufer in that year published his pamphlet on the history of tobacco in Asia, he ended it by praising smoking. "Of all the gifts of nature, tobacco has been the most potent social factor, the most efficient peacemaker, and greatest benefactor to mankind. It has made the whole world akin and united it into a common bond. Of all luxuries it is the most democratic and the most universal; it has contributed a large share toward democratizing the world. The very word has penetrated into all languages of the globe, and is understood everywhere." Though smokers can today still be counted in the hundreds of millions worldwide, this sentiment is no longer one we embrace. Pleasure and health now go in different directions.

As the global community of smokers grew in the seventeenth century, though, they were uninhibited in expressing their delight at discovering the pleasures of tobacco and have left behind many signs of their debt to its pleasures. One of the more exuberant and unexpected is a tobacco ballet that the townspeople of Turin, Italy, staged in 1650. The first act of the ballet opens with a troupe of townspeople dressed up in native costumes, dancing together and singing their praises to God for having given humankind such a wonderful herb. The dramatist may have acquired the idea for this scene from illustrations of native customs in books about the Americas, which were popular with European readers. (Such exotic public displays of native customs were a fashion unto themselves, especially if one had actual Natives to perform them. Johann Maurits, who used the fortune he made from plantations in Brazil to build the palatial residence in The Hague that is now the Mauritshuis museum, included in the opening ceremonies a dance by eleven Brazilian Indians on the cobbled square out front.) In the second act of the tobacco ballet, another troupe of townspeople appears. This group is dressed in costumes from all over the world. Surely the pantomime would have called for someone to be in Chinese costume. There was a Chinese smoking on the Van Meerten plate, so there probably was one in the Turin ballet. The show ends with these representatives of world cultures making their way together to a School for Smoking, where they sit down and beg the first troupe to instruct them in the virtues of tobacco.

WEIGHING SILVER

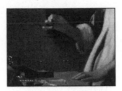

EIGHT YEARS HAVE passed since Johannes Vermeer painted *Officer and Laughing Girl* and *Young Woman Reading a Letter by an Open Window*. His wife, Catharina Bolnes, has spent most of those years pregnant, and if I am right in seeing her as the model in those paintings, she appears to be pregnant again when her husband brings her into his studio to pose for *Woman Holding a Balance* (see plate 6). Catharina is looking older. Now in her early thirties, she is no longer girlish in posture or manner, and more the mistress of her emotions. Then she was absorbed in the excitements of youth; now she calmly concentrates, without seeming effort, on the task before her. Vermeer has darkened the studio to subdue the animation in his earlier versions of this room by closing the lower shutters and letting the drape over the upper window block out much of the light from outside. Catharina holds a balance. Her hand is positioned precisely at the painting's vanishing point, but the focus of our attention is on her face. Serenely composed, almost a mask, its untroubled concentration draws our gaze. Our eyes may dart to the strings of luminescent pearls and the shining gold chain slung carelessly over the edge of her jewelry case, but they return to her.

The only suggestion of movement is the painting of the Last Judgment in the Flemish style hanging on the wall behind Catharina. Her head and upper torso are framed by an apocalyptic vision of Christ with his arms raised, summoning the dead to arise and be judged by him. His heavenly throne glows directly over the woman's head, and mortals on either side of her look to the heavens and clamor to be saved. Contrary to the animation and violent motion of this picture, Catharina appears as calm and untroubled as the whitewashed stretch of wall beside the heavily framed canvas. The painting-within-the-painting is there to guide the viewer to the theme of moral discrimination. The conscientious must carefully weigh their conduct just as Christ will weigh good and evil at the Final Judgment. Vermeer may even have intended that we observe Catharina's gentle posture and think of the Virgin Mary, who intercedes on behalf of poor sinners so that they too may enter heaven.

The allegory of judgment is obvious. But let us set aside the painting's iconography and direct our attention instead to what the real woman in this painting is actually doing. She is holding a balance preparatory to weighing something, but what? This painting was once known as *Woman Weighing Pearls*, but that title doesn't fit. There are one or two strings of pearls on the table, but they have been casually set aside; no individual pearls are waiting to be weighed. The only things on the table that she might put in her balance are the coins along the edge of the table to her left: four small gold coins and one large silver coin. This is a painting of a woman about to weigh money. Contemporaries would have seen this more clearly than we do, as this was a common subject for Dutch painters at this time. Indeed, Vermeer may have taken the subject, and even the design, of this painting from a less successful picture by his fellow Delft artist Pieter de Hooch.

When Vermeer's painting was put up for sale in the auction of his son-in-law's collection in 1696, it was called *Young Lady Weighing Gold*. This catalog title brings us closer to the subject, *gelt* being the Germanic word for "money." Weighing coins is not something we do today, but it was an essential part of economic transactions in the seventeenth century. Silver and gold coins of the time were softer than they are today, and use gradually wore down the metal, reducing the weight of silver or gold each coin contained. The careful householder therefore had to weigh her coins to know how much they were really worth. This problem would have been negligible were there a standard currency in use, but one had yet to be established. The United Provinces had a standard unit of account, the guilder, but there were no actual guilders in circulation in the 1660s when Vermeer painted this picture, only silver ducats (one of which weighed 24.37 grams). The guilder (weighing 19.144 grams of fine silver) had been issued in the mid-sixteenth century, but was thereafter superseded by other coins, some Spanish and some Dutch. Fortunately for the burgeoning commercial economy, the substitution of one type of coin for another did not interfere with the main purpose of money, which is to calibrate the relative value of objects. The real constant in these calculations was the price of the precious metal in the coin, not its face value. Still, no European state allowed its merchants to set prices by weight in unminted silver, which was the Chinese practice at this time. In the Dutch Republic, every commodity had a price in guilders, even when there were no guilders in circulation, and had to be paid for in coin. In 1681, the States of Holland, the provincial government for the Delft region, decided to revive the guilder (resetting its value at 9.61 grams of fine silver). The much larger silver ducat continued to be used elsewhere in the Netherlands for another decade, until at last the entire Republic went over to guilders.

We cannot see the silver coin on Catharina's table well enough to identify it. The estimated date of the painting (1664) argues in favor of this being a ducat, not a guilder. We can corroborate this by considering its sole visible characteristic, its size. It is much larger than the gold coins beside it. Unlike silver coins, which were minted in many weights and denominations, most gold coins circulating in the United Provinces were of one type, the gold ducat (weighing 3.466 grams). A gold ducat was worth roughly two silver ducats. Given a silver-to-gold ratio of about twelve to one, it should therefore have weighed about a sixth of a silver ducat. This seems roughly to be the size differential between the silver and gold coins laid out on the corner of the table, circumstantial evidence that Catharina's silver coin is indeed a ducat.

Knowing something about Dutch currency does not lead us away from the theme of moral discrimination that imbues the painting. As the woman weighs her coins, so she measures her own behavior in the light of the divine judgment awaiting her at the resurrection. It is worth knowing that some artists used the image of a woman weighing coins to condemn the contemporary obsession with silver, not just the sin of worldliness. But that is not the sense of this painting. Vermeer is not inviting us to condemn Catharina. He bathes her in light, making her a figure of trust and conscience. She handles money, but her calculating of the family's wealth is as honorable and wholesome as the fecundity of natural increase that her pregnancy signifies. Vermeer's depiction is positive, in keeping with the new ethic of accumulation in seventeenth-century Holland. The capitalist economy was in formation, and making money was a virtue, so long as it was made by fair means. This, at least, is what the Dutch middle class now believed. Even Christ in this painting seems to bless Catharina's accountancy.

The large silver coin on Catharina's table is our next door into the mid-seventeenth-century world. At the end of the corridor on the other side of this door we will catch a glimpse of the single most important global commodity of the time—silver. Silver played an enormous role in the economy of this period, shaping the lives of all who were touched by it, including Catharina's.

VERMEER LIVED TOWARD THE END of what has been called the silver century, which began around 1570. At no previous time had so much of this precious metal been circulating in travelers' satchels, on pack animals, in riverboats, and, most of all, in the cargo holds of the Chinese junks and European carracks restlessly plying the waters of the globe. Silver was suddenly available in unheard-of volumes, and suddenly everything was being bought and sold according to its standard. That a thing could be "sold for its weight in silver," the price that a mid-seventeenth-century English writer claimed Virginian tobacco cost at the turn of the century, was an expression calculated to amaze ordinary people. The cost of something in silver could also be taken as the height of folly, as a character in a Thomas Dekker play of 1600 observes when he satirizes a keen smoker as "an ass that melts so much money in smoke."

The power that silver exerted on the world was something of a mystery to those who actually thought about it. It could be put to decorative purposes, yet its actual uses were limited. Most people wanted to acquire it, but they did so only to acquire other things. Its own value was purely arbitrary.

To contemporary moralists from Europe to China, silver created the illusion of wealth but was not itself wealth. It was, in the words of Paolo Xu, the Catholic convert in the Ming court, "merely the measure of wealth." It was superfluous to the production of real value. The ruler who was concerned about the welfare of his people should be concerned that they had enough food, clothing, and land, not that they had enough silver. The problem with this maxim was that it no longer applied in a fully commercialized economy. If everything could be bought and sold for silver, then silver *was* all you needed. In a partially commercialized economy, on the other hand, which is the economy that most people in the seventeenth century inhabited, silver was useless when its supply dried up or famine drove prices beyond the reach of ordinary people, which still regularly happened. But once silver was present in the economy, most people had no choice but to use it, whether to buy their food or pay their taxes. They also had no choice but to acquire it by selling things or their own labor. Silver became unavoidable.

The percolation of silver down into everyday transactions in Europe and China occurred as these economies were expanding, which created a huge demand for it. Chinese needed to import silver to compensate for their inadequate money supply, and Europeans needed to export it to buy their way into the Asian market. These needs created a demand for silver that stimulated supply from two major sources: Japan and South America. It was around this structure of supply and demand that the global economy of the seventeenth century took form. Silver was the perfect commodity that appeared at just the right time, linking regional economies into a web of interregional exchange that set the patterns for our own global predicaments.

Where did the silver in Catharina's coin come from? Japan was a major producer of silver in the seventeenth century, and Dutch merchants handled much of its exported bullion, as they alone were permitted to trade in Japan. But almost none of it found its way back to Europe. The Dutch profited from it strictly within the intra-Asian trade. So the silver in Catharina's coin was likely not Japanese. There were much closer silver mines in Germany and Austria, though these accounted for barely 5 percent of world production, and most of their output was drawn into cash-poor Eastern Europe. So it is unlikely the silver was German. That leaves the only other major world source of silver, Spanish America, either New Spain (today's Mexico) or Peru (which in the seventeenth century encompassed today's Bolivia).

For the sake of marking a clear trail, let us suppose it came from the Bolivian part of Peru, more specifically from the mining city that was more productive than any other in the first half of the seventeenth century. Let us suppose it came from Potosí.

Potosí sits above the tree line at an altitude of four thousand meters, a zone that the people of the Andes declared to be *puna*, "uninhabitable." A great beehive of a mountain, called Cerro Rico, or the Rich Hill, stands on the barren, windswept plain. The place would have remained forever *puna* were it not for the thick veins of high-grade silver running through the mountain. Before the Spanish Conquest, the Indians had mined this silver, but there was a limit to their need for precious metals. The same could not be said for the Spanish. The first Spaniards brought here by Indians in 1545 thought their wildest dreams had come true. Although the conditions on the high plain are harsh, nothing could deter them from exploiting the mountain's treasure. At first they used recruitment to get Indians to mine the silver, but once the Indians discovered how dangerous and unprofitable the work was, the Spaniards instituted the *mita*, a system of forced labor dragooning Indians into labor service from as far away as eight hundred kilometers to work in the mines.

Almost overnight, Potosí became the largest city in the Americas. The early decades, when the ore was rich and easy to dig, saw the city grow to 120,000 by 1570. People from all over Europe and South America showed up to live on this barren site and produce the silver or supply the goods and services a city demands. The productivity of the mines could not continue at that initial level, but even with their slow decline through the seventeenth century, the population continued to grow, approaching 150,000 in 1639. Thereafter it gradually dwindled, falling below the 100,000 mark in the 1680s.

While the boom lasted, mine owners made incredible fortunes. The phrase "as rich as Potosí" entered the English language. No one lived in the shadow of the Rich Hill and remained untouched, though whether one did well or badly depended on a complex array of factors that included ethnic status, social ties, capital, and pure luck. As fortunes were made and lost, violence did much of the sorting among those who were caught between extreme wealth and extreme poverty: violence between Spaniards and Indians, between Spanish-born and American-born (known as Creoles), and between ethnic factions, especially between the Basques, who tended to control the ore refineries, and everyone else. One small incident or affront to honor could throw the entire city into turmoil. When in 1647 the American-born Mariana de Osorio on her wedding day rejected the Basque to whom her Andalusian parents betrothed her in favor of a Creole who had been wooing her through the Creole manager of her father's refinery, a virtual civil war erupted between Basques and Creoles that dragged on for years.

Potosí did far more than enrich the men who controlled it and pit the rest in deadly struggles against each other. It enriched Spain first of all, but it also financed the consolidation of the Spanish Empire in South America, funded its reach across the Pacific to the Philippines, and drew the formerly separate economies of the Americas, Europe, and Asia into a de facto condominium. This happened without anyone intending that it should. Silver gained a global life of its own, as individuals improvised in the face of opportunity and compulsion to keep the bullion flowing.

Before the silver could be transported, it had to be coined at the Potosí mint into reals.[1] The greater portion went to Europe by two different routes, the official route and the "back door." The official route, under the control of the Spanish crown, ran west over the mountains to the port of Arica on the coast, a journey by pack animal that took two and a half months. From the coast of Peru it was shipped north to Panama, whence Spanish ships carried it across the Atlantic to Cadiz, the port serving Seville, the center of the world silver trade. The back door route was technically illegal but so profitable that it siphoned off as much as a third of Potosí's silver production. This route went south down to the Rio de la Plata, the River of Silver, into Argentina, the Land of Silver. It arrived in Buenos Aires, where Portuguese merchants transported it across the Atlantic to Lisbon. There it was exchanged for commodities that were in demand in Peru, particularly African slaves. Much of the silver that reached Lisbon and Seville moved quickly to London and Amsterdam, but it did not tarry for long there. It passed through them and on to its final destination, the place that Europeans would later call "the tomb of European moneys": China.

China was the great global destination for European silver for two reasons. First of all, the power of silver to buy gold in Asian economies was higher than it was in Europe. If twelve units of silver were needed to buy one unit of gold in Europe, the same amount of gold could be bought for six or less in China. In other words, silver coming from Europe bought twice as much in China compared to what it could buy in Europe. Adriano de las Cortes makes this point when he describes sixty-eight ceremonial stone arches spanning the main street of Chaozhou in his record of his year of captivity in China. He expects his reader to be astonished at the lavishness of this scene, then explains that the cost in silver of building them is much lower in China than in Spain ("the largest of them did not cost more than two or three thousand pesos") precisely because the purchasing power of silver in China is much higher than in Spain. Compound this advantage with generally lower production costs in China, and the profits to be gained from taking silver to China and buying commodities to sell in Europe were enormous.

The second reason for China's being the destination for silver was that European merchants had little else to sell in the China market. With the exception of firearms, European products could not compete with Chinese manufactures in quality or cost. European manufactures offered little more than novelty. Silver was the one commodity that did compete well with the native product, for silver was in short supply there. China had silver mines, but the government severely restricted production, fearing that it could not control the flow of silver from the mines into private hands.[2] It also declined to mint silver coins, restricting coinage to bronze cash in the hope that this would keep prices low. These measures could do nothing against the economy's need for silver, however. As that economy grew, the demand for silver grew. By the sixteenth century, prices in China for anything but the smallest transactions were calibrated by weight of silver, not by unit of currency—which is why Chinese would immediately have understood what Catharina Bolnes was doing in *Woman Holding a Balance*. Weighing silver was part of everyday economic transactions in China.

The Chinese thirst for silver was so strong that most of the Spanish reals that Dutch merchants brought into the Netherlands simply went out again in the direction of Asia. The demand was for pure silver, but reals were circulating as something like an international currency in Southeast Asia, and Chinese merchants were happy to take them. The coins were trusted because Spanish mints kept their silver content steady at 0.931 fineness, though the ultimate fate of the reals that reached China was to be melted down. Only when war and embargo strangled the flow of reals to Holland did Dutch governments mint their own coins. The silver ducat on Catharina's table was introduced in 1659 to meet just this sort of shortfall.

The Dutch shipped a vast amount of silver to Asia during the seventeenth century. On average, the VOC sent close to a million guilders' worth to Asia every year (roughly ten metric tons by weight). That annual volume tripled by the end of the 1690s. The cumulative value was stunning. In the half century from 1610 through 1660, the headquarters of the VOC authorized the export of just slightly under fifty million guilders—almost five hundred tons of silver. It is hard even to imagine such a mountain of silver. Add to this an equivalent volume of silver that the VOC was shipping from Japan to China in the three decades after 1640, and the mountain of silver grows by at least half as much again.

What did all this silver buy for the Dutch? It paid for commodities unavailable in Europe that sold well in the home market: chiefly spices in the early years, which were edged aside by textiles later in the seventeenth century, and supplemented by tea and then coffee in the middle of the eighteenth. Looking into Dutch paintings of the seventeenth century, we see it also bought beautiful things such as porcelain bowls. One of the puzzles of this trade is that the invoice value of the goods officially returning in the holds of VOC ships (which of course fails to account for "private" cargo such as the ceramic load of the *White Lion*) was a quarter of the value of the silver going out. This shortfall did not dismay the Company, for the VOC sold what came back to Europe at prices that amply repaid the original investment. The rest of the silver was used in part to pay for the huge costs of running the Dutch colonial empire in Southeast Asia, and in larger part to buy commodities that the Company sold elsewhere within Asia for a profit. The bulk of the silver, in other words, was the capital that the VOC used to buy its way into the Asian market, stimulating intraregional as well as global trade. Who could have guessed that silver from Potosí would gain such power—and end up on Catharina's table?

Silver flowed east from Potosí to Europe and then from Europe to Asia, but that was not the only route it took to China, nor even the most important. Twice the volume of silver that went east also went west, first to the coast and then up to Acapulco, from where it crossed the Pacific to Manila in the Philippines. At Manila, the silver was traded for Chinese goods and then shipped to China. A river of silver linked the colonial economy of the Americas with the economy of south China, the metal extracted on one continent paying for goods manufactured on another for consumption on a third.

The flowing river worked to the advantage of many Spaniards and many Chinese, but not all. Spanish royal officials regularly complained that "all of this wealth passes into the possession of the Chinese, and is not brought to Spain, to the consequent loss of the royal duties." To staunch the flow, King Philip imposed restrictions on the amount of silver that could be sent across the Pacific. What defeated Philip was the fact that the profit on purchases made in Manila was far higher than the profit on goods brought from Spain. There was a political imperative to strengthen Spain's ties across the Atlantic, but there was an economic imperative driving silver across the Pacific. And so Manila became the nexus where the European economy hooked up to the Chinese economy: the place where the two hemispheres of the seventeenth-century globe joined.

When the Spanish first arrived in Manila in 1570, they found a trading port there under the control of a Moro rajah named Soliman. The Moros were a seaborne Muslim trading community that had moved up from the south over the preceding half century, expanding their control of trading ports throughout insular Southeast Asia. This made them the chief rivals of the Spanish. The first Spanish commander who went to Manila tricked Soliman into granting him territory at Manila. He used an old ruse, borrowed from the *Aeneid*, of asking for a piece of land no bigger than an ox hide. As a Chinese writer indignantly reports the story several decades later, "The Franks tore the ox hide into strips and joined them end to end to a length of a dozen kilometers which they used to mark out a piece of land, and then insisted that the rajah fulfil his promise. He was surprised but could not go back on his word as a gentleman and had to grant permission." Shortly thereafter the Spanish assassinated Soliman and burned the rest of the Moros out of Manila.

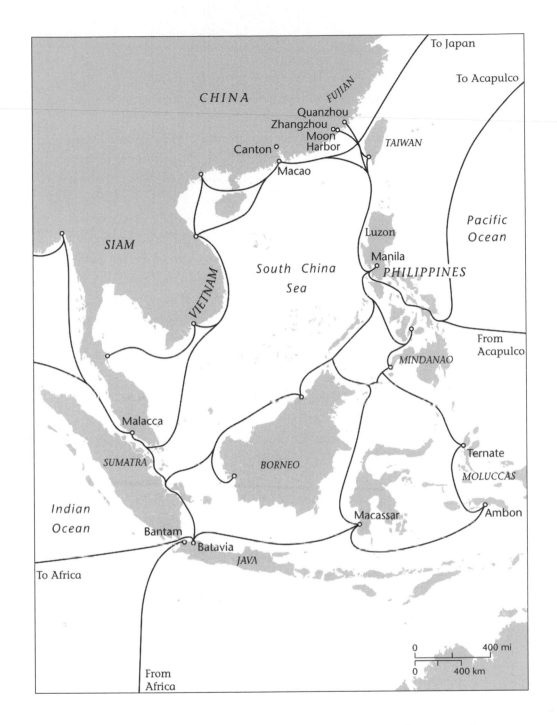

TRADE ROUTES AROUND THE SOUTH CHINA SEA

The phrase "losing the country for one ox hide" entered the Chinese lexicon as a shorthand for being swindled by Europeans; it was still in use in the nineteenth century.

The first Spaniards in Manila found some three hundred Chinese merchants already there, dealing in silk, iron, and porcelain. Relations started out well, each side sensing that the other might be a profitable trading partner. In fact, the timing was perfect. For the preceding half century, China had closed its borders to maritime trade in order to discourage the rampant piracy along the coast, much of it in Japanese hands. Merchants from the southeastern province of Fujian did dare to sail abroad, following the arc of islands from Taiwan down through the Philippines to the Spice Islands, but they did so at the risk of execution if caught. The Chinese state had no imperial ambition to follow its merchants' path, much less support their adventures. Its ambition was quite the opposite: to prevent the private wealth and corruption that could only come from foreign trade.

This was the situation until 1567, when a new emperor came to the throne in Beijing and lifted the ban on maritime commerce. It was a sign that the pressure of foreign demand was having its effect. Overnight, pirates became merchants, contraband goods became export commodities, and clandestine operations became a business network linking ports of Southeast Asia, including Manila, to Fujian's two major commercial cities, Quanzhou and Zhangzhou. Zhangzhou's port, Moon Harbor, became the main portal through which the bulk of the commodities going out, and the silver coming in, tied China to the outside world.

If this was an empire, it was an empire purely of trade, not of conquest. The Spanish imagined their future in East Asia rather differently. Two years after the killing of Soliman, a Spaniard in Manila petitioned the king of Spain for permission to lead eighty men to China to conquer that country. Philip II (after whom the Philippines had been named while he was still crown prince) had the good sense not to be persuaded. A second proposal arrived the following year for an invasion force of sixty men. Three years after that, Francisco

Sande, then governor of the Philippines, corrected these estimates and declared that Spain would need four to six thousand soldiers, plus a supporting Japanese armada, to conquer China. Still, he thought conquest possible, given his generally contemptuous view of Chinese. They are "a mean, impudent people, as well as very importunate," Governor Sande insisted. "Almost all are pirates, when any occasion arises, so that none are faithful to their king. Moreover, a war could be waged against them because they prohibit people from entering their country. Besides, I do not know, nor have I heard of, any wickedness that they do not practice; for they are idolaters, sodomites, robbers, and pirates, both by land and sea."

Nine years later, another proposal to conquer China raised the invasion force to ten to twelve thousand Spaniards, five to six thousand Filipino "Indians," and as many Japanese as they could muster. This proposal also advised sending an advance force of Jesuit missionaries to infiltrate the country, collect intelligence, and set up networks of collaborators. China held "all that the human mind can aspire or comprehend of riches and eternal fame," trumpeted the men who presented this proposal, "and likewise all that a Christian heart, desirous of the honour of God and in his faith, can wish for, in the salvation and restoration of myriad souls." Conquering China was not about "sordid lucre," the petitioners assured King Philip, but "honorable deeds." Much was at stake and time was of the essence. "The chance is slipping by, never to return," they warned. "The Chinese are each day becoming more wary, and more on their guard. They are laying in munitions of war, fortifying themselves and training men—all of which they have learned, and are still learning, from the Portuguese and our people." The final argument made for invasion is, for us, the oddest one of all: that China was in danger of falling into Muslim hands. Once Muslims controlled China, the petitioners warned, Spain would be cut out of the Chinese market forever. The memory of the expulsion of the Muslims from Spain in 1492 was still strong, and the competition between the Spanish and Ottoman empires was fierce enough that this appeal might have overridden calmer consideration.

It didn't. King Philip not only turned down the proposal; he forbade the governor from forwarding any more such foolish schemes to him. It was not possible for Spain to conquer China as it had conquered South America or the Philippines. The wealth of China would have to be tapped through trade, not conquest.

THE BASE FROM WHICH THIS trade was carried out was Manila. The Spanish rebuilt the coastal harbor town into a heavily fortified city. The area inside the massive stone walls was an enclave exclusively for "Spaniards," the term for all Europeans. They were permitted to bring into Manila with them their servants, guards, and slaves (despite a papal decree of 1591 emancipating all slaves in the Philippines), but the Chinese with whom they conducted business should remain outside. Initially, Chinese came seasonally to Manila, arriving with the spring winds and returning to Moon Harbor in the fall. As the volume and complexity of the trade grew, the Chinese agitated for permission to stay through the year, a practice they called "cramming winter." The Chinese government forbade merchants from staying year-round, but that rule was no match for the business incentive for cramming winter. The Spanish agreed to the request, but set the upper limit on those who crammed winter at six thousand. In 1581, they decided further to restrict Chinese to a ghetto, in imitation of the practice of restricting Jewish residence in European cities.[3] The Chinese ghetto consisted of a town surrounded by a wooden palisade, to which all Chinese were to be confined at night. The Spanish called it the Alcaiceria, the Silk Market, from the Arabic word for silk (*cer*, from the Chinese *si*). The local Tagals called it the Parián, which in Tagalog means "a place (*an*) where haggling (*pali*) goes on."

The Spanish forbade the Chinese from building in stone. That material they considered far too fine for such people, which is why the overcrowded Parián regularly burned down. But it was just as regularly rebuilt, each time on a grander plan, so that by 1637, a Spanish visitor to the Parián could declare his admiration for "the fine order in which they live." The site was moved several times with each rebuilding, but it always stayed close to the walls of Manila—"under the range of its artillery," as a Dominican priest was pleased to report to the king in 1666. The Dominicans were assigned the task in 1594 of converting the Chinese to Christianity, and within the Chinese enclave they built the Church of the Three Kings for their ministry. They were permitted to build in stone, which meant that whenever the Parián burned, the church regularly "escaped from the midst of this fire of Sodom," as one priest put it when the Parián went up in flames in 1628. (He declared that the fire "was the punishment of Heaven for the so horrible sins by which those heathen Chinese provoke the wrath of God.") Few Chinese converted, for that meant having to cut their hair in the European style and wear a beaver hat. Most were not prepared to cross that far into Spanish culture. Among those who were, one was selected to be headman of the Parián. After the fire of 1628, however, the governor of Manila replaced the Chinese headman with a Spanish official, known as the Chinese Protector.

The population of the Parián grew to twenty thousand, according to an official figure, though the actual number of Chinese in and around Manila may have been higher by at least half as much again. The Spanish could not have built their colony without them. The merchants who transported export wares from China were the minority, after all; the rest of the Chinese who came were the people who made it possible for the Spanish to live as they did. They were the grain dealers and vegetable farmers, the tailors and hatters, the bakers and chandlers, the confectioners and apothecaries, the carpenters and silversmiths. They supplied the paper on which the Spanish wrote, caught the fish they ate for supper, and transported the goods they acquired. The Spanish would not have been able to live as officers, priests, and gentlemen without them. They were called the Sangleys, a Spanish corruption of a Chinese term—though which term is under dispute. The standard etymology derives Sangley from *shengli*, "making profit," but others have proposed *shanglü*, "traveling merchants," or *changlai*, "come regularly"—which is what the Chinese did, to the enormous benefit of the Spanish community. "The fact is," Governor Antonio de Morga conceded in 1609, "without these Sangleys, the City cannot get along or maintain itself, because they are masters of all trades, and good workers who labor for moderate wages."

To poor Chinese from Fujian, Manila was Gold Mountain (this name was given, for similar reasons, to cities on the west coast of North America in the nineteenth century; it can also be translated as Money Mountain). They were fearless in going to sea to get a piece of it. Their daring impressed a Chinese coastal official named Zhou Qiyuan writing in 1617. "These petty traders view the huge waves under the open sky as though they were standing at their ease on a high mound, gaze at the topography of strange regions as though they were taking a stroll outside their own homes, and look upon foreign chieftains and warrior princes as though they were dealing with minor officials," he observes with awe. "They are at their ease on the ocean's waves and treat their boats as though they were fields"—fields being where wealth should properly come from. Zhou does note that these men are apt to respond violently to any attempt to interfere with trade and are utterly indifferent to the laws and courts that seek to restrain and punish them, but he was in general so impressed with their courage to go to sea and pursue their fortunes that he could not withhold his admiration. "These polers and punters are the sea-leopards of the rolling ocean."

In the spring of 1603, an official from the imperial household charged with collecting maritime customs duties in Fujian, an avaricious eunuch by the name of Gao Cai, decided to learn the truth of the rumors about Manila's gold mountain by sending a delegation to investigate. This was an extraordinary move, as Chinese law forbade its officials from crossing a border or sending a delegation out of the country without express permission. Gao could afford to ignore such rules. He was the emperor's personal appointee, charged with raising as much silver as he could for the emperor's private purse. (Zhou Qiyuan and other regional officials finally got Gao recalled for corruption a decade later, though it would take street riots to do it.)

The delegation's visit surprised and worried the Spanish colonists. Some feared that the story of fact-finding was a cover, and that the Chinese delegation was actually there to reconnoiter in advance of a military invasion. Others scoffed at the idea, recognizing that China did not aspire to having a Spanish-style colonial empire. One Spanish administrator who took this view thought the idea was being put about by schemers who hoped "to see the peace disturbed, and to have the opportunity to seize something" from the Chinese living in the Parián. The governor formally welcomed the delegation, but stayed on his guard. He worried that something odd was afoot.

When a fire broke out in the hospital for non-Europeans later that spring and Chinese volunteered to enter the city to fight the fire, the nervous governor turned them down and let the fire burn. The Chinese were offended by Spanish distrust; they were also suspicious as to why the governor allowed the hospital to burn down. The Spanish archbishop, who had recently arrived in Manila and had not yet gotten a feel for the delicacy of the situation, made things worse that summer by delivering an ill-timed sermon accusing the Chinese of sodomy and witchcraft. The tension between the two sides exploded into violence that fall. Twenty thousand Chinese, poorly armed and unprepared for the attack, were massacred by frantic Spanish soldiers and Native warriors. A provincial official in Fujian lodged a protest, only to be told that the Spanish retained the right to quell rebellion, and that he "should consider what he should do, if any similar case happened in China." The Ming government dropped the case, concluding that the incident occurred outside its jurisdiction and that the Chinese who died had effectively abandoned their status as subjects of the emperor by no longer living within the realm. Trading resumed the next season, yet the memory of the outbreak continued to haunt relations between the two sides for the rest of the century.

The memory of the 1603 massacre cautioned the Chinese government against opening the door of trade with the outside world too wide, but it did nothing to deter more Chinese from coming.

According to a report the Chinese minister of war made to his emperor in 1630, a hundred thousand Fujianese were going to sea every spring, and it was poverty that was driving them—a point he made to argue against closing the border, lest these hundred thousand resort to other, less salubrious ways to make a living. By 1636, according to an agent of the Spanish crown, the Chinese and Japanese living in and around Manila numbered thirty thousand.

Manila greatly mattered to everyone who traded there. It was the point of commercial contact between the economies of seventeenth-century Europe and China, and once silver was flowing, not even a massacre could break the contact. Each side brought to the table what the other wanted to buy and could afford, and took from it what it could use. Every spring, one great Spanish ship—called the Manila galleon in the Philippines, the China ship in Mexico—crossed the Pacific from Mexico loaded with silver. And every spring from China came thirty to forty junks crammed with "silks, cottons, china-ware, gunpowder, sulphur, iron, steel, quicksilver [mercury], copper, flour, walnuts, chestnuts, biscuits, dates, all sorts of stufs [textiles], writing-desks, and other curiosities."[4] The trade coaxed many Chinese into the business. As Zhou Qiyuan notes, "merchants step onto ships and go out by the western and eastern sea routes to trade." The western route hugged the coastline from Fujian down to Vietnam, and the eastern ran out to Taiwan and then south to the Philippines. "The cargo they carry is precious and remarkable, the wonderful items are beyond description, and there is no doubt that what they gain in gold and silver runs to the hundreds of thousands."

The risks for the Spanish were high. A Manila galleon had to spend two or three months crossing the Pacific to reach the Philippines, then it faced an even longer return. It had to depart for Acapulco before July, lest typhoons catch it in the treacherous channels through the Philippine Islands. So the trade was a fragile arrangement. The loss of one Chinese junk had only modest impact on the exchange, since the commodities were distributed over several dozen vessels whereas if one Spanish galleon sank on the voyage out, the entire trading season had to be canceled, producing severe losses on both sides. This happened frequently enough to be a real concern. From the beginning of the trade to 1815, fifteen galleons were lost as they sailed west from Acapulco. Twenty-five went down on the more difficult return voyage.

A seventeenth-century Italian traveler, Francesco Careri, has recorded the horrors of the eastbound crossing of "almost the one half of the Terraqueous Globe." A galleon had to battle "the Terrible Tempests that happen there, one upon the back of another." If storms did not destroy the ship, then there were "the desperate Diseases that seize People, in 7 or 8 Months, lying at Sea sometimes near the Line [the equator], sometimes cold, sometimes temperate, and sometimes hot, which is enough to Destroy a Man of Steel, much more Flesh and Blood, which at Sea had but indifferent Food." The indifferent food could cause scurvy—Spaniards called it "the Dutch disease"—if it didn't run out and threaten crews with starvation instead. The crews of two galleons in the 1630s warded off the problem of starvation by throwing 105 people overboard so that the rest might survive. The most chilling case was the *San José*, found in 1657 after more than a year at sea, drifting southward off the coast below Acapulco, laden with corpses of the starved and the dehydrated, and a cargo hold full of silks.

For the mountain of treasured goods the Manila galleons carried back to Mexico, the Spanish exchanged their own mountain of silver. The amount of silver that was officially registered for export at Acapulco started at about three tons a year in the 1580s and 1590s, expanded to close to twenty tons a year in the 1620s, then settled at around nine or ten tons a year. In the first half of the seventeenth century, official records suggest that Spanish galleons carried just short of three quarters of a million kilograms of silver to Manila. Add in the smuggled silver and the total at least doubles. Not all this silver went to Fujian. Some got diverted to Macao and passed through Portuguese hands—recall that the *Guía*, wrecked on the south China coast in 1625, was carrying silver from Manila to Macao. But the bulk of it went to Fujian and disappeared into the Chinese economy. According to the current best estimate, in the first half of the seventeenth century, China imported five thousand tons of silver, roughly half of it from Japan and the rest from mines of Spanish America. A portion of that came east from Europe via the Indian Ocean, but the bulk of it was shipped directly west across the Pacific.

The importation of silver on this scale highlighted the awkward distance in China between public policy and private commerce. On the one hand, the Ming court did everything it could to restrict the mining of silver, fearing the corruption and the social instability it believed would arise within mining communities. On the other hand, merchants were importing vast quantities of silver into south China. When the writer Feng Menglong was serving as a county magistrate in northern Fujian in the 1630s, he strengthened the military cordon around the seven silver mines in the county, which had been closed by imperial order a century earlier. How ironic that Feng should be exercising his vigilance to keep vagabonds from digging in the old silver pits, while at the other end of the province merchants were bringing in American silver by the ton. But that was the internally contradictory situation in which China found itself in the first half of the seventeenth century. The government worked to discourage the private accumulation of wealth among the socially marginal for fear that this wealth might feed the forces of rebellion, while private mercantile families amassed vast fortunes by trading abroad.

Silver flowed easily into the Chinese economy because it was needed to supplement the small bronze coins that were used for small transactions. It was the standard form of money; it was also the form in which the Ming regime collected taxes. The amount of silver coming into China was so great that the Chinese believed its supply was endless. They also assumed that the foreigners, by controlling that supply, were in the enviable position of buying whatever they wanted at no real cost to themselves. Chinese converts to Christianity, in fact, suggested this very strategy to Franciscan missionaries. "As people by nature love profit, if you give silver to everyone, there won't be a single person who doesn't follow" your teaching. Pedro de la Piñuela, the Franciscan missionary who inserts this conversation into a model dialogue, offers the expected response first. "This is not following a teaching; it is following silver." But then he turns to the practical problem that his order doesn't have an endless supply of silver to hand out. "If people come for the sake of silver, then the situation is such that when the silver runs out, they will go. Since there is a limit to the silver from the West, and since people's avarice is inexhaustible, then once the silver you give them runs out, won't their desire for the Way, like the silver, run out as well?" And run out, or at least down, it would, as we shall see.

While the supply lasted, silver gilded the Chinese world. It created a potential for accumulation and liquidity that encouraged ostentatious spending and social competition. Those who could afford the new culture of wealth embraced its arrival and took pleasure in spending vast amounts of silver on expensive goods, antiques, and mansions. This new wave of luxury spending excited a powerful backlash just after the turn of the seventeenth century, however. Among conservative elites, silver became a lightning rod for frustrations and an occasion for dire warnings about the decay of the age. Magistrate Zhang Tao was one of those appalled by the silver economy. In 1607, Zhang was posted to an inland county south of the Yangzi River that happened to be home to some of the greatest commercial families of the age. It was a bad match. By 1609, Zhang was fulminating in a local publication about easy money, flamboyant display, and moral poverty. The ethical foundations that once held society together were crumbling, and the reciprocal duties that had once sustained village life were no longer observed. He blamed it all on the lust for silver, the one overwhelming passion that now consumed people's hearts. Silver could not be an innocent medium for storing wealth. By its very nature, as something without fixed use or real value and infinitely exchangeable for all other goods, silver gave the rich free rein to amass personal fortunes while depriving the poor of the means to survive. The unfortunate result was that "one man in a hundred is rich, while nine out of ten are impoverished." The result, in Zhang's baleful summary was, that "the Lord of Silver rules heaven and the God of Cash reigns over the earth."

Blaming silver may have felt satisfying, but by the turn of the seventeenth century, any proposal to curb the use of silver was pointless. Silver was so thoroughly a fact of daily life that no one gave it any thought, except when he didn't have enough silver to acquire what he needed to subsist. When that happened—and it happened often enough in the later years of the Ming, when colder temperatures and epidemics threatened the dynasty's survival—they too were willing to cast silver as the villain in the economy. Zhang Tao's frustration at the power of the Lord of Silver may be linked to his very first experience as a county magistrate. When he arrived to take up his post in 1607, he found the price of rice rising because the spring rains had washed away the local crop. In normal times, the price of rice per Chinese "peck" (*dou*, a unit volume equal to 10.75 liters) stayed under half a "mace" (one *qian* was a unit of silver weighing 3.75 grams). But as the spring wore on, Zhang watched the price almost triple to 1.3 *qian* (4.6 grams). At that point, he stepped in and released the stocks of rice in the county granary at below-market rates. This intervention forced down the market price and eased the crisis for long enough for the circulation of commercial grain to resume at close to regular prices. Zhang regarded the local reliance on silver as the cause of the problem. In his view, were there no silver in the local economy, the price of rice would not have risen to the level it did.

Was the increase in the stock of silver circulating in China driving up prices? Economic logic argues that an increase in money supply should have had an inflationary effect, but it is difficult to detect this from the available evidence. What is not difficult to detect is the wild price inflation during the mounting subsistence crises of the early 1640s. Before the seventeenth century, a local crisis might double or even triple the price of rice, but no more. The brief exceptions came in the 1540s and again in the 1580s, when the price went beyond an informal price ceiling of 6 grams of silver per decaliter. In the 1620s, that ceiling started to move. In 1639, according a Shanghai resident, a peck of rice was commanding a price of 1.9 mace (6.6 grams per decaliter). "However," the same memoirist goes on to note, "it was nothing like what happened in the spring of 1642." The value of currency collapsed, driving a peck of white rice up to 5 mace (17.5 grams per decaliter). The price in Shanghai stabilized for a few years in the elevated range of 7 to 10 grams per decaliter, then in 1647 shot up to 14 grams. These prices were only for those who had the silver to pay them, of course. For those who had none, the only currency that could buy rice was children. In a market southwest of Shanghai in 1642, the human price of a peck of rice—barely enough to feed one person for a week—was two children. China did not experience another crisis in the value of money this severe until the twentieth century

What devastated China in the 1640s was not its monetary system so much as the impact of cold weather, and with it, virulent epidemics, falling grain production, and huge military spending to hold back the Manchus to the north. Nonetheless, people at the time felt that money played a part. Some of the great minds of the years following the collapse of the Ming dynasty in 1644 blamed silver (that "perfidious metal," as one called it) for harmful, negative economic behavior, such as hoarding, that undermined stability for the poor and encouraged wasteful extravagance among the rich. As for silver's effect on state fiscal administration, according to one analyst of the period, "Depending on silver to enrich the state is like resorting to wine to sate one's hunger." Silver had attained a role it never should have had.

Economic historians have recently suggested that another factor may have been at work—that prices were being forced up in the late 1630s and early 1640s not by the long-term increase in the supply of silver, but by a short-term contraction. The flash point was Manila.

THE TRADE BETWEEN THE SPANISH and the Chinese in Manila always had balanced on a delicate pivot. Small crises of supply or liquidity could excite a larger crisis of confidence, shutting the whole operation down. This is what began to happen in 1638. *Nuestra Señora de la Concepción*, the largest ship the Spanish had ever built, was the east-bound galleon leaving Manila that summer. Monsoons delayed its departure, and when the *Concepción* finally did sail, its commander strangely decided to take the incoming route just above the equator, rather than follow the standard northerly route up to Japan and then head east from there to the coast of California. The ship was loaded with a declared cargo worth four million pesos. It also carried a large undeclared cargo. Although the Spanish governor of the Philippines had recently been taking an active interest in reducing smuggling on the galleons lest exports go untaxed, in this sailing he had a direct interest in letting it go undeclared.

Sebastián Hurtado de Corcuera was posted to Manila as governor in 1635 after eight years' service in Peru, first as a garrison commander (he had previously distinguished himself as a member of the council of war in Flanders fighting the Dutch), then as treasurer. His transfer to Manila took him through Acapulco, where he was stunned at the scale of corruption around the galleon trade. Writing back to Philip IV the following year, he observes, "I think it would be better to use angels rather than men" to run places such as Acapulco. Unless "the most disinterested and zealous in Your majesty's service" are appointed, "the royal treasury will pay for it, for in order to make 1,000 pesos an official must steal 10,000 from the king's vassals and the treasury suffers." Three years later, hoping to beat Acapulco at its payoff game, Corcuera prevented a proper manifest of the cargo on the *Concepción* from being compiled. Without a manifest, he figured, the inspector in Acapulco would not be able to take his usual cut.

Corcuera's concern to protect the cargo of the *Concepción* went too far, for he overlooked competent senior officers and entrusted the galleon to his favorite nephew, Pedro, a young man with no experience in navigation or command. Pedro's nominal authority collapsed as soon as the ship was out of Manila harbor. On 20 September 1638, the *Concepción* was threading its way through the Mariana Islands, which lie about a quarter of the way between the Philippines and Hawaii (no

European would discover those islands until James Cook wandered into them a century later). The officers were so busy arguing among themselves that the galleon went off course and struck a submerged reef, spilling its cargo across the coral beds. Of the four hundred people on board, a few dozen got to shore and lived to tell the tale. The ship's cargo, which Corcuera had been so anxious to keep hidden, was beyond salvaging. Beachcombers today can still pick up shards of Ming porcelain along the shore where the ship went down.

The destruction of the *Concepción* could have been borne more easily had the same disaster not repeated itself. It did so the following spring when the incoming galleon *San Ambrosio*, laden with silver, foundered off the east coast of Luzon. The outbound galleon back to Mexico that summer also sank, this time off the coast of Japan. These three sinkings crippled trade in Manila. The entire system teetered on the edge of collapse. In terms of silver production in Spanish America, the timing could not have been worse, for the supply of silver that funded the transpacific exchange had begun to contract. Silver production in Potosí was already slipping in the mid-1610s, and by the 1630s it was not possible to produce enough silver to cover all the purchases that Spanish merchants were making in Manila. Desperate at the prospect of declining revenues, the municipal councillors of Potosí sent someone to Madrid to plead with the Spanish court for financial help. Potosí "until recently has supported the full weight of the Monarchy with its great riches," their representative declared in an open letter. Grant the silver producers of Potosí some sort of fiscal concessions to keep production going, the councillors pleaded.

The downturn in South America coincided with new restrictions on Europeans trading with Japan, the other major source of silver for China. The Portuguese based in Macao had enjoyed a lock on this trade for decades, but when Japan came under a centralized authority in the 1620s, it chose to restrict foreign access. The new Tokugawa regime banned Japanese from going abroad as of 1635, and pressured the Portuguese to stop bringing Europeans to Japan, especially missionaries, whom the Tokugawa regarded as agents of sedition. The

Tokugawa severely restricted Christianity in 1637, declaring that foreign missionaries who entered the country did so on pain of death. A Jesuit close to Governor Corcuera went in disguise to Japan later that year, but was soon exposed, tortured, and beheaded for flouting this law. When a Portuguese ship showed up in 1640 in the hope of reopening trade, most of the crew were executed, leaving a few to return to make it clear back in Macao that no more Portuguese would be welcome. Macao never fully recovered from this loss and dwindled into a colonial backwater. Thenceforth, the only Europeans permitted to continue trading in Japan were the Dutch, and then only from a tiny island in the harbor of Nagasaki under tight restrictions.

To make matters worse for Manila, when a new emperor came to the throne in China in 1628, his government, tired of Dutch piracy, reimposed its earlier prohibition on maritime trade. For two years, trade at Manila stagnated, then revived to former levels. But when the ban went back into effect in 1638, the traffic to Manila fell from its record high of fifty junks in 1637 to sixteen. The faction in Beijing that favored an open border gained the upper hand at court the following year and got the maritime prohibition lifted, but then when thirty well-stocked junks showed up in 1639, the sinking of the *San Ambrosio* meant that there was not enough silver to buy the cargoes. On top of that, for three years running, the viceroy of New Spain had been trying to staunch the flow of silver by clamping down on Chinese imports into Acapulco. He viewed the swapping of silver for cheap Chinese imports as a drain on his economy that benefited no one but the merchants in Manila. This was another reason why Corcuera made sure there was no manifest for the goods on the *Concepción*. He was trying to get around the new restrictions.

The upshot of these circumstances was that close to ten tons of anticipated silver failed to arrive in Manila. Trade was at a standstill. The fine balance collapsed at the village of Calamba southeast of Manila on the night of 19 November 1639, when several hundred Chinese farmers burst into the house of Luis Arias de Mora. These farmers had volunteered to come into the jungle to build rice paddies for the

Spanish in exchange for tax breaks, but conditions were deplorable. Resources were nonexistent, and the promised tax holiday was never honored. When disease swept through the Chinese community, the farmers turned on Mora. Mora, the former Chinese Protector of Manila, was now the hated administrator of this agricultural colony. He had used his position to squeeze the Chinese for all he could get. He was aware of the discontent, but had no reason to suspect anything that night, and was sound asleep when the mob arrived. The farmers dragged him outside, denounced his oppression, and put him to death. The insurgents then set off on a march to Manila to appeal for clemency and demand redress for their sufferings.

This small outbreak of violence might have been contained, had the Chinese delegation that rushed down from the Parián to mediate been able to gain full cooperation from the Spaniards sent to suppress the uprising. During the parley, however, a junior Spanish officer attacked one wing of the insurgents, possibly without realizing that a cease-fire was in place. The Chinese fought back, and then the rest of the Spanish forces threw themselves into battle. The war that was being averted was on again. As soon as word of the insurgency spread, Chinese all over Luzon rose up and joined the rebels. The insurgents gathered across the Pasig River across from Manila and prepared for their assault. Chinese living in the Parián strove to maintain their neutrality, but on 2 December they joined the insurgents.

The governor responded by ordering all Chinese inside Manila and the nearby port town of Cavite put to death. The warden of Cavite, Alonso Garcia Romero, chose to implement the order stealthily. He invited all Chinese in Cavite to close their houses and gather in the enclave of royal buildings for their own protection. He also invited priests from all the religious orders to come and hear confessions from the Christian Chinese and baptize the non-Christians. He then announced to the Chinese who had obediently assembled that they were to be taken in groups of ten to greater safety within the walls of Manila. In fact they were being taken out for decapitation. Some thirty such groups of ten had been processed when someone noticed a guard cutting off the purse of one of the departing Chinese. Suddenly the warden's behavior looked like a trick to take their money (no one quite yet realized it was a trick to take their lives), and an uproar ensued. The Chinese turned on their guards, who fled but closed and barricaded the only exit from the outside. A squad of arquebusiers surrounded the building, entered, and shot every Chinese inside. A Spanish chronicler, who assumed that the Chinese were plotting to rise up and murder all the Spaniards in Cavite, declared the Cavite massacre to have been "a great mercy of God." He estimated the death toll at thirteen hundred. Only twenty-three Chinese managed to escape the massacre.

The Chinese insurgents laid siege to Manila, but the city was well fortified and the Spanish had no difficulty holding out. After three weeks, they took the offensive, launching an attack across the Pasig River. The Chinese had to fall back, and eventually were routed from the area. As they passed through one burned village, Spanish soldiers found a singed but otherwise unharmed statue of Christ in the ruins of a church. They presented it to Corcuera, who declared the statue's salvation from fire a miracle, and raised it at the head of his forces: God was on their side. A few days later, a Chinese Christian convert in a village across the Pasig River exhumed a statue he had buried of Emperor Guan, the god of war and the patron saint of merchants (see plate 8). He should have burned the statue when he converted, but decided instead to bury it behind his house against future uncertainties. When he was exhumed, according to what Spanish investigators later learned, Emperor Guan promised to aid his followers in battle. It was a promise his followers could not bring to fruition. As long as the Chinese were outgunned by their adversaries and orphaned by their ruler, the god of commerce could not prevail over the god of empire.

The Spanish eventually cornered the remnants of the Chinese insurgency and asked a Jesuit priest to negotiate their surrender. The insurgents, insisting that "they did no harm where they were not harmed," agreed to end hostilities on the condition that the Spaniards allow them to go down to the coast and return to China. Corcuera refused. His condition for accepting their surrender was just the opposite: that they *not* leave the Philippines. The governor understood that Manila's wealth and power depended on the Chinese being there. He needed them to return to Manila and resume the old arrangements if the colony were to survive. Not only did the Chinese lack leverage, but they too could appreciate the value of returning to the way things were. On 24 February 1640, eight thousand combatants laid down their arms. They were marched back to Manila in a victory parade before the city walls. The Spanish cavalry led the parade followed by their indigenous allies, who were followed in turn by the defeated Chinese. At the end of the march rode Governor Corcuera, and directly in front of him, held aloft on a pole, the fire-blackened statue of Christ that had been recovered from the burned church.

SILVER DID NOT CAUSE THE massacre of thousands of Chinese in the Philippines. Yet these events would not have occurred had the bridge of precious metal flowing across the Pacific not collapsed. The rupture inflamed anxieties on both sides, allowing one small incident to snowball into a massive conflict. The violence that wealth is capable of provoking is invisible in *Woman Holding a Balance*. Preparing to weigh her coins, Catharina Bolnes is untroubled by the frenzy of acquisition and conflict that silver was fueling in the wider world.

Not everyone who weighed silver in the seventeenth century could be so dispassionate. Fulgencio Orozco was already fifty years old when he arrived in Potosí in 1610 looking to make money. Although a nobleman, he was too poor to repay a debt of 800 pesos and unable to assemble a dowry for his daughter, for which he needed another 2,000 pesos. Orozco's social status gave him an entrée with the elite families of the town, one of whom was able to recommend him for a position as a foreman in an ore refinery. It was the sort of job that an American-born Creole rather than a Spanish-born gentleman would take, but Orozco was desperate and willing to work any job that would earn him silver. Despite his best efforts, the job paid him barely enough to cover his own costs. His impatience to earn more drove him to leave the refinery in search of quicker methods. After struggling for twenty months in Potosí and finding himself still no closer to earning his daughter's dowry, Orozco became deranged and suicidal. He ended up in the royal hospital, damning Christ for abandoning him in his time of need and ranting at the devil for not keeping up his end of a bargain that Orozco had thought he had struck to get rich.

Orozco's rants drew a crowd of spectators, who decided he was possessed and sent for an Augustinian priest, Antonio de la Calancha, to exorcise the devil inside him. Orozco refused his help, and became so angry at some of the zealous bystanders imploring the devil to leave his body that he grabbed the priest's crucifix and smacked one of them on the forehead. The police arrived to disperse the crowd, which only added to the mayhem. Brother Antonio performed an exorcism without any apparent effect, and then performed a second. This only drove Orozco to greater frenzy. He kept trying to get the priest to realize that the devil was not inside him, but standing by the head of his bed. There was nothing in him to exorcise.

Brother Antonio had reached his wits' end. He turned on his patient and demanded, "Why is someone like you, a nobleman, raving like a heretic or a Jew?"

"You wish to know why I abhor Christ?" Orozco shot back. "It is because He gives riches to worthless men and common folk, while He afflicts me, a gentleman whose obligations are heavy, with poverty. Since I came to this Peru to earn money for my daughter's dowry, He has repeatedly taken away everything I have earned, forcing me to witness with my own eyes others earning money where I have lost it. Is there anyone in this city who has worked as hard as I and yet acquired nothing, and when I am witness to the fact that with less effort than my own, in less time and more easily, many have succeeded in laying hands on thousands?"

Orozco's despair was not just in finding himself poor, but in discovering that effort, honest intentions, and gentlemanly status had nothing to do with success in a commercial economy. Money did not end up in the hands of those who deserved it, and class was no protection. For Orozco, Potosí had become what it had been for the Andean Natives: *puna*, uninhabitable. Calancha tried to shift the argument by observing sympathetically that, whereas good people might become rich because God wanted them to, most people in Potosí got rich through theft, usury, and fraud. God might reward the virtuous with riches, but riches did not necessarily go only to those blessed by God. Potosinos in particular, being "zealous in the pursuit of riches, and somewhat given to venery," rarely were among the blessed. This might seem like an impolitic admission from a priest who preached a doctrine of divine reward for the good and punishment for the evil, but that theology was always hedged by the conviction that God worked in mysterious ways, that it was not for humans to judge such matters, and that all such credits and debits would be weighed and sorted at the Last Judgment.

At this point, Calancha abandoned theological reasoning and offered Orozco a deal. Suppose the people assembled around his hospital bed—and this group now included eight to ten priests of the Inquisition, who were keenly interested in the rumor that Orozco was spouting heresy—raised the 2,800 pesos to cover his needs? Would he agree to spurn the devil and seek God's forgiveness? Orozco fell quiet but stayed noncommittal. He needed to see the money. To demonstrate their good faith, four or five priests went off to draw the silver from funds controlled by the Inquisition and have it weighed at the assaying office in the exact amount Orozco required. They even checked how much it would cost to have the silver delivered back to Spain before they returned to Orozco's bedside.

The offer worked. When the sacks of silver were delivered to his bedside that evening, the madman repented, praising God and confessing his sins to the priest. Exhausted, he lost the power of speech later in the evening and died in the small hours of the morning. At a cost of 2,800 pesos plus courier charges, it was an expensive conversion, but the Church (which, like every other institution in Potosí, accumulated a substantial share of silver) expressed itself satisfied with the transaction. Charity had worked its magic. A debt had been paid, a dowry secured, and a soul saved. And the agent through which all this was achieved—the agent as well of the man's despair and death—was the silver dug out of Potosí, the very same substance waiting for Catharina to calmly assess its value.

JOURNEYS

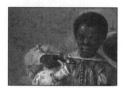

THE CARD PLAYERS (see plate 7) is easily recognized as a midcentury Dutch painting, but one is unlikely to mistake it for a Vermeer. The familiar elements are present: windows on the left, diagonally laid marble squares, a line of Delft tiles where the wall meets the floor, a Turkish carpet pushed aside on a table where two people converse, a delftware jug imitating Chinese blue-and-white, a wineglass held up, a map of the province of Holland on the wall. Add the officer in red military coat and beaver hat flirting with the young woman, and it seems like Vermeer's *Officer and Laughing Girl* all over again. But it isn't. The painting has all the elements of a Vermeer, yet it lacks the precision of draftsmanship and the care in composition that can turn a generic scene into a dynamic painting.

The artist is Hendrik van der Burch, a painter of good reputation who worked in the same circles as Johannes Vermeer and possibly to much the same level of commercial success. The two men were rough contemporaries on the Delft art scene. Born near Delft five years before Vermeer, he moved to the city when he was fifteen. He studied painting there and joined the guild of St. Luke when he was twenty-one—exactly the same age at which Vermeer joined five years later. No documents prove the two artists knew each other, but it is impossible that they did *not*, since Van der Burch's sister or stepsister married the prominent Pieter de Hooch, whose paintings Vermeer certainly knew. It is harder to prove a link between *The Card Players* and *Officer and Laughing Girl*. The courting officer was a common subject. Vermeer likely executed his painting first by a year or two, though by then Van der Burch was living in Leiden or Amsterdam, so he may never have seen *Officer and Laughing Girl*.

Despite similarities of subject matter and style, no Vermeer interior prepares us for the figure who stands dead center in Van der Burch's picture. Vermeer painted no children, he painted no servant boys, and he painted no Africans. Van der Burch gives us all three in a ten-year-old African boy in fancy doublet and earrings, doing his mistress's bidding. Not only that, but he is looking straight at the artist—and at us. The man and woman are busily engaged in their game with each other, just as the little girl to one side is engaged in hers with the lapdog. The African boy alone is unengaged in these games, and looks at us almost knowingly. It is an odd pose for someone pouring a glass of wine. He should be looking at the wineglass. Even more odd is the position of the glass. Close inspection shows that he is holding the glass with his left hand. But from a superficial glance at the painting, the viewer could think that the woman is holding it between her thumb and forefinger—which was the polite way to hold stemware in the seventeenth century. The only indication that she isn't holding the glass is the card in her hand, though you have to look closely to see it.

To me, the placement of the wineglass directly over her hand suggests that Van der Burch originally intended that she should hold it for her page boy to fill. That would make the principal act of exchange in the painting between the white mistress and her black servant, a favorite pairing in seventeenth-century paintings of upper-class women. But Van der Burch changed his mind, deciding that the principal act of exchange should be between the woman and her suitor. The wineglass she receives from the boy is no longer the center of the painting; the playing card she gives to her suitor takes its place. At that point, it was too late for him to remove the boy. So there the young African stands pouring wine from a jug, but with the glass full and no wine actually flowing from the tipping jug. No wonder the boy is able to take his eyes from the task and look at us.

As we look at him. We would never know from Vermeer's oeuvre that there were Africans in Delft. Van der Burch shows that there were. Africans had been coming in small numbers to Europe since the fifteenth century, but their numbers were increasing noticeably in the Low Countries in the seventeenth century. Africans arrived as sailors, laborers, and servants in the port cities of Antwerp and Amsterdam, but most of all as slaves. The laws of those cities permitted slaves to petition the city authorities for manumission from slavery once they had entered their jurisdictions. Few, it seems, did. The legal distinction may not anyway have made much difference to the real life of Africans in Flanders or the Netherlands, who had little alternative to employment outside domestic service and were as good as bound to the master or mistress who acquired them, even if the law judged them to be legally free.

Van der Burch was not the exception among Dutch painters in including a black servant in his painting. Many Dutch artists painted Africans, usually within domestic settings, indicating that these slaves were not kept apart from the white families that owned them. In fact, those who owned black child servants (and they are usually boys) wanted to show off what they possessed. It was not unlike having an artist put a favorite Chinese vase into the painting you commissioned. It signaled your wealth, your good bourgeois taste, and your knowledge that these were meaningful signs in the social world in which you thrived. If you were a woman and your black slave was a boy, his copresence in a painting also highlighted your color, your complexion, your gender, and your superiority.

The boy in *The Card Players* is the door within this painting that opens onto a wider world of travel, movement, servitude, and dislocation. This wider world was seeping into everyday life in the Low Countries, bringing real people from real places far away. As for this particular boy, we know nothing beyond the fact of his presence in this picture. If he wasn't born in Delft, he was probably one of the unlucky ones who found himself caught in the net of trade and capture that moved people as readily as it moved things. Still, to be alive was to be one of the lucky ones. So many drawn into the whirlpool of global movement never made it out alive. Even those who went by choice rather than by force often were not spared. The toll of the seventeenth century fell on both.

To reckon the human costs of the restless movement that scattered people across the seventeenth-century globe, we will follow five journeys that dumped people in places and situations far from where they were born: three men in Natal on the southeast coast of Africa, seventy-two men and boys on an island off the coast of Java, a Dutchman on the Korean island of Cheju, an Italian on the coast of Fujian, and two homeward-bound Dutch sailors on the island of Madagascar. Over their journeys hangs the figure of Van der Burch's black boy, the one who made it safely to Delft but never made it home. We shall end with a journey story dear to seventeenth-century Christians, the journey of the magi, to think about why Vermeer hung a painting of this subject in his house.

THE LAST TIME ANYONE SAW them, the three men watched their shipmates cross the broad river before them and recede into the African distance heading, they hoped, in the direction of Mozambique. The huge fat man on the litter, which his bearers had set under a makeshift canopy, was a Portuguese. Attending him were a Chinese and an African. The names of the African and the Chinese are forgotten. Slaves of empires rarely get their names entered in the public record unless they commit crimes that the annals of colonial justice consider worth preserving. But we do know the name of the Portuguese reclining on the litter, for he was their owner: Sebastian Lobo da Silveira.

Lobo—his name means "wolf"—had the reputation of being the most obese man in Macao in the 1640s. In February 1647, he was sent back to Portugal to face trial. He had arrived in Macao nine years earlier to take up the lucrative position of captain general, a post that gave him command of all maritime trade between Macao and Japan. Lobo paid handsomely back in Lisbon for a monopoly that he expected in turn to pay him handsomely in Macao. Portugal had a monopoly on the trade between China and Japan, since the governments of both countries were generally hostile to direct trade but permitted the Portuguese to act as middlemen. A single return run between the Portuguese colony of Macao and the Japanese port of Nagasaki, carrying Chinese silks in one direction and Japanese silver in the other, could double your capital, so long as the Dutch did not capture your ship. But Lobo's timing was bad. He had the misfortune to buy his post in 1638, just before Japan banished Portuguese traders from Japan for failing to observe the ban against missionaries entering the country. A Portuguese captain who tested the ban in 1639 was expelled. Another who tried in 1640 was executed along with most of his crew. Thenceforth only the Dutch, who happily agreed not to smuggle Catholic proselytizers into Japan, were permitted to trade in Nagasaki. There were no more runs from Macao, and no more easy profits for the Wolf.

Blocked from trading with Japan, Lobo turned to other schemes, such as obliging wealthy Macanese merchants who needed his good opinion to loan him large sums he had no intention of paying back. Adding insult to injury, he enjoyed flaunting his wealth and snubbing public convention. He went about Macao in a ridiculous "Moorish costume of rich gold and sky blue silk, with a red cap on his head." His rapacity put him in conflict with the Senate, a body consisting of the leading merchants of the town. That conflict eventually led to street battles in which the antagonists actually brought artillery into play against each other. When the crown administrator tried to get the situation in hand at the end of the summer of 1642, Lobo had him kidnapped, locked in a private dungeon for eight months, and finally beaten to death.

The disorder that erupted in the streets of Macao here at the far southern edge of China was nothing compared to the chaos engulfing the cities of north China at that moment, where rebel bands were fighting government armies and, at least as often, each other, in the struggle to win supremacy over the faltering Ming regime. In 1644, one of these rebel leaders, a postal guard made redundant by the collapse of central funding, mounted a daring raid on Beijing and took the capital. Finding himself abandoned by those who had sworn to uphold his reign, Emperor Chongzhen, the one who tried to get Portuguese gunners to Beijing despite the objections of some of his courtiers, hanged himself from a tree at the north end of the Forbidden City. China was not to be taken so easily by one of its own, however. Within six weeks, a joint Sino–Manchu army swooped down on Beijing from the Great Wall and drove the rebel leader from his tenuously held prize. The Manchus then staged a coup by putting a young prince of their own on the throne and declaring him to be the first emperor of the Qing dynasty. The Ming dynasty was now officially over.

That same year, a new governor arrived in Macao from the Portuguese colony of Goa. Charges had been filed against Lobo in Lisbon, and the new governor's job was to indict him. It would take two and half years before the governor was at last able to bundle the Wolf onto a carrack bound for Europe. The ship left Macao in February 1647. With Lobo went his devoted brother, his Chinese bond servant, and an African slave loaned to him for the duration of the voyage. Their ship never made it around the Cape of Good Hope. It went aground somewhere short of the cape, in the region now known as Natal. Those who made it ashore reckoned that their best chance of survival lay in trekking north toward Mozambique, but it was not a solution that suited Lobo's constitution. The merchant was so grossly overweight and physically ruined by his extravagant lifestyle that he could walk only a few steps at a time. His brother had a hammock made from fishing lines and convinced the cabin boys to carry him in this device for a handsome daily wage.

Within a day, the porters tired of their employment and decided to leave the Wolf in the company of several nuns who could go no farther. Lobo's brother stepped in and promised rich rewards to sixteen sailors to take over the work, along with the threat that they might be held responsible for failing to fulfill the king's command to return Lobo to Lisbon. So off they went, leaving the nuns behind. After a week of heavy carrying and dwindling food supplies, no price could buy cooperation. On the south bank of a wide river they could not possibly lug him across, the sailors put up a small cloth awning and left Lobo there. His Chinese bond servant and African slave had no choice but to remain with him, their prospects no better than his. Lobo's brother tarried with them for a few hours, then set off after the others. He made it back to Portugal. The three men he abandoned were never heard of again.

Africans were seen in seventeenth-century East Asia, but Chinese were a rarer sight outside of that region. Ming law forbade Chinese from leaving the emperor's realm and imposed capital punishment on anyone who left without authorization, should he return. But for over two centuries, many had been going to Southeast Asia to trade and work, and had managed to slip back into China without dire consequences. Most officials looked the other way so long as the maritime traders who came and went were not exporting military materials such as gunpowder. Servitude to foreigners was another matter.

Ever since the Portuguese set up their colony on the tiny peninsula of Macao in 1557, Chinese had been going there to find work. Many went freely, but some ended up there as bonded labor, either because they had sold themselves into bondage to pay off debts or because they had been kidnapped. Bond service was legal in Ming China, so long as it was entered into willingly and by written contract. Human trafficking with foreigners, however, was against Chinese law, and provincial officials in Canton were vigilant on this point. The ban against human trafficking was important enough to be listed as the second of five basic regulations to which the Portuguese were forced to agree to after a round of negotiations with Chinese officials in 1614. (Another of the regulations forbade the Portuguese from having Japanese servants, "Dwarf Slaves," in Macao either.) Two years later, these regulations were inscribed on a large stone tablet erected in the center of town, lest anyone conveniently forget what they had agreed to respect. Chinese persons could not be bought and sold.

Regardless of what was carved in stone, Chinese officials realized that no legal barrier could stop the flood of poor Chinese heading out to scrape a few flakes off the gold mountain of Macao. Ordinary people had no interest in respecting the quarantine that the Ming state would have liked to impose between Chinese and foreigners, especially when the benefits of going out to Macao so clearly outweighed whatever moral duty these regulations were supposed to uphold. "Every year they go," one official complained, "every year we do not know how many." The Chinese government's concern was not so much ideological as fiscal. The problem with letting Chinese leave the country was that they then disappeared from their home county tax registers. One more Chinese bond servant in Macao was one fewer taxpayer. The rector of the Jesuit college in Macao sided with the Chinese officials by speaking out against trafficking in Chinese children, yet this did nothing to stop the flow of the people whose labor and services kept the colony going.

Had Lobo's ship made it back to Lisbon, his Chinese bond servant would have become one of Europe's rare Chinese. A few had gone ahead of him, some as Christian acolytes for the Jesuits to train, some as curiosities to show to great monarchs and enlightened scholars. As the ship didn't make it, Lobo's servant was left stranded between his master's world and his own. Once the Wolf was dead, his bond service was finished—as were his chances of survival. He was about to become one of the many whom the whirlwind of seventeenth-century trade picked up in one place and scattered to another.

GOING TO SEA WAS A risky business. Merchant corporations in Europe were building ships ever bigger so that they could accommodate ever-larger cargoes and better withstand attack at sea as they sped around the globe on ever-tighter schedules. But the bigger the ship, the less deftly it could maneuver its way through offshore channels, run up on a beach without harm when a storm struck, or evade a smaller but more nimble attacker. As a result, the seventeenth became the great century of shipwrecks. It was a simple matter of numbers. In the first decade of the seventeenth century, 59 Dutch ships and 20 English ships sailed for Asia. Skip a decade to the 1620s, and the numbers increase to 148 Dutch and 53 English. The more ships went out on the ocean, the more ships sank. Add to numbers the pressure of competition. Ships' captains began to sail at faster speeds and took greater risks in their attempts to outrun their competitors. As a result, more crews and passengers were getting thrown onto coasts evermore far flung and finding themselves in unimagined situations where they had to use their wits to survive. More cultures were being thrown up against each other and having to negotiate swiftly the visible differences of skin color, dress, gesture, and language that tend to mark the boundaries between who we are and who you are.

The year 1647 happens to have been a particularly bad one for Dutch ships making the passage around the Cape of Good Hope. Four months earlier, the *Nieuw Haarlem*, on the return leg of its fourth round-trip to Batavia, foundered near the cape, stranding its passengers there for almost a year before rescue came. Once they were back in Amsterdam, the survivors lobbied the VOC to let them return to the southern end of Africa and colonize it. The VOC was not keen to get involved in occupying territory overseas beyond what was needed to conduct trade. Unlike the Spanish and Portuguese, who projected their trade power as an imperium of military control, the Dutch simply wanted to come and go as free traders. After five years of intensive lobbying, some of the survivors were able to go back and settle in the place where they had been washed ashore in 1647. It was the first Dutch settler expedition to the cape, the first thread in the fabric of white settlement and black servitude in South Africa that would take three centuries to weave and several tumultuous decades late in the twentieth century to unravel.

Maritime ventures created fortunes for a lucky few and fueled the dreams of the rest. Some men willingly indentured themselves to long voyages from which the likelihood of winning riches—even of returning—may not have been good, but which was better than staying

at home. Even for those who did stay home, there was vicarious pleasure in dreaming about sailing abroad for riches, and the schaden-
freude of knowing that death and destruction lay at every turn for
those who did so. So much could go wrong on long sea voyages. Disease, dehydration, and starvation regularly devastated crews at sea.
Storms could tear a ship apart and leave not a plank to indicate that it
or those who sailed on it had ever existed. Unfamiliar coastlines consistently misled navigators and uncharted rocks tore out ships' bottoms, tilting passengers into the waves and dumping cargoes on sea
bottoms. And as Adriano de las Cortes discovered, making it to shore
was no guarantee of survival if the local inhabitants had learned to be
suspicious of traders and their guns, or avaricious for whatever goods
they might carry.

It is hardly surprising, then, to learn that the seventeenth-century
imagination was much gripped by tales of disaster at sea. From the beginning of the century, writers in all genres were happy to supply
readers with such stories. Even William Shakespeare got caught up in
the demand for shipwreck tales late in his career, though if he churned
out *The Tempest* merely to please public taste, he ultimately wrote what
today is regarded as one of his most enthralling plays. Of the shipwreck tales that publishers rushed into print in the early decades, none
sold as well as Willem Bontekoe's *A Memorable Description of the East
Indian Voyage*. Bontekoe regales the reader with six years of hair-
raising adventures starting in 1619, when he captained the *Nieuw
Hoorn* so disastrously across the Indian Ocean. He claims he wrote the
account for his family and friends back in Hoorn (he was one of three
brothers who captained VOC ships), doubting that anyone else would
be interested in reading it, and tells the readers to blame the publisher
for taking his manuscript from him and putting it into print, should
they judge the book substandard. Two decades had passed since the
events Bontekoe describes, but that did not dismay a public avid for
this kind of story. The book was a wild commercial success.

Unexpected disaster struck the *Nieuw Hoorn* on the journey out.

On the Indian Ocean crossing, a sailor upset a lantern that started a fire. The crew did what they could, but the blaze quickly got out of hand and burned its way to the gunpowder stores and detonated the ship's supply. The explosion killed many crewmen and drowned many more. Some were able to escape to the ship's two lifeboats before the explosion tore the ship apart, but Bontekoe stayed on board to the last. The force of the explosion threw him clear of the ship. Wounded and dazed, he had enough life left in him to grab hold of a floating mast. The survivors in one of the lifeboats eventually fished him out of the sea. Seventy-two men and boys then drifted eastward for two weeks with nothing but the ocean around them. As their food supply dwindled, the sailors eyed the cabin boys for food. Fortunately for all on board, the lifeboats drifted onto an island off the coast of Sumatra before hunger took their lives.

The disaster had not been Bontekoe's fault, and yet Jan Coen, the recently appointed VOC governor at Batavia and one of the company's more effective leaders, rebuked him once he reached the Dutch colony. The VOC had been developing a new route across the Indian Ocean but Bontekoe had failed to take it. Rather than go around the cape and up to Madagascar and then head east, which placed ships in unfavorable currents and howling winds, VOC ships were encouraged to head south from the cape and pick up the westerlies. These winds would carry them smartly across the bottom of the Indian Ocean. Before going too far east and smashing onto the rocky western coast of Australia, the ships were to cut north to Batavia. Bontekoe had skipped the cape and taken the old route. He justified his choice in his log with the observation that "all our people were still in good health, and we did not lack water; therefore we let all sails out." In the end, though, his journey was far longer than it needed to be. The new route cut the eleven-month journey from Amsterdam to Batavia by three or four months. Bontekoe could have been in Batavia three months before the explosion ever happened.[1]

The survivors of the *Nieuw Hoorn* stumbled onto an island that they soon realized was anything but deserted. Shortly after going ashore they found a campfire that had recently been put out, with a small stack of tobacco leaves piled beside it—evidence that the Malays on this island had already been inducted into the joys of smoking. The islanders had also learned not to expose themselves to newcomers but to slip from sight and assess their strength and disposition before making direct contact. The Malays showed up the next morning to parley. Three of the Dutch sailors who had been to Asia before knew enough Malay to make themselves understood. The first question the Malays asked was whether the men were carrying firearms. The Dutch had lost all their arquebuses when their ship exploded, but they were canny enough not to reveal that they were unarmed, telling their hosts that their guns were stashed in their boats. Their questions showed the sailors that the Malays knew a considerable amount about Dutch trade, as did their willingness to take Dutch coins in exchange for food. The islanders knew the name of Governor Jan Coen in Batavia. They also knew that Dutch traders carried valuable goods, and so attempted an ambush the following day. The attack failed, though at the cost of several Dutch lives.

Bontekoe and his men fled back to sea in their lifeboats and eventually connected with Dutch ships that carried them to Batavia. There they got work on VOC ships sailing the waters around Southeast Asia. Three years later, in June 1622, Bontekoe took part in the failed Dutch attack on Macao, in which a cannonball from Giacomo Rho's gun made a lucky hit and ignited the attackers' gunpowder casks. The explosion, as Bontekoe delicately phrases it, "placed our men in a quandary." Unable to capture the town, the Dutch withdrew and spent the rest of the summer on the ocean blockading the Portuguese and harassing Chinese shipping. If the VOC could not have Macao, they could force the Chinese into opening a separate trading relationship elsewhere on the coast—which is why the survivors of the *Nossa Senhora da Guía* three summers later found themselves threatened by militiamen when their ship ran aground. The Red Hairs had taught coastal people one lesson above all: fear Europeans.

That summer of skirmishes continued into the fall, when four sailors and two cabin boys from Bontekoe's ship got marooned on the coast. The six were manning a boat assigned to guard a captured Chinese ship when a storm blew up and drove them ashore. They survived the shipwreck and managed to hold on to their arquebuses. Even though their soaked guns could not be fired, they wielded them in a threatening manner to warn off anyone who approached. On their second day ashore, they were able to obtain fire from a house to relight the guns' matches. When later that day they came upon half a dozen Chinese bodies on a beach, shot by other Dutchmen, they had good reason to fear that the locals would be looking for reprisal. Soon enough the Dutch sailors were surrounded, though the crowd remained at a cautious distance, watching them. To make sure the Chinese kept that distance, the Dutchmen fired their guns into the air to warn them from getting any closer. They reported with some satisfaction that the Chinese "were mightily shaken" by the sound—but surely they had seen arquebuses before. They also said that the Chinese "gazed at them with wonder." These Dutchmen may have been the first real Red Hairs these Chinese had ever seen.

The locals were armed with only knives and pikes, and not keen to pick a fight. Instead of challenging the Red Hairs, they decided it would be safer to mollify and contain them. They gestured them toward a village temple and made signs that they would be fed. The Dutchmen were on their guard, lest this was a trick. It wasn't. The Chinese must have reckoned that starving men might behave less rationally than men who had full stomachs. After the meal, the Dutchmen withdrew and went down to the shore in the hope of attracting the attention of a passing Dutch ship. It was fortunate that they they did not have to fight, as "they had not four shots of powder left in their bandoleers." They passed an anxious night on the beach, and following morning constructed a makeshift raft and escaped to sea and rescue.

The six men and boys were fortunate to survive their adventure. For ordinary folk like these who found themselves hitched to the stars of their globe-sailing captains, the odds barely favored survival. The toll on those serving under Bontekoe's command through the following winter and spring—and this says nothing about the even greater toll on Chinese lives—was discouragingly steady. Hendrick Bruys of Bremen died of a poisoned Chinese arrow on 24 January 1623. Claes Cornelisz of Middelburg died on 17 March. The following night they lost Jan Gerritzs Brouwer of Haarlem, promoted to second mate less than six weeks earlier. The worst case has to be the nameless young man who died on 19 April. Four days earlier he climbed out of the hold of a captured junk tethered to Bontekoe's ship to pee over the side just as his mates were testing a newly installed cannon behind him. The ball-shot went right through his leg. The ship's surgeon amputated the young man's leg four days later to stop the infection, but he was dead within an hour.

For those who managed not to die, illness and injury were there to wear them down. By the end of Bontekoe's tour of duty that May, he still had ninety men, but barely half of them were well enough to work. Still, that was enough of a crew for Bontekoe's last exploit along the China coast: intercepting a Chinese junk heading for Manila with 250 passengers and cargo intended for that year's Acapulco trade. Bontekoe seized the ship and all its cargo, which he wrote was worth "thousands," and carried the luckless passengers and crew to the Pescadore Islands in the Strait of Taiwan where the Dutch needed construction labor to build fortifications for a trading base. Chinese officials later convinced the Dutch to abandon this base and withdraw to Taiwan. The laborers were not repatriated, however, but shipped off for sale at the slave market in Batavia. This sort of piracy was why, as a Japanese interpreter in Nagasaki observed, "whenever Chinese ships bound for Nagasaki sighted Red Hair ships, they behaved like a mouse does when it sees a cat." In service to the VOC doctrine that the inherent

right of all nations to trade justified seizing cargo from those who denied it, Bontekoe was one of the cats.

NOT EVERY DUTCHMAN STRANDED ON an Asian coast returned to his
ship. Four years after Bontekoe captured his last junk, a Dutch sailor
found himself stranded beyond the far north end of the Chinese coast
on the Korean island of Cheju. Nothing was heard of Jan Janszoon
Weltevree for twenty-six years. In 1653, the VOC ship *Sparrow Hawk*
was on its way from Taiwan to Nagasaki with a load of pepper and
sugar and twenty thousand deer skins. A powerful storm engulfed the
ship for five days, blowing her off course and onto Cheju Island. Of
the crew of sixty-four, thirty-six men survived the wreck. They too
were not heard of until eight of the thirty-six escaped by sea to the
Dutch outpost in Nagasaki thirteen years later. They carried with
them the report that a Dutchman named Weltevree had been living
in Korea for thirty-nine years.

   Weltevree had sailed to Asia on the *Hollandia*. After reaching
Batavia in July 1624, he found work on a smaller ship, the *Ouwerkerck*.
As no Dutch-built VOC ship by that name sailed from Holland during this period, the *Ouwerkerck* must have been built in Batavia for the
intra-Asian trade. The ship was bound from Taiwan to Nagasaki in
July 1627 when a Chinese junk heading for Moon Harbor on the Fujian coast crossed its bows: another mouse, falling into the paws of another cat. The junk was carrying a hundred and fifty passengers back
to Fujian after the trading season in Manila, presumably laden with
American silver. The ship was unarmed and easily taken. The Dutch
captain brought half the Chinese passengers to the *Ouwerkerck* and
transferred sixteen of his own sailors to the junk to take charge. The
plan was to sail the ships to Taiwan, empty the junk of its cargo, then
transfer the hapless passengers south to Batavia as slave labor. When a
storm struck before the ships reached Taiwan, the cat lost its mouse.
The captain of the *Ouwerkerck* abandoned hope of finding his prize
and instead headed south to prey on Portuguese ships heading to
Japan. If he could not steal American silver from Chinese ships, he

could steal Chinese silks from Portuguese. Soon enough a convoy of five Portuguese ships came into range. The captain did not know that the five had been refitted for combat and were sailing in disguise to lure unsuspecting Dutch ships into attack. The *Ouwerkerck*'s attack backfired. The captain and his crew of thirty-three were captured, and the ship was towed to Macao for public burning.

The junk that the *Ouwerkerck* had captured was blown in the opposite direction and washed up at the south end of Korea. Three of the Dutchmen, including Weltevree, went ashore at Cheju Island to find water. While they foraged, the Chinese on board regained control of their ship and sailed away, abandoning those who had gone ashore. The "pirate," as the modern historian who has reconstructed Weltevree's story calls him, "had been done in by his victims."

Weltevree must have handled his first encounter with Koreans with dexterity, for not only did the Koreans not decapitate him, as the Chinese had done to some of Las Cortes's fellow shipwreck survivors, but they recruited him for his technical skills. The sole condition of his employment was that he not leave the country. Now that he was in Korea, he had to accept that he was there for good. His two fellow castaways died fighting against a Manchu invasion in 1635, but Weltevree survived, and indeed flourished, as a royal gunsmith. The arquebuses carried by the Koreans who apprehended the *Sparrow Hawk* crew may well have been manufactured under his supervision.

Weltevree did more than just adapt to his new circumstances in Korea: he prospered. He worked hard, rose in rank, married a Korean woman, and had children who were assigned to carry on their father's trade as gunsmiths. By the time the *Sparrow Hawk* wrecked on the coast of Cheju, Weltevree had been speaking and presumably reading Korean for twenty-six years. Having spoken no Dutch for that long, when confronted with the Dutch sailors, he found it awkward to speak to them. As one of the *Sparrow Hawk* survivors later recorded, they were surprised that "a Man of 58 Years of Age, as he then was, could so forget his Mother-tongue, that we had much to do at first to understand him; but it must be observ'd he recover'd it again in a month." Weltevree had crossed so far over the language barrier with his host culture that he found it difficult to cross back when the need arose. He may have learned other Asian languages, for one of his duties was to take charge of foreign sailors and fishermen—mostly Japanese and Chinese—who were shipwrecked on the coast. He shared command of the newly shipwrecked Dutch sailors with a Chinese sergeant, in fact, and they may well have communicated with each other in a language other than Korean.

Weltevree integrated himself into Korean society so well that Koreans came to accept him as one of them. The Korean official who introduced him to the *Sparrow Hawk* survivors laughed when they expressed delight in finding a Dutchman. "You are mistaken," the Korean told them, "for he is a *Coresian*." Weltevree may have looked Dutch to the Dutchmen, but to the Koreans he had become something else. The Dutchmen who found him a generation later could scarcely imagine such a transformation. His entry into Korea had been a matter of necessity at the time, but by the time the *Sparrow Hawk* struck the coast, Weltevree had no wish to leave. He had attained a position of much greater importance than he ever could have achieved back home, and in that condition survived into his seventies surrounded by his sons. His life as a Korean turned out far better than his life as a returned Dutchman would have been.

When the survivors of the *Sparrow Hawk* learned in their first interview with the Korean king that they would not be permitted to return to the Dutch post in Japan, they were shocked. Repatriation was the shipwreck convention in Europe, and they had expected it to be respected in Asia.

"We humbly beseech your Majesty," the Dutch sailors addressed the king through Weltevree, "that since we have lost our Ship to the Storm, you would be pleas'd to send us over to Japan, that with the assistance of the Dutch there, we might one Day return to our Country, to enjoy the Company of our Wives, Children and Friends."

"It is not the custom of Corea to suffer strangers to depart the Kingdom," the king replied. "You must resolve to end your Days in my Dominions. I will provide you with all Necessaries." The king saw no reason to alter standard procedure, as foreigners who left Korea might take back strategic information that could be used against the king in the future.

The king then became the ethnologist and ordered them to sing Dutch songs and dance Dutch dances so that he could witness European culture firsthand. After the performance, he gave them each a set of clothes "after their Fashion," as one of the survivors put it, and assigned them to serve in the royal bodyguard. Henceforth they would live as Koreans. Some learned to function well in the Korean language, but most were not content with their new position. Two years later, the ship's master and a gunner approached a Manchu ambassador visiting Korea to ask that he take them back to China, whence they understood they could be repatriated. The Koreans, learning of this appeal, were adamant that this should not happen. They bribed the Manchu ambassador to get the two Dutchmen back and threw them in prison, where they eventually died. Eleven years after this incident, another eight, unwilling to accept their life sentence, escaped by boat to Japan. They were the ones who carried the story of Weltevree, otherwise thought lost at sea, to the outside world.

That left eight of the original crew to live out their lives as "Coresians." Among them was a sailor named Alexander Bosquet. This man had had several identities before being stranded in Korea. He started life as a Scot, possibly one of the Scottish exile community in France; then went looking for work in the Netherlands, where he changed his name to Sandert Basket; then sailed to Asia as a ship's gunner for the VOC. He ended up finally in Korea—where he must have been obliged to adopt yet another name, this time a Korean one. Bosquet/Basket managed to be Scottish, French, Dutch, and Korean by turns. How many of the other "Dutchmen" on the *Sparrow Hawk* started out as something else or ended up as something else again?

WELTEVREE NEVER MEANT TO LAND on Korean soil. Nor had he any intention of staying there when he did, though in time he accepted the sovereignty into which he had fallen. China handled such affairs differently, as we have seen. Adriano de las Cortes and the survivors of the *Guía* were permitted to repatriate after clearing themselves of the suspicion of being pirates. But there were other Europeans who did enter China with the intention of staying: missionaries.

There were two ways to take up permanent residence in China. One was to petition the regional authorities for permission, which the Jesuits successfully did starting in the 1580s. It was understood on both sides that, by entering China of their own will, they were agreeing to remain in China for the remainder of their lives. From the Chinese point of view, the only reason a foreigner would come and then leave, other than to bring tribute, was to spy. The other way to enter China was to sneak in unnoticed, which is what missionaries of the Dominican order started to do in the 1630s. These two ways into China—by the "front door" through Macao (the Jesuits' route), and by the "back door" along the Fujian coast (the Dominicans')—happen to be the same two paths by which tobacco first entered China.

The Jesuit strategy of working with the political authorities in China was based on the hope that their support would translate into open toleration and popular acceptance. The most successful of the early Jesuits was the Italian missionary Matteo Ricci, who entered China from Macao in 1583. After spending a decade improvising his dress and conduct, Ricci worked out an accommodative relationship with Chinese customs and beliefs that enabled him to find his way into elite society—and after 1604 to collaborate with Paolo Xu on translation projects. Their success encouraged the Jesuits to follow this path of accommodation. By the time of Xu's death in 1633, there were roughly a dozen Jesuit missionaries working throughout the realm.

The Dominicans' strategy was the diametric opposite of the Jesuits' accommodative posture. They were suspicious that accommodating, both politically and theologically, compromised the integrity of Christian doctrine. The Dominicans preferred to sidestep officialdom and embed themselves in local social networks below the radar of the state. This is why, when an Italian Dominican named Angelo

Cocchi landed on an island off the Fujian coast on the second day of 1632, he was not another hapless shipwreck victim seeking repatriation, but someone who intended his journey to end exactly here in China.

Angelo Cocchi was fortunate to have reached China. By all rights he should have died before reaching land. He and his party of twelve had bought passage on a ship that was leaving Taiwan two days earlier. Cocchi had been on the island for the previous three years heading a Dominican mission that had been founded five years earlier. (The Spanish would shortly abandon their little foothold and leave Taiwan to the Dutch.) Juan de Alcarazo, the Spanish governor of the Philippines, asked him to open trade negotiations with the Chinese governor of Fujian, Xiong Wencan. Cocchi had agreed readily, for the request handed him a long-sought opportunity to go to China. His dream to convert the Chinese may have dawned on him as early as 1610, when the thirteen-year-old Florentine boy entered the Dominican order as a novice. Perhaps the idea took form over the next decade of study in Fiesole and Salamanca, or when he left Cádiz for Panama in 1620, or when he took ship in Acapulco for Manila in 1621. The idea was certainly upon him by 1627, when he was ordered to learn the Fujian dialect in Cavite, the port of Manila where all Chinese, and possibly his former teacher, would be systematically massacred in 1639.

On 30 December 1631, Angelo Cocchi took passage on a Chinese junk sailing from Taiwan to Fujian. His multicultural retinue included a fellow Dominican from Spain, Tomas de la Sierra, two Spanish guards, seven Filipinos, a Mexican, and a Chinese interpreter. Whatever they were bringing with them in the way of presents, supplies, and rumored silver was too great a temptation for the sailors of the vessel. The crew wasted no time. On the first night at sea, they attacked the foreigners, intending to kill them all and take their possessions. Five Filipinos, the Mexican, and the Spaniard were killed. The rest retreated to a cabin and barricaded themselves inside. Each side spent the following day waiting out the other. The next night, New

Year's Eve, the boat was boarded by yet another gang of pirates, who stripped it of everything it carried, massacred the entire crew, and left the boat to drift. Did they not know that an Italian, a Chinese, two Spaniards, and two Filipinos were hiding below deck? It seems not, for they would have been sure to equate foreigners with silver and fight them for it.

On the morning of New Year's Day, 1632, Angelo Cocchi emerged cautiously from the cabin in which he and five traveling companions, two of them wounded, had barricaded themselves for two nights and a day. They found their junk drifting off the coast of Fujian and completely deserted, except for the bodies of the slain that still lay on the deck. They managed to land the junk on an island, from which local fisherman conveyed them to the mainland, perhaps out of honest pity, though more likely because they got the junk in exchange for their aid. They were then transferred to the prefectural seat of Quanzhou, one of the ports that handled the trade with Manila, from where they were sent on to Governor Xiong in Fuzhou, the provincial capital. Xiong received Cocchi politely but was not about to grant him residence or even open discussion about trade. Instead, he reported Cocchi's arrival to Beijing and asked for instructions. He also ordered that the pirates who had boarded Cocchi's ship be apprehended and executed—which they were, despite Cocchi's plea to spare their lives.

The court responded four months later with an order that the survivors of the *Guía* would have been delighted to receive so quickly: these people were to be sent back. European missionaries were allowed to enter China so long as they observed the four conditions the Jesuits respected, thanks to Matteo Ricci's improvisation: arrive through legal channels, dress Chinese, speak Mandarin, and conduct yourself according to Chinese norms. Cocchi failed on all counts (was his Chinese substandard, or was the dialect he learned in Cavite unintelligible?) and was ordered out of the country. Rendition to the Philippines was precisely what Cocchi did *not* want. He wanted to stay in China; he desired to devote the rest of his life to spreading

Christianity among the Chinese; he wanted never to return to Manila, much less to Florence.

When the day arrived for Cocchi to board the boat that was arranged to take him back to Manila, a Japanese Christian who wanted to go to the Philippines took his place. The substitution was arranged through Luke Liu. Liu was a Chinese Christian from Fuan, a neighboring county seat where the Jesuits had already established a mission and won ten converts. What a Japanese Christian was doing in Fuzhou, and how he fooled the authorities, are puzzles without answers, but the ruse worked. After making the switch, Liu whisked Cocchi out of the capital and off to Fuan, where together they set about transforming Cocchi's appearance and speech into those of a Chinese.

Cocchi managed to stay out of sight of the provincial authorities. They would have apprehended and exiled him had they known he was there. Even so, he worked publicly enough to convert several people and build two churches. He was so certain of his ambition to build a Dominican presence in Fujian that, within a year, he and his followers devised a plan to smuggle more missionaries from Manila, again via Taiwan. This time the boat was sent from China for the purpose and was manned by four Chinese converts to make sure nothing went amiss. The plan went off without a hitch. In July 1633, Cocchi welcomed two Spanish priests (one of whom, Juan de Morales, had previously led a failed mission to Cambodia) to Fuan. None of this would have been possible without Cocchi's Chinese associates, and yet they would not have become involved had Cocchi failed to gain their trust and devotion. Four and a half months later, at the age of thirty-six, Angelo Cocchi suddenly fell ill. He died in the very place where he had long intended his life to end, if not quite this soon.

COCCHI, LIKE WELTEVREE, MADE THE choice never to go home. Both men survived the choice they made, at least initially, and both began to fashion new lives for themselves in their new circumstances, one as a priest, the other as an employee of the king's arsenal. Theirs were not the only circumstances through which Europeans who ended up in foreign lands far beyond Europe made the decision not to go back. There were others.

The ship on which Weltevree had first sailed to Asia, the *Hollandia*, returned to Europe in 1625 with a load of pepper. Two of its crew on that voyage chose not to complete the journey. We know about them because, by coincidence, none other than Willem Bontekoe captained Weltevree's *Hollandia* on its return. Bontekoe once again was a magnet for misfortune, for storms ravaged the *Hollandia* during its Indian Ocean crossing. By the time the ship reached the island of Madagascar, it had to limp into the Bay of Sancta Lucia for repair, including the raising of a new mast.

Sancta Lucia was a mooring that Dutch mariners in this situation regularly used, so the Malagasy people living around the bay were well familiar with Europeans. Bontekoe sent some of his men ashore to "have speech with the inhabitants"—indicating that at least one side spoke the language of the other. The Malagasy agreed to let them land and repair their ship, and even volunteered to help drag the timber needed for making a new mast from the interior of the island out to the coast. Working side by side bred familiarity, so much so that over the three weeks the crew spent at Sancta Lucia, "the men often wandered away to seek pleasure." As Bontekoe bluntly puts it, "the women were keen to have intercourse with our men." His sole concern was that the men not absent themselves too much from their jobs, though he also realized that sexual intercourse boosted their morale. "When they had been with the women," he noted, "they returned meek as lambs to their work." The visitors found clear evidence that this was not the first time Dutch sailors had slept with the local women. Though Bontekoe notes that the Malagasy are "mostly black" with hair "curled like sheep's wool," he also observes that "we saw here many children who were almost white, and whose fair coloured hair hung from their heads." He doesn't need to explain further. The crew of the *Hollandia* were about a decade behind the first Dutch fathers of Malagasy Creole children.

As the ship was preparing for departure on the morning of 24 April, after close to a month's sojourn at Sancta Lucia, Bontekoe discovered that two of the men on night watch were missing. Hilke Jopkins and Gerrit Harmensz had not only disappeared, but had taken one of the ship's boats with them. As Bontekoe put it, Jopkins and Harmensz "ran away to the blacks." Perhaps the evidence of earlier coupling had encouraged Hilke Jopkins to take his chances locally and not return home to Friesland, and Gerrit Harmensz not to go back to his family in Norden. Is it even reasonable to assume that either man had a home or family in Europe? Having sailed east years earlier, a choice that was for many a last resort, they may well have had nothing to return to. Why not make a new life where there seemed some chance of happiness, or even just survival?

Bontekoe sent a company of soldiers out to apprehend the deserters and return them to the ship. Their labor was needed. Jopkins and Harmensz were spotted at one point, but with the connivance of the Malagasies, they could not be caught. The search achieved nothing except to delay the *Hollandia*'s departure by one more day. Bontekoe gave up and left them to the life they had chosen.

Jumping culture was not as easy as jumping ship. It involved giving up the language, food, beliefs, and etiquette of one's birthplaces in favor of those of an adopted land. Such matters were different for the rich, who had a stake in the way things were at home. Jopkins and Harmensz were poor men, and the conditions of life for the poor were much the same everywhere. Holland's poor might eat different grains from Africa's poor, but starch still made up the bulk of their diet. They might dress themselves in this homespun rather than that homespun, but rough cloth was rough cloth. They might pray here to this deity rather than there to that god, but they knew that the afterlife was pretty much beyond their management in any case. All they could do was pray and hope for the best.

The key actors in this drama of escape were not the European men, even though Bontekoe assigned them the leading role in his memoir. They were the Malagasy women. Had the women been unwilling to help the Dutchmen, Jopkins and Harmensz could not have dreamed of surviving at Sancta Lucia. They could have survived without sex, of course, but not without the resources and know-how the women provided, and the position within kinship networks that relations with them provided.

The same calculations were going on all over the world. Champlain actually encouraged his men to find Huron wives, including those who had legal wives back in France. There was no better way to ensure their survival than by embedding them among those best able to support them and facilitate trade. On one side, missionaries in New France denounced these cross-racial unions as immoral. On the other, Huron men wondered how their women could tolerate such ugly mates. As one Huron said after meeting his first Frenchman, "Is it possible that any woman would look favourably on such a man?" But they had no other reason to object, for traders on both sides benefited from the practice: these unions gave them preferential access to trade goods. Canadian historian Sylvia van Kirk has called these Natives "women in between." Interposed between two distinctly different cultural formations, they were able to relate to both, bridging from one to the other and enjoying influence and prestige as a result. Once the balance between French and Native tilted in French favor, however, the channel they had opened was shut. By then, European women were arriving in New France in sufficient numbers to drive Native women from the marriage market and reimpose racism as a social principle of Canadian society.

These relationships existed in what American historian Richard White calls a "middle ground," the space in which two cultures meet and must learn to interact. This space of intersection survives so long as neither culture has the power to overwhelm the other. As long as it does survive, both cultures are in a position to adjust their differences and negotiate a reasonable coexistence. Through war, trade, and marriage, the French and the Hurons sustained this sort of middle ground through the first half of the seventeenth century. The Malagasies and the Dutch were engaged in the same strategy at Sancta Lucia. There, too, neither side was in a position to force its will on the other, except at the cost of breaking the profitable bond between them. In this linking of cultures, castaways and captives had many roles to play. They taught and learned languages, gave and took knowledge, made whatever sense they could of the new customs and ideas they encountered and then interpreted them to the other side.

This middle ground depended on each side seeing the necessity of compromise. Shakespeare in 1611 intuited the fragility of this relationship when he wrote *The Tempest*. All too soon, as Caliban rages to Prospero, his shipwrecked European master, what began as kindness—"Thou strokedst me, and made much of me"—turned to enslavement and deculturation. "You taught me language," the fictional Caliban bitterly reminds Prospero, "and my profit on't is, I know how to curse." Shakespeare's imaginary character expresses the despair that real Natives came to feel over their loss of language and culture. As one Algonquin complained to a French missionary who was converting his fellow tribesmen, "It is you who overturn their brains and make them die." The consequences of exposure were unstoppably swift. "It is all done so quickly," the contemporary Montagnais poet, Armand Collard, has written. "You have no time to react and so you submit." The middle ground closes and with it the choice to meet strangers as equals.

To be in Holland was similarly not a choice Van der Burch's boy got to make. All he could do was submit and figure out how to improvise in his new surroundings. Looking at how he carries himself in the manner of a Dutch servant, he seems to have managed all right. And yet there is the hint of something in the frank look he casts our way, a hint perhaps of his mindfulness that this is not his place.

VERMEER DIDN'T PAINT ANYONE WHO wasn't born within twenty-five kilometers of Delft. The only time he considered painting people who weren't purely Dutch was in his early twenties, when he took on the classical and biblical subjects that a student painter of that time was expected to paint. In the previous generation, Rembrandt van Rijn in Amsterdam and Leonaert Bramer in Delft had transformed biblical scenes into visually dramatic subjects establishing a style within which the young Vermeer had no choice but to start working. The challenge for seventeenth-century painters of scenes from the distant past was how to compose them in such a way that closed the natural gap between the world the viewers saw around them and the world as it might have looked in another time and place. The painter wanted his viewers to feel that they were there, actually seeing what was going on. Was that best achieved by making the biblical past look just like the Dutch present, or by making them different? Was the demand of realism better served by avoiding such playacting and dressing your figures in contemporary Dutch garb and remaining faithful to the architectural details of Dutch buildings? If not, then should a painter fill his canvas with Oriental details picked up from contemporary Near Eastern culture? Was this a more powerful device to get viewers to suspend their disbelief?

Painters of the generation of Bramer and Rembrandt were brilliant in developing a hybrid look that Orientalized some features while retaining a strong touch of the familiar. Vermeer's instinct went in the opposite direction: not to try for a faux-historical realism, but to translate historical moments into the present. When he paints the figure of Jesus in his early *Christ in the House of Mary and Martha*, he depicts him in the conventionally indeterminate drapery that artists of the time tended to put on Jesus. Mary and Martha, though, he dressed more or less as though they were Dutch women. So too, the sparsely indicated room where they are sitting looks suspiciously like a Dutch home. Already at the age of twenty-two, Vermeer was shying away from the Near Eastern touches in which his elders indulged. Within two years, he gave up this sort of fake historicizing entirely and painted nothing but the real world of everyday Delft.

If Vermeer gave up painting biblical scenes, he was not averse to hanging them on his wall, as Catholic households in Protestant Holland did to remind themselves of their more literal interpretation of Christian belief. Among the artwork listed in the inventory of his possessions drawn up after he died was a "painting of the Three

Kings" depicting the journey of the three magi to Bethlehem to worship the newborn Jesus. The painting was in his bequest to his mother-in-law, Maria Thins, who remained firm in her Catholic faith. It hung in the main hall of the house. This position gave it a prominence that suggests it was a painting intended to be seen, perhaps because of its devotional significance (attacks on the cult of the magi by Luther and Calvin may have inspired particular loyalty from Catholics keen to honor the role of adoration in worship) or because it was an object of some monetary value. As there is nothing more we can learn about this painting, let us suppose it is the one three kings painting by a Delft artist of this period that still exists, and that Vermeer could plausibly have seen: Leonaert Bramer's *The Journey of the Three Magi to Bethlehem.*

Bramer was the senior painter in Delft throughout Vermeer's life. Born there in 1595, Bramer spent a decade learning his craft in France and Italy before returning home in 1628 and establishing his practice as a fine painter. He was also an excellent sketch artist: porcelain painters in town transferred his drawings to delftware. Bramer was a friend of the Vermeer family, perhaps through Vermeer's father, who dealt in art and may have sold some of his work. Some have suggested that Bramer could have been Vermeer's first painting teacher. Vermeer's craftsmanship points to a strong technical education, making Bramer, thirty-seven years his senior, a reasonable candidate. At the very least, the elder painter was the young man's mentor if not his actual teacher, for he was one of the delegation of two who called on Maria Thins on Vermeer's behalf to ask her to give up her objection to a marriage between her daughter Catharina and the twenty-three-year-old painter.

Bramer painted *The Journey of the Three Magi to Bethlehem* in the late 1630s, when Vermeer was still a child. The central figures are the three kings, or the three wise men, as we know them now—Caspar and Melchior on foot and well lit, Balthasar on camelback and in shadow—following three angels toward Bethlehem. It is dusk and the angels carry torches to light the way. Accompanying the three magi is a retinue of attendants trailing off into the gloom behind them. The magi are dressed in lavish fur-lined robes and carrying gold vessels containing the incense and myrrh that Matthew mentions in his Gospel. The only element missing is the baby Jesus. The three wise men have not yet reached Bethlehem, but they approach.

When a writer or painter tells a story, especially a religious story, he selects from a large treasury of such stories. In the case of a painting, he must also choose one part of the story to tell. One scene must convey the whole story. So when Bramer decided to represent the birth of Jesus, he had many decisions to make. He could have painted the story in the Gospel of Luke about the angel Gabriel appearing to the shepherds rather than the story in Matthew about the three magi, for example; or he could have painted the magi in the more conventional posture of presenting their gifts to Jesus in the manger, rather than carrying them en route to Bethlehem. Given the choices Bramer had to make, we have to ask the question that Renaissance historian Richard Trexler asks again and again in his history of the cult of the three magi. What was emerging or evolving at the time the story of the three wise men was being told "for which the magi story provides a discourse"? To focus on Bramer, what was he trying to talk about by choosing to depict the journey of the magi in this way? Or, to return to the device I have used throughout the book, where are the doors in this painting, and down what corridors do they lead?

For me, the doors in this painting are the people. When he did a biblical scene in a faux-Orientalist realist style, a Dutch painter found himself obliged to depict people who were not, in fact, Dutch. Since Bramer was not interested in achieving realism by transposing Bible stories into Delft, he had to decorate his characters with Near Eastern details. These would lure his viewers back to biblical times. The most consistent touch in his *Journey of the Three Magi* is the turban, a standard cliché for setting a biblical scene. All three magi have turbans, though Melchior has taken his off and carries it loosely in his right hand. In addition, Balthasar's black servant and at least one of the attendants are in turbans. Evoking simultaneously the contemporary Near East and the distant past, the turban blends the Oriental present with biblical time into a pastiche that doesn't need to worry about historical realism. Bramer has used clothing to achieve the same effect: an eclectic mix of nonstandard ecclesiastical vestments; fur-lined Oriental robes; and indeterminate drapery that appears real, while evoking the distance of time and place that puts the scene back in the biblical era.[2]

Underneath the robes and turbans, however, are the people wearing them. This is where we might begin to detect what Bramer was trying to express when he produced this picture: people of many origins thrown together on a journey and heading toward an outcome that is not yet in view. The ethnic variety of the convoy is signaled most vividly by Balthasar, the black African. Theological reasoning had long accepted that Balthasar might have been black, but the iconography of the three kings only caught up to the theology in the 1440s, when the first African slaves were arriving in Lisbon. In no time, European artists were painting Balthasar black (some were even painting over the white Balthasars in older paintings). In Bramer's painting, the black king is difficult to see. He is turned away from us. A black servant is next to his camel, but he too is indistinct—which may reflect a lack of Africans in Delft that Bramer could use as models. Perhaps he had to make these figures up from his memory of the Africans he saw in Italy. As for the other two magi, Bramer makes the ruddy-faced Caspar look completely and hopelessly Dutch (was he working within the tradition that allowed an artist to paint in his patron as one of the magi?), but he has exoticized the bald and bearded Melchior, giving him what could be read as Jewish or Armenian features. Two attendants reacting to a rearing horse look so Dutch as to be straight out of Rembrandt, but the white-skinned angels are of indeterminate ethnicity.

Are we as viewers supposed to notice these details? If the whole point of the painter's artifice is to make us think that what is happening in the picture is actually happening, we are not. The last thing a realist painter wants to do is to leave any of his tools lying about the scene, a badly drawn figure, say, or an anachronistic detail that couldn't belong to that place and time. Such details disrupt the viewing experience and remind us that what we are looking at is just a picture. But every picture, not just a poorly executed one, is attached to the place and time of its making. No picture can escape the tension between what is going on inside the frame and what is happening out in the world—which is, after all, where the artist and his viewers live—and what was happening in Bramer's time was an unprecedented mixing of people, hence the multicultural odyssey in his painting. The scene may be biblical, but the artist was not abandoning his social experience and common knowledge when he assembled these figures. Nor need we abandon ours, which is why it is worth paying attention to the ethnic signs of the characters in the painting and suspecting that the variety of people we are seeing is a variety that Bramer experienced in his own time.

The ostensible purpose of a three kings painting is to celebrate the recognition of Christ's birth and reinforce the viewer's pious adherence to the truth of that recognition. That is the first meaning of the painting. But the second, lived meaning of a three kings painting belongs to the place and time the painter made it, and that second meaning keeps shifting as we, the viewers, move through place and time and look for doors that we can open. This is especially so with a painting from four centuries ago. An artist of our own time wouldn't paint the story in this style, so the details catch our eye, hinting at secrets now lost to us.

What we see in the painting—people of different cultural origins who have banded together to journey through a dim landscape toward the promise of a future that remains unrevealed—is I think not a bad description of the world in the seventeenth century. It may not have been what Bramer intended, yet he too lived in a real world, and in that real world the defining boundaries of cultures were perforating under the pressure of constant movement. People were journeying around the globe, from the wealthy few merchants handling high-value commodities over long distances, to the impoverished multitude of transport workers and service personnel who followed in their wake.

This is the knowledge that retrospection gives us as we think about the three kings painting that hung in the main hall of Vermeer's home. Our urge to place it within a wider historical context sends us well beyond Vermeer's intentions. Perhaps he hung the painting for an entirely devotional purpose: to make a Catholic version of Christian faith daily visible, at least to his mother-in-law. If the painting really were by Bramer, he might have hung it in honor of the mentor who convinced Maria Thins to let him marry her daughter. But why stop at the first door, when we have the knowledge to step right through the painting and come out the other side into the town of Delft, where well-dressed men who traded in precious metals, exotic manufactures, and spices worth their weight in silver brought with them a ragged multitude of Europeans, Moors, Africans, Malays, possibly even the odd Malagasy picked up in Sancta Lucia—all of whom improvised their way as best they could into survival.

Here is one of them now, attending his mistress as she entertains her gentleman caller in an upstairs room in Delft: a black boy, who never meant to be where he was, who will never find a way back to his place of beginning, and whose descendants most likely will end up blending into Dutch society as though he had never been black.

ENDINGS: NO MAN IS AN ISLAND

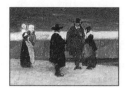

N O MAN IS an Island, entire of itselfe." The line comes from
Devotions upon Emergent Occasions by the English poet and the-
ologian John Donne. Donne wrote these meditations on the burdens
of Christian faith in 1623 while deathly ill, at a time when he faced
one of the many "occasions of emergency" in his life. His seventeenth meditation ("Perchance hee for whom this Bell tolls") contains the fragments of Donne's writings best remembered today,
including "No man is an Island." Donne does not end the image of
the island there, but takes the metaphor and inserts it into a wider vision. "Every man is a peece of the Continent, a part of the maine; if
a Clod be washed away by the Sea, Europe is the lesse, as well as if a
Promontorie were." Donne then turns to the moral purpose to
which the image is building and declares: "Any man's death dimin-
ishes me, because I am involved in Mankinde." At the close of this
meditation, he returns to the tolling bell with which he began.
"Therefore never send to know for whom the bell tolls," he con-
cludes. "It tolls for thee."

When Donne wrote this passage, he was meditating on the state of
his soul, not on the state of the world. He feared his own death, but
with that fear found himself struggling with the spiritual responsibility
for the welfare of every lost soul, not just his own. To a historian looking back on 1623, the metaphor of island and continent—an inten-
tionally resonant choice for English islanders who, among other
threats, feared attacks from the continent—stands out more powerfully

than the theology on which it rests. The language Donne has chosen
to use is the language of geography, one of the rapidly changing new
fields of seventeenth-century research. The trend within that academic discipline at the time he was writing—which was to assemble
a global system of knowledge of the oceans and continents coming to
European attention, and to compile an ever-more complete map of
the world—gives him a model to think about the spiritual links that
every member of the human community has with every other, ex-
tending outward in a universal web. As his spiritual world was filling,
so too more and more of the mundane world was coming onto the
map. The metaphor of island and continent would have occurred
naturally to Donne at this moment, when Europeans were moving
across the face of the globe in ever-greater numbers and bringing
their new knowledge back to Europe—or to Asia, for that matter,
where seventeenth-century cartographers in China and Japan also began drawing surprising new images of the world.

Donne's imagination in 1623 fixed on other timely images as well.
One he employs in the same meditation is the image of translation.
He declares that death is not a loss but a translation of the soul into
another form. "When one Man dies, one Chapter is not torne out of
the booke," Donne writes, "but translated into a better language; and
every Chapter must be so translated." Death comes in many forms,
and so "God emploies several translators"; not only that, but "God's
hand is in every translation."

Donne's point was theological, but he was a poet who thought in
images that rose to his attention from the age in which he lived. The
translator was one of those images. Within the space of Donne's own
life, the English and Dutch had organized East India companies, the
EIC and the VOC, to mount trade expeditions all over the globe.
Wherever their ships and people went, as Bontekoe put it on arriving
at Madagascar in 1625, they had to "have speech with the inhabitants."
Fortune, even survival, depended on someone on board knowing how
to speak to the local people. Donne declares that God employs many
translators; so too these trading corporations had to hire many

translators to interpret between the needs of one side and the demands of the other, and often to move among several languages at once. The number of translators can only have increased as networks of trade expanded and their experience of trading in disparate locations deepened. By the 1650s, over forty thousand people were departing decennially on VOC ships for Asia. Thousands more were leaving on other ships. Many of them picked up at least one form of local pidgin in the places where their travels dumped them. Many of them became translators.

Sometimes the accidents of travel forced a sailor such as Jan Weltevree to become fluent in a foreign language without his ever being given a choice in the matter. Others actually chose to study a foreign language so that they could translate themselves into new contexts. When the Italian missionary Angelo Cocchi crossed from Taiwan to Fujian at the end of 1631, he took a Chinese translator with him. Cocchi had studied Chinese in Manila, but he anticipated the cost of failing to communicate his message once he got to China, which was, at a minimum, expulsion from the country. For translation is not just about knowing the right words for things in another language; it is about transposing ideas between languages, and knowing how to shape the expectations that words create.

And what about Cocchi's Chinese translator? How did he come to study Spanish? Was he a long-term resident of the Parián who picked up the language by virtue of living in the Spanish colony of Manila? Did he convert to Christianity and learn Spanish in the course of his contact with missionaries? Did he actually study the language, or was it something he acquired through daily use? However he mastered the language, he ended up translating into Chinese, not for a Spaniard but for an Italian, who in turn had learned that language while at seminary in Salamanca. By 1631, no trading company and mission could do without "several translators," many of whom were adept at moving among multiple languages.

There is one other metaphor in Donne's seventeenth meditation that stands out to readers today. Donne was a man obsessed with his own sinfulness, which he sought to use as a goad for climbing to faith. To work this transmutation, he advises himself and his readers to reverse the values they normally assign to things like contentment and affliction. "Affliction is treasure," Donne tells us, and the more one has of it, the better. But it must be properly channeled to be of any use. And here he interprets this unsought treasure as silver. "If a man carry treasure in bullion, or in a wedge of gold, and have none coined into currant Monies, his treasure will not defray him as he travells. Tribulation is Treasure in the nature of it, but it is not currant money in the use of it, except wee get nearer and nearer our home, Heaven, by it." The only thing that convinces us to convert the silver bullion of our affliction into the coin of religious understanding, says Donne, is the sound of the tolling bell, the prospect of death.

How intriguing that Donne should turn to the relationship between bullion and coin for a metaphor for tribulation and redemption! Silver was constantly swapping forms as it moved through currency zones around the globe. In some zones, such as China, bullion was the form in which silver was wanted. In other zones, silver by law had to circulate in what Donne calls "currant money." In Spanish America, it had to be in the coin of the realm, the real. In the Dutch Republic, as we have seen, the coin of several realms could circulate, from the real to the guilder, depending on supply. In the trading zone of the South China Sea, silver could be traded in a mixture of bullion and Spanish reals. When Willem Bontekoe asked two Chinese on the Fujian coast to bring pigs to his ship on 8 April 1623, he gave them 25 reals and they willingly took the coins. Bullion would have been fine too, for all they wanted was the silver, but Bontekoe had none. Like most European states, the United Provinces banned the use of unminted silver so as to control the volume of money in circulation. If you wanted to use your silver as money in Europe, you had to have it in coin. Beyond these historical particulars, though, there looms the simple fact that in 1623, when Donne was in search of images to express the accumulation of afflictions that might provoke the sinful to piety, that infinitely accumulatable substance, silver, was what suggested itself to his fevered mind.

Silver and translation. Isolated islands and linked continents. Donne had no idea he was installing doors to his century when he composed his text, but there they are: casual openings onto corridors leading us back to his world. Like Vermeer, I suspect, Donne was so absorbed in making sense of his own existence that he had no reason to try imagining what people in later ages might like to look for in his work. Both men were struggling with the present, and that was more than enough burden. Neither was preparing a dossier for the history to come. Of course, we are no different. We are just as absorbed in the present, and just oblivious to the doors we are leaving behind for those who come after us and might want to make sense of their world—a world we cannot imagine—by thinking about where it came from.

If Donne in 1623 was excited to discover that no person was an island, it was because, for the first time in human history, it was possible to realize that almost no one was. No longer was the world a series of locations so isolated from each other that something could happen in one and have absolutely no effect on what was going on in any other. The idea of a common humanity was emerging, and with it the possibility of a shared history.[1] The theology underpinning Donne's sense of the interconnectedness of all things is Christian, but the idea of mutual interconnection is not exclusive to Christianity. Other religious and secular logics are capable of supporting the same conclusion, and equally effective at provoking an awareness of our global situation and our global responsibility. As across Donne's continent, so in Indra's web: every clod, every pearl—every loss and death, birth and coming into being—affects everything else with which it shares existence. It is a vision of the world that, for most people, became imaginable only in the seventeenth century.

The metaphors that have surfaced in traditions all over the world are needed now more than ever, if we are to persuade others, and even ourselves, to deal with the tasks that face us. This is one motive for this book: knowing that we as a species need to figure out how to narrate the past in a way that enables us to acknowledge and come to terms with the global nature of our experience. It is a Utopian ideal—an ideal we haven't realized and might never attain, and yet pervades our daily existence. If we can see that the history of any one place links us to all places, and ultimately to the history of the entire world, then there is no part of the past—no holocaust and no achievement—that is not our collective heritage. We are already learning to think ecologically in this way. Indeed, global warming in our era mirrors to some degree the disruptive impact of global cooling in Vermeer's, when people recognized that changes were afoot, even that these changes were affecting the entire world. Late in life, the shipwrecked Dutch gunsmith Jan Weltevree reminisced to a Korean friend about his childhood in Holland. He told him that when he was growing up, the elderly had a saying for foggy days when the cold damp got into their joints: "Today it is snowing in China." Even as climate change was turning the world topsy-turvy, people were sensing that what was happening on the far side of the globe was no longer happening just there but, now, here as well.

THE STORIES I HAVE TOLD in these pages have revolved around the effects of trade on the world, and on ordinary people. But between the world and ordinary people is the state, which was powerfully affected by the history of trade and had powerful effects in turn. Trade and movement during the seventeenth century strengthened the state. At least in Europe, the private realms of monarchs, who once commanded the loyalty of their fief lords, were turning into public entities serving the interests of firms and populated by citizens earning private wealth. The formation of the Dutch Republic is but one example of this transformation. Even in countries that remained monarchies, such as Britain, violent civil war intervened to transmute the absolute ruler into a constitutional monarch respecting commercial interests. Polities could not resist drawing on the immense new economic power of corporate trading, thereby becoming stronger themselves—and more fractious.

The Peace of Westphalia in 1648, which conventionally marks the emergence of the modern state system, involved several treaties that brought an end to the long-running wars among the newly powerful states competed across the split between Catholicism and Protestantism, including the Eighty Years' War between Spain and the Netherlands (one of which banned the Dutch from entering the port of Manila). The new system established norms of state sovereignty that are regarded as underpinning the world order today: that states are the fundamental actors in the world system, that each state enjoys inviolable sovereignty, and that no state has the right to intervene in the affairs of another state. States were no longer the domains of monarchs now but public entities that concentrated and deployed resources for national ends. We have the global transformations of the seventeenth century to thank for this new order, if thanks are due.

The states that rose to global power after Westphalia were well positioned to take advantage of global trade, and none more so than the Dutch Republic with its powerful array of well-regulated monopoly corporations. And yet, by the end of the century, the Dutch were being pushed aside by the English as the leading global trading power. There are many reasons for this eclipse, among which is the French invasion of the Netherlands in 1672. Jealous of Dutch overseas trade, the French dispatched a land army into the Low Countries far larger than anything the Dutch could field. The ultimate Dutch defense was to open the dikes, but it was a Pyrrhic victory from which the Dutch Republic was not able fully to recover. That defeat helped prop open the door for British imperial expansion, enabling Britain to surpass the Netherlands as the dominant global trading power in the eighteenth century.

The growth of the British Empire was due to many factors, not least of which was the creation of the opium trade, through which the English East India Company linked its territorial control of India with markets in China where it was buying tea and textiles. The Company's success must in turn be linked to the leadership vacuum on the subcontinent around the death of the great Moghul empire-builder Aurangzeb in 1707. With no one of his persistence and personality to hold the Moghul empire together, the EIC was able to maneuver itself into a hegemonic position in India and, from there, to dominate the trade with China. Imperial conquest and trade monopoly went hand in hand through the eighteenth century to give the British an unrivaled position in global trade. The VOC lasted until the end of the century, but the Dutch were never able to recover the leading position in the world economy they had held in the seventeenth century. Britain's victory over France at the battle of Waterloo in 1815 completed the ascendancy of Britain at home—and banished Napoleon to St. Helena long after sailors needed it as a stopping point in the South Atlantic.

The history of the state followed a different course in Asia, though a similar intensification of state operations can be seen. Both the Tokugawa regime in Japan and the Qing dynasty in China strengthened their bureaucratic administrations, exerting a tighter control than previous dynasties. Indeed, Europeans were so impressed with the Qing administration that they regarded China as a model of state bureaucratization—which is why the word that the Portuguese borrowed from Sanskrit to refer to Chinese officials became the universal term for powerful state bureaucrats, "mandarins." Japan responded to the rise in global trade by closing its borders to all but a few specially designated Dutch and Chinese merchants, otherwise pursuing an autarkic economic model. Qing China allowed limited maritime trade through Canton (upriver from Macao), but the Manchu rulers were drawn more to continental expansion than to maritime power. The British and Chinese empires held each other at bay with limited monopoly trading positions until the nineteenth century, when EIC traders undercut China's political economy by bringing to Canton boatloads of Indian opium, draining vast amounts of silver out of China and tilting the balance of payments in British favor. A shift in military power followed. It has taken China most of the last two centuries to recover from the collapse of its own imperial pretensions and begin to reconstruct itself as a world power.

LET US CLOSE THIS BOOK by looking back at three of the characters we have met along the way and asking what happened to them: Manila governor Sebastián Corcuera, *Treatise on Superfluous Things* author Wen

Zhenheng, and our painter and guide throughout this book, Johannes Vermeer.

Governor Corcuera believed that his victory over the Chinese in Manila in 1640 should have bought him enormous credit, not just to his position as governor but to the royal finances that were his responsibility. It didn't. For four years before the uprising, Corcuera had been locked in a battle with the entire ecclesiastical establishment in the Philippines, and with none more fiercely than the archbishop of Manila, whom the governor regularly banished and by whom he was just as regularly excommunicated. At the heart of the struggle was the silver trade. Despite the river of privately traded silver that flowed into the colony, the governor ran a hugely expensive administration that was hopelessly underfunded. The problem, from Corcuera's perspective, was the enormous financial privileges that the Catholic Church enjoyed in the Philippines. Reducing these privileges, Corcuera reasoned, would reduce his deficit. King Philip warned him against making any changes—possibly recalling that a previous governor had been assassinated by the priests for meddling with the Church's expectations for income.

The clergy was not willing to treat Corcuera's suppression of the Chinese insurgency as a justification for giving in on his fiscal demands. Rather, they went on a counterattack by insisting that he was responsible for the uprising in the first place. The reason the farmers of Calamba rose in rebellion was entirely due to Corcuera's desire to increase royal revenues, they reported back home. If he hadn't been pushing so hard on revenues, the farmers would have not been in such desperate straits, and the other Chinese would not have had the grievances that drove them into open revolt. The governor's priestly enemies were not content to say that he was overzealous in doing his job. They insisted that this was all for Corcuera's own benefit, and that his campaign for fiscal responsibility was an elaborate tactic to hide the fact that he was the biggest embezzler of all.

The cost of the suppression obliged Corcuera to press even harder for revenue. One device he used was doubling the price that Chinese merchants had to pay for trading licenses. The plan was to punish Chinese traders for supporting the insurrection, but it backfired when the Chinese passed the increase in their fees on to their customers. As a result, prices went up all over Manila. "Where shoes were worth two reals before, they are now worth four," or half a peso (piece-of-eight), the king's fiscal agent in Manila complained in 1644. "It now costs four or five pesos to have a garment made where before it cost two. The same thing is true in everything else," he complained. "It all originated and proceeded from the year of 1639, with the increase of their burden for the general license." Corcuera had put himself in the unfortunate position of making the Spanish pay for his victory, not the Chinese.

Unable to break the opposition against him, Corcuera asked to retire from his post. This he could not do until his replacement arrived, as it was up to the new governor to review his predecessor's books before allowing him to depart. And as the Church had filed fifty-nine charges of impeachment against him, Madrid decided in 1641 that Corcuera should be held in prison pending the full review. His replacement did not arrive until 1644, which meant that Corcuera was under comfortable house arrest for three years awaiting judgment. After a year investigating his case, the new governor found him guilty on some counts (the loss of the Spanish toehold on Taiwan to the Dutch was added to his crimes) and innocent on others. He referred the case to Madrid for final judgment. Corcuera had supporters at home, and they issued a fresh round of countercharges against the Church to further complicate matters. His case was no closer to resolution.

Of the fifty-nine charges laid against Corcuera, one was that he had purloined objects of precious metal belonging to the king and shipped them back to Spain to build his personal fortune. Included in the list was a solid gold plate and ewer set, intended as a gift from the king of Spain to the emperor of Japan in the hope of opening trade relations. The gold plate and ewer somehow disappeared, and Corcuera was charged with having sent the set back as his personal property on the *Concepción*, the outbound ship that sank in the Marianas in

1638. He vigorously denied the charge, and nothing came to light, as he had prevented a thorough manifest from being compiled. Eventually, the authorities in Madrid threw up their hands and declined to find for or against Corcuera. All charges were dismissed, and Corcuera resumed his service to the Spanish empire. He was appointed magistrate of Córdoba, and ended his career and his life in the prestigious post of governor of the Canary Islands.

No gold plate and ewer ever surfaced at the time to stand as evidence against Corcuera. But 350 years later, it did. When marine archaeologists in the 1980s surveyed the coral bed where the *Concepción* went down, they found on the ocean floor the rim of a gold plate—the best evidence yet that Corcuera was guilty as charged.

WEN ZHENHENG, THE CONNOISSEUR OF superfluous things, might have risen to high office like Corcuera, had he been able to pass the state examinations. He succeeded in passing the qualifying county exams in 1621, but couldn't seem to discipline his writing into the formulas that examiners liked and that he needed to imitate if he were to proceed toward an official appointment. The 1620s was not a propitious decade to seek official advancement anyway. Notoriously corrupt eunuchs around the throne effectively throttled and bled the administration, and anyone who sought a post in government had to go along with this state of affairs or face impeachment, or worse. After failing the prefectural exams again in 1624, Wen stepped out of the examination rat race and turned his attention to the things he loved: playing music, staging operas, and building gardens in Suzhou, the center of high culture and consumption in the late Ming. The family's immense wealth allowed him to live the life of the aesthete that he had championed in his *Treatise on Superfluous Things*.

Wen had a talented brother, Zhenmeng who passed the highest exams in 1622 and pursued a bureaucratic career that brought renewed honor to the Wens, but political calamity to himself when he opposed the eunuch faction. He died in 1636, leaving the responsibility of leading the family to Zhenheng. After the obligatory year of mourning, Wen Zhenheng felt he had to follow his brother's example. He secured a minor post in Beijing, where he soon got on the wrong side of court politics and ended up briefly in prison. Two years later, he was appointed to serve with one of the armies defending the northern frontier of the Ming against the Manchus. This was 1642, the worst year of the dynasty, with Manchu forces massing on the border and making lightning raids into Chinese territory, and plague crossing from Mongolia and devastating much of north China. It was a disease episode of extraordinary virulence; in some places struck by the plague, entire villages died.

Wen managed to evade the appointment and found an excuse to retire home to Suzhou in the south. He was engaged in building a new garden for himself when the Manchu conquerors reached Suzhou in 1645. He died during the takeover of the city. What place would a sixty-year-old man of his temperament have had in the new order?

Wen Zhenheng's biography is but one of any number that could be told for Chinese scholars who got caught in the collapse of the Chinese world in the mid-seventeenth century. Yang Shicong, the vice-minister who noted the appearance of tobacconists on every street corner of Beijing, lived a similar fate. Yang did not quit the capital when Wen did in 1642. He remained right up to the time a rebel army captured the city in the spring of 1644, when the last emperor tried to kill his daughters rather than allow them to fall into the rebels' hands and was later found hanging from a tree behind the palace. Yang's daughter and two concubines followed the imperial example and committed suicide, but Yang's servants prevented him from taking his own life and smuggled him out of the fallen capital so that he could join the resistance. He returned home, but had to flee farther south when the Manchus invaded. The armies did not catch up with him as they did with Wen, but agents of the Manchus eventually did, approaching him to abandon his loyalty to the Ming and serve the new regime. He rejected their offer and died shortly thereafter in self-imposed exile in the south.

For people such as Yang Shicong and Wen Zhenheng, the seventeenth century may have been bringing the world together, but its effects on their place and time were more than they could bear.

JOHANNES VERMEER, TOO, FACED HARDSHIPS in the last years of his life. The family had never been prosperous, but they had managed to survive on Vermeer's painting and his art dealing, along with Maria Thins's properties and investments. When France invaded the Netherlands in 1672, the art market on which Vermeer relied for his financial solvency collapsed. Dealing in art was a line of business that did well when the economy flourished. The abundance of cash in the Dutch economy favored the production of these wonderfully superfluous things. Householders were mad about hanging paintings on their walls and through the mid-seventeenth century bought art as never before—which is one of the reasons art museums all over the world have so many seventeenth-century Dutch paintings. The disappearance of surplus cash from the Delft economy in the 1670s was catastrophic for artists such as Vermeer, whose survival depended on sales. When purchases and commissions dried up, the only way for him to support his family was to take loans. The last loan on record, contracted from a merchant in Amsterdam (who may have been buying painting futures by offering it), was for a thousand silver guilders, an enormous and unrepayable sum. The pressure of these hardships muted his muse. Of the three paintings that survive from these later years, all of which show women self-consciously playing musical instruments, only one begins to match the brilliance of the earlier work.

Suddenly on 15 December 1675, at the age of forty-three, Vermeer died. In a petition to the Delft municipal authorities for support a year and a half later, Catharina testified that his death had been due to the financial collapse brought about by "the ruinous and protracted war." Her husband had found himself "unable to sell any of his art and also, to his great detriment, was left sitting with the paintings of other masters that he was dealing in, as a result of which and owing to the very great burden of children, having nothing of his own, he had lapsed into such decay and decadence, which he had so taken to heart that, as if he had fallen into a frenzy, in a day and a half he had gone from being healthy to being dead." The suddenness of his death suggests that a deadly infection laid him low. Despite her elaborate explanation, Catharina was probably right in believing that his depressed condition sapped his resistance. If so, then what killed Vermeer may well have been the same thing that gave him his career the first place: Delft's place in the economic networks that stretched around the world. When those networks flourished, Vermeer's carefully crafted masterpieces earned him the means to support his family and the time to take as long as he liked to finish a painting. When it collapsed and the only way to get silver was to borrow it, desperation and death ended both his life and his work.

Vermeer was buried the following day in the Old Church, somewhere near the spot I visited. Fortunately for the family, Maria Thins had bought the grave fifteen years earlier when the family was flush. She had no intention to find herself at death's door without a place to rest. What she had not expected was to find her son-in-law preceding her into it. Nor was Johannes the first. He and his wife had already buried three children there. When the gravediggers lifted the paving stone to bury the artist, they found the body of the child they had interred two years earlier still intact. They carefully removed the little body, lowered Vermeer's coffin into the grave, then laid the child to rest on top of its father. This time the bell tolled for Vermeer. The great era of Delft painting had come to an end, yet the doors that trade and travel and war had opened not just in that town, but all over the globe, remain so still.

ACKNOWLEDGMENTS

This was not an obvious book for a specialist in Chinese history to write, but world history has to be written from some promontory of expertise, and China is as good a place as any, perhaps better, to track the global changes of the seventeenth century. The idea for writing this history grew out of my experience teaching a world history course at Stanford University and the University of Toronto. As the ideas for the book developed, I was invited to present some of them at the Center for Chinese Studies at the University of California, Berkeley; the Center for Early Modern History at the University of Minnesota; the Department of History at the University of Manitoba (the Henry A. Jackson Memorial Lecture); the Center for Historical Studies at the University of Maryland; and at the China Studies Group at the University of British Columbia.

Partial funding for this project was generously provided by the project on Globalization and Autonomy under the direction of William Coleman at McMaster University, Ontario. The Globalization and Autonomy group also gave me an interdisciplinary context within which to develop my ideas. I have also been blessed with support received over many years from the Social Sciences and Humanities Research Council of Canada. I completed the manuscript while enjoying a fellowship from the John Simon Guggenheim Memorial Foundation.

Among those who have helped me shape the ideas and logic of this book, often without knowing they were doing so, I would like to thank Gregory Blue, Jim Chaplin, Tim Cheek, Craig Clunas, Paul Eprile, Shin

Imai, Ken Mills, Ken Pomeranz, Richard Unger, Danny Vickers, and Bin Wong. For answering queries from me on topics far from my own expertise, I am grateful to Greg Bankoff, Liam Brockey, Patricia Bruckmann, Jim Cahill, Timothy Francis, Geoffrey Parker, Jane Stevenson, Maggie Tchir, and Hsing-yuan Tsao. Susan Galassi hosted my visit to the Frick Collection in New York to view *Officer and Laughing Girl* at close quarters, and Ilse Boks of the Gemeente Musea Delft kindly supplied me with the photograph of the Van Meerten plate, the subject of chapter five. Eric Leinberger drew the maps.

Without the constant encouragement of my literary agent, Beverly Slopen, and my editors at Bloomsbury Press, Peter Ginna, Katherine Henderson, and Elizabeth Peters, I'm not sure this book ever would have appeared. My final thanks go to Fay Sims for constantly reminding me that I should be writing for readers like her.

Appendix: Chinese and Japanese Publications

Advantages and Disadvantages of the Various Regions of the Realm
(*Tianxia junguo libing shu*)
A Brief Account of Macao (*Aomen jilüe*)
Case Summaries from Mengshui Studio (*Mengshui zhai cundu*)
Collected Writings from Jade Hall (*Yutang wenji*)
Compendium of Archives and Documents on the Macao Question in
the Ming-Qing Period (*Ming-Qing shiqi Aomen wenti dang'an wen-
xian huibian*)
Compendium of Pictures and Writings (*Tushu bian*)
Comprehensive Gazetteer of Guangdong (*Guangdong tongzhi*)
Comprehensive Gazetteer of Guizhou (*Guizhou tongzhi*)
The Complete Works of Master Jingyue (*Jingyue quanshu*)
The Condolence Collection (*Zhuai ji*)
Continuation of My Record of Extensive Travels (*Guangzhi Yi*)
Dew Book (*Lu shu*)
Diary from the Water-Tasting Studio (*Weishui xuan riji*)
Further Deliberations on My Record of Extensive Travels (*Guangzhi yi*)
Gazetteer of Jining Subprefecture (*Jining zhouzhi*)
Gazetteer of Songjiang Prefecture (*Songjiang fuzhi*)
Illustrated Account of the Eastern Foreigners (*Dongyi tushuo*)
Investigations of the Eastern and Western Oceans (*Dongxi yangkao*)
Jottings from the Hall of Benevolence (*Renshu tang biji*)
Miscellaneous Notes from Zai Garden (*Zaiyuan zazhi*)
Miscellaneous Records from the Wanping County Office (*Wanshu zaji*)

New Standard History of the Tang Dynasty (*Xin Tang shu*)

Notes on Rare Historical Sources from the Ming–Qing Period (*Ming Qing xijian shiji xulu*)

Pharmacopoeia of Edible Wild Plants (*Shiwu bencao huizuan*)

A Popular History of Smoking in China (*Zhongguo xiyan shihua*)

Provisional Gazetteer of Shouning County (*Shouning daizhi*)

Questions and Answers on First Meeting (*Chuhui Wenda*)

Sights of the Imperial Capital (*Dijing jingwu lüe*)

Smoking Manual (*Yanpu*)

Standard History of the Ming Dynasty (*Ming shi*)

Studies in the Early History of the Opening of the Port of Macao (*Aomen kaipu chuqi shi yanjiu*)

Supplement to the Agricultural Treatise, annotated edition (*Bu nong-shu jiaozhu*)

A Survey of the Age (*Yueshi bian*)

The Swords of Canton (*Yuejian pian*)

Tobacco Manual (*Yancao pu*)

Toward a History of the National Language: A Festschrift in Honour of Professor Doi Tadao (*Kokugoshi e no michi: Doi sensei shōju kinen ronbunshū*)

Treatise on Superfluous Things, annotated (*Zhangwu lun jiaozhu*)

Twilight Tales of Nagasaki (*Nagasaki yawagusa*)

Unedited Records of the Chongzhen Reign (*Chongzhen changbian*)

Veritable Records of the Tianqi Reign of the Ming Dynasty (*Ming Xizong shilu*)

The Woof of the Earth (*Di wei*)

RECOMMENDED READING AND SOURCES

This bibliography provides a record of the sources on which I have drawn to write *Vermeer's Hat*, both original sources from the seventeenth century and later studies by twentieth-century scholars. Sources in Asian languages are cited first by an English translation of the title, followed parenthetically by the original title in Chinese or Japanese. For those who wish to read further in some of the subjects on which this book touches without having to burrow into the detailed references that follow, I recommend these eight books:

Anthony Bailey's *Vermeer: A View of Delft* (New York: Henry Holt, 2001) is a thoughtful and thoroughly engaging biography of Johannes Vermeer. John Michael Montias's more scholarly *Vermeer and His Milieu: A Web of Social History* (Princeton, NJ: Princeton University Press, 1989) exhaustively examines every piece of evidence the author, an economic historian, could discover relating to Vermeer in the Delft archives. This book is a historian's dream.

For delightful short essays on the histories of major commodities and global markets over the past half millennium, see Kenneth Pomeranz and Steven Topik, *The World That Trade Created: Society, Culture, and the World Economy, 1400 to the Present* (Armonk, NY: M. E. Sharpe, 1990).

On Ming China, the author's *The Confusions of Pleasure: Commerce and Culture in Ming Society* (Berkeley: University of California Press, 1998) provides a broad social and cultural history. Craig Clunas relies on Wen Zhenheng's guide for connoisseurs, *The Treatise on Superfluous*

Things, to analyze Ming culture in his *Superfluous Things: Material Culture and Social Status in Early Modern China* (Cambridge, MA: Polity, 1991). Still the most engaging account of a Jesuit missionary in Ming China is Jonathan Spence, *The Memory Palace of Matteo Ricci* (Harmondsworth: Penguin, 1985).

Marc and Muriel Vigié's *L'Herbe à Nicot: amateurs de tabac, fermiers généraux et contrebandiers sous l'Ancien Régime* (Paris: Fayard, 1989) is a delightful cultural history of smoking in the seventeenth century. For a survey of the topic in English, I recommend V. G. Kiernan, *Tobacco: A History* (London: Hutchinson Radius, 1991).

THE EPIGRAPH IS FROM GARY Tomlinson, *Music in Renaissance Magic: Toward a Historiography of Others* (Chicago: University of Chicago Press, 1999), p. 20.

CHAPTER 1. THE VIEW FROM DELFT

I began my acquaintance with Vermeer through Ludwig Goldscheider, *Vermeer* (London: Phaidon, 1958, 1967). On Vermeer's life and work, in addition to John Montias's *Vermeer and His Milieu* and Anthony Bailey's *Vermeer*, I have benefited from reading Gille Aillaud, Albert Blankert, and John Montias, eds., *Vermeer* (Paris: Hazan, 1986); Arthur Wheelock, *Vermeer and the Art of Painting* (New Haven, CT: Yale University Press, 1995), and his edited volume, *Johannes Vermeer* (Washington, D.C.: National Gallery of Art, 1995); Ivan Gaskell, *Vermeer's Wager: Speculations on Art History, Theory and Art Museums* (London: Reaktion Books, 2000); Wayne Franits, *The Cambridge Companion to Vermeer* (Cambridge: Cambridge University Press, 2001); and Bryan Jay Wolf, *Vermeer and the Invention of Seeing* (Chicago: University of Chicago Press, 2001); also the Web site http://www.essentialvermeer.com.

On the Netherlands during Vermeer's lifetime, see Jonathan Israel, *The Dutch Republic: Its Rise, Greatness, and Fall, 1477–1806* (Oxford: Oxford University Press, 1995); see p. 621 for population figures. On the history of seventeenth-century Dutch art and culture, see E. de Jongh, *Questions of Meaning: Theme and Motif in Dutch Seventeenth-Century Painting*, trans. Michael Hoyle (Leiden: Primavera, 2000); and David Kunzle, *From Criminal to Courtier: The Soldier in Netherlandish Art 1550–1672* (Leiden: Brill, 2002). On Delft's history, see Ellinor Bergrelt, Michiel Jonker, and Agnes Wiechmann, eds., *Schatten in Delft: burgers verzamelen 1600–1750* [Appraising in Delft: Burghers' Collections, 1600–1750] (Zwolle: Waanders, 2002); and John Montias, *Artists and Artisans in Delft: A Socio-Economic Study of the Seventeenth Century* (Princeton, NJ: Princeton University Press, 1982).

On Yuyuan garden in Shanghai, see *Gazetteer of Songjiang Prefecture* [*Songjiang fuzhi*], (1630), 46.59b.

"Paintings as puzzles" is taken from James Elkins, *Why Are Our Pictures Puzzles? On the Modern Origins of Pictorial Complexity* (New York: Routledge, 1999).

View of Delft is presented in Epco Runia and Peter van der Ploeg, *In the Mauritshuis: Vermeer* (Zwolle: Waanders, 2005), pp. 42–59; their discussion of boat types on pp. 48–49 is particularly instructive. For a bird's-eye view of the Oost-Indisch Huis on a seventeenth-century map, see H. L. Loutzager et al., *De Kaart Figuratief van Delft* [A Pictorial Map of Delft] (Rijswijk: Elmar, 1997), pp. 177, 197.

On Delft's connections to the wider world, see Kees van der Wiel, "Delft in the Golden Age: Wealth and Poverty in the Age of Johannes Vermeer," in *Dutch Society in the Age of Vermeer*, ed. Donald Haks and Marie Christine van der Sman (The Hague: Haags Historisch Museum, 1996), pp. 52–54.

On the Little Ice Age, the shift in the herring fishery, Pieter Bruegel's winter scenes, and the frost killing of orange trees in China, see H. H. Lamb, *Climate, History and the Modern World* (London: Methuen, 1982), pp. 218–23, 227–30. Data on canal freezing in the Netherlands, compiled by Jan de Vries, appear in H. H. Lamb, *Climatic History and the Future* (Princeton, NJ: Princeton University Press, 1985), p. 476, n. 1.

On the plague, see William McNeill, *Plagues and Peoples* (New

York: Doubleday, 1976). Plague episodes in Amsterdam (after 1578) are noted in N. W. Posthumus, *Inquiry into the History of Prices in Holland* (Leiden: Brill, 1946), vol. 1, p. 641. For Venice, see Carlo Cipolla, *Fighting the Plague in Seventeenth-Century Italy* (Madison: University of Wisconsin Press, 1981), p. 100.

The estimates of the numbers of Dutch leaving the Netherlands come from Jaap Bruijn, Femme Gaastra, and I. Schöffer, *Dutch-Asiatic Shipping in the 17th and 18th Centuries* (The Hague: Martinus Nijhoff, 1987), vol. 1, pp. 143–44. Vermeer's cousins being in the Far East is noted in Montias, *Vermeer and His Milieu*, p. 312.

The quote from Francis Bacon is featured in Joseph Needham, *Science and Civilisation in China*, vol. 1 (Cambridge: Cambridge University Press, 1954), p. 19. On the effect of guns on the changes of the seventeenth century, see Jack Goody, *Capitalism and Modernity: The Great Debate* (Cambridge: Polity, 2004), pp. 77–78.

On transculturation, see Fernando Ortiz, *Cuban Counterpoint: Tobacco and Sugar* (1940; repr. Durham, NC: Duke University Press, 1995), pp. 98, 103.

European influence on late Ming art has been suggested by James Cahill, *The Compelling Image: Nature and Style in Seventeenth-Century Chinese Painting* (Cambridge, MA: Harvard University Press, 1982), pp. 82–86; and Richard Barnhart, "Dong Qichang and Western Learning—a Hypothesis," *Archives of Asian Art* 50 (1997–98), pp. 7–16. On possible Chinese influences on Vermeer, see Bailey, *Vermeer*, p. 177.

Pearls in Vermeer's paintings are examined in Runia and van der Ploeg, *In the Mauritshuis: Vermeer*, pp. 66–67. On Chinese taste in pearls, see Gu Yanwu, *Advantages and Disadvantages of the Various Regions of the Realm* [*Tianxia junguo libing shu*] (*1662*) (Kyoto: Chūbun shuppansha, 1975), 29.126a; see also Sung Ying-hsing, *Chinese Technology in the Seventeenth Century*, trans. E-tu Zen Sun and Shiou-chuan Sun (University Park: Pennsylvania State University Press, 1966), p. 296.

Song Yingxing's comments come from his preface to Sung Ying-hsing, *Chinese Technology in the Seventeenth Century*, p. xi. The epitaph to Willem Schouten appears in Willem Ysbrantsz Bontekoe, *Memorable Description of the East Indian Voyage, 1618–25*, trans. Mrs. C. B. Bodde-Hodgkinson and Pieter Geyl (New York: Robert M. McBride, 1929), p. 157. The Chinese comment of 1609 is quoted in my *Confusions of Pleasure: Commerce and Culture in Ming China*, p. 153.

CHAPTER 2. VERMEER'S HAT

On the officer's hat, see Wheelock, *Vermeer and the Art of Painting*, p. 58. On Vermeer's use of maps, see James Welu, "Vermeer: His Cartography," *The Art Bulletin* 57:4 (Dec. 1975), pp. 529–47; Evangelos Livieratos and Alexandra Koussoulakou, "Vermeer's Maps: A New Digital Look in an Old Master's Mirror," *e-Perimetron* 1:2 (Spring 2006), pp. 138–54. For an early look at the Balthasar/van Berckenrode family of cartographers, see Edward Lynam, "Floris Balthasar, Dutch Map Maker and His Sons," *Geographical Journal* 67:2 (Feb. 1926), pp. 148–161.

The primary source for the battle is Samuel Champlain's own account, first published in 1613 and again, with slight alterations, in 1632. The first appears in bilingual text in *The Works of Samuel de Champlain*, ed. H. P. Biggar (Toronto: University of Toronto Press, 1922), vol. 2, pp. 65–107; the second is in vol. 4, pp. 80–105. With the exception of the opening passage, which can be found on pp. 97–99 of vol. 4, all direct quotes from Champlain in this chapter are taken from vol. 2, with minor alterations to remove euphemisms. The 1609 conflict is fully described in Bruce Trigger, *The Children of Aataensic: A History of the Huron People to 1660* (Montreal: McGill-Queen's University Press, 1976), ch. 4. For more recent scholarship on Champlain, see *Champlain: The Birth of French America*, ed. Raymonde Litalien and Denis Vaugeois, trans. Käthe Ross (Montreal & Kingston: McGill-Queen's University Press, 2004). As I was finishing this book, I was pleased to discover that Christian Morissonneau in "Champlain's Dream" in that volume came independently to the same conclusion regarding China's place in Champlain's calculations.

For Olive Dickason's view of 1609 as a decisive moment in Native-white history, see her *Canada's First Nations: A History of Founding Peoples from Earliest Times* (Toronto: McClelland and Stewart, 1992), p. 122. For a view skeptical of its significance, see W. J. Eccles, *The Canadian Frontier, 1534–1780* (rev. ed., Albuquerque: University of New Mexico Press, 1983), p. 25.

On the Champlain and Huron wampum belts, see Tehanetorens, "Wampum Belts" (Onchiota: Six Nations Indian Museum, 1972; Ohsweken, Ont.: Iroqrafts, 1993), pp. 11, 59.

For Indian words and names, I generally follow the usages in *The Cambridge History of the Native Peoples of the Americas*, ed. Bruce Trigger and Wilcomb E. Washburn (Cambridge: Cambridge University Press, 1996), vol. 1. Etymologies of tribal names have been taken from John Steckley, *Beyond Their Years: Five Native Women's Stories* (Toronto: Canadian Scholars' Press, 1999), pp. 15–16, 63, 243–45.

On the history of the arquebus, see Carl Russell, *Guns on the Early Frontiers: A History of Firearms from Colonial Times Through the Years of the Western Fur Trade* (Berkeley: University of California Press, 1957; Lincoln: University of Nebraska Press, 1980), pp. 1–18. The early history of guns in Japan is treated in Noel Perrin, *Giving Up the Gun: Japan's Reversion to the Sword, 1543–1879* (Boston: David Godine, 1979), pp. 5–31. The demand for Dutch firearms is noted in C. R. Boxer, *Jan Compagnie in Japan, 1600–1850* (The Hague: Martinus Nijhoff, 1950), p. 26.

On torture in Native culture, see Georg Friederici, Gabriel Nadeau, and Nathaniel Knowles, *Scalping and Torture: Warfare Practices Among North American Indians* (Ohsweken, Ont.: Iroqrafts, 1985). Georges Sioui's observation is from his *For an Amerindian Autohistory: An Essay on the Foundations of a Social Ethic* (Montreal & Kingston: McGill-Queen's University Press, 1992), p. 52.

On the history of beaver hats, see Hilda Amphlett, *Hats: A History of Fashion in Headgear* (1974), pp. 106–109; Bernard Allaire, *Pelleteries, manchons et chapeaux de castor: les fourrures nord-américaines à Paris* [The Fur Trade, Muffs and Bearer Hats: North American Furs in Paris] (Québec: Septentrion, 1999). On the fur trade, see Harold Innis, *The Fur Trade in Canada* (Toronto: University of Toronto Press, 1956); Paul Phillips, *The Fur Trade* (Norman: University of Oklahoma Press, 1961); Raymond Fisher, *The Russian Fur Trade, 1550–1700* (Berkeley: University of California Press, 1943).

The destruction of natural habitat in fifteenth-century Europe is noted in David Levine, *At the Dawn of Modernity: Biology, Culture, and Material Life in Europe After the Year 1000* (Berkeley: University of California Press, 2001), pp. 153–55.

Queen Elizabeth's letter to the emperor of China is mentioned in Morissonneau, "Champlain's Dream," p. 260.

On Champlain's quest for saltwater in 1603, see *Works of Samuel de Champlain*, vol. 1, pp. 156–62.

Champlain's maps are examined in Conrad Heidenreich and Edward Dahl, "Samuel de Champlain's Cartography," in *Champlain: The Birth of French America*, pp. 312–32; see also Christian Morissonneau, "Champlain's Place-Names," op. cit., pp. 218–29.

The standard account of the travels of Jean Nicollet (also spelled Nicolet) as having paddled to Green Bay is repeated in my *Confusions of Pleasure*, p. xv. I now accept the correction that Nicollet went to Lake Nipigon rather than Green Bay, as proposed by Gaétan Gervais in his "Champlain and Ontario (1603–35)," in *Champlain: The Birth of French America*, p. 189. For early maps that name Green Bay as Baye des Puans, see Derek Hayes, *Historical Atlas of the United States* (Vancouver: Douglas & McIntyre, 2006), pp. 38, 41, 90, 92, 94.

A post-contact epidemic among the Winnebagoes is mentioned by Wilcomb Washburn in *The Cambridge History of the Native Peoples of the Americas*, vol. 1, pt. 2, p. 409.

For "glorious Vests, wrought & embroidered on cloth of Gold," see John Evelyn, *The Diary of John Evelyn* (Oxford: Claendon, 1955), vol. 2, pp. 460–61, writing of what he saw in 1664.

De la Franchise's poetic dedication to Champlain's *On Savages* of 1603 appears in *Works of Samuel de Champlain*, vol. 1, p. 86.

CHAPTER 3. A DISH OF FRUIT

Most of the information about the *White Lion* is taken from the excavation report of the Groupe de Recherche Archéologique Sous-Marine Post-Médiévale, *The Ceramic Load of the 'Witte Leeuw' (1613)*, ed. C. L. van der Pijl-Ketel (Amsterdam: Rijksmuseum, 1982). The price of pepper is from Posthumus, *Inquiry into the History of Prices in Holland*, vol. 1, p. 174. Information about the voyages of VOC ships comes from Bruijn, et al., *Dutch-Asiatic Shipping*, vol. 1, pp. 74, 86, 89, 91, 188, 192; vol. 2, pp. 12, 18, 22, 26; and vol. 3, pp. 8, 12–13, 16–17. A complete catalog of VOC ships is available online at www.vocsite .nl/schepen.

The Portuguese carracks are listed in A. R. Disney, *Twilight of the Pepper Empire: Portuguese Trade in Southwest India in the Early Seventeenth Century* (Cambridge, MA: Harvard University Press, 1978), p. 172. Van der Pijl-Keter identifies the *Nossa Senhora do Monte da Carmo* as the *Nossa Senhora de Conceição*.

Information on Dutch maritime trade has been taken from C. R. Boxer, *The Dutch Seaborne Empire: 1600–1800* (New York: Knopf, 1965), pp. 22–25; Kristof Glamann, *Dutch-Asiatic Trade, 1620–1740* (1958; rev. ed., Gravenhage: Martinus Nijhoff, 1981), pp. 16–20, 57–59, 112–18, 134, 153; Els Jacobs, *In Pursuit of Pepper and Tea: The Story of the Dutch East India Company* (Amsterdam: Netherlands Maritime Museum, 1991), pp. 11–12, 51–53, 73–74, 84–95; Dietmar Rothermund, *Asian Trade and European Expansion in the Age of Mercantilism* (New Delhi: Manohar, 1981), especially pp. 27–30; and Niels Steensgaard, *The Asian Trade Revolution of the Seventeenth Century: The East India Companies and the Decline of the Caravan Trade* (Chicago: University of Chicago Press, 1973), pp. 101–113. The close to 3 percent growth rate in Dutch imports is given in Kevin O'Rourke and Jeffrey

Williamson, "After Columbus: Explaining Europe's Overseas Trade Boom, 1500–1600," *Journal of Economic History* 62:2 (June 2002), p. 419. The *Wapen van Delft* voyages are noted in A. J. H. Latham and Heita Kawakatsu, eds., *Japanese Industrialization and the Asian Economy* (New York: Routledge, 1994), app. 2.1. The effects of this trade are explored in Violet Barbour, *Capitalism in Amsterdam in the 17th Century* (Ann Arbor: University of Michigan Press, 1963), pp. 35–41; and Om Prakash, "Restrictive Trading Regimes: VOC and the Asian Spice Trade in the Seventeenth Century," in *Emporia, Commodities and Entrepreneurs in Asian Maritime Trade, c. 1400–1750*, ed. Roderick Ptak and Dietmar Rothermund (Stuttgart: Franz Steiner, 1991), pp. 107–126.

The *Red Lion* in Japan in 1609 is mentioned in Boxer, *Jan Compagnie in Japan*, p. 27. For the two ships named *China*, see Bruijn et al., *Dutch Asiatic Shipping*, vol. 2, pp. 22–23, 196.

On the history of Dutch porcelain imports, see T. Volker, *Porcelain and the Dutch East India Company, 1602–1682* (Leiden: Brill, 1954); Maura Rinaldi, *Kraak Porcelain. A Moment in the History of Trade* (London: Bamboo, 1989); Christian J. A. Jörg, "Chinese Porcelain for the Dutch in the Seventeenth Century: Trading Networks and Private Enterprise," in *The Porcelains of Jingdezhen*, ed. Rosemary Scott (London: Percival Foundation of Chinese Art, 1993), pp. 183–205; and John Carswell, *Blue & White: Chinese Porcelain Around the World* (London: British Museum Press, 2000). On Sino-Persian interaction in porcelain design, see Lisa Golombek, "Rhapsody in Blue-and-White," *Rotunda* 36:1 (Summer/Fall 2003), pp. 22–23.

The development of porcelain production in Europe is described in Hugh Honour, *Chinoiserie: The Vision of Cathay* (New York: Harper & Row, 1961), pp. 103–5.

Grotius's quotations are taken from *The Freedom of the Seas*, trans. Ralph Van Deman Magoffin (Toronto: H. Milford, 1916), pp. 12–13; see also Hamilton Vreeland, *Hugo Grotius, the Father of the Modern Science of International Law* (New York: Oxford University Press, 1917), pp. 47–58.

The 1608 porcelain order is mentioned in Volker, *Porcelain and the*

Dutch East India Company, p. 23. The Portuguese commissioning of export porcelain is treated in Rui Guedes, *Companhia das Índias: porcelanas* [Company of the Indies: Porcelains] (Lisbon: Bertrand, 1995). For the cargo of the *Nassau*, see "Cargo van twee Oost-Indische Shepen" [Cargo of Two East India (Company) Ships] (Amsterdam: Gerrit Jansz, 1640), on display at Amsterdam's Maritime Museum.

Wen Zhenheng's comments in this chapter are taken from his *A Treatise on Superfluous Things, Annotated* [*Zhangwu lun jiaozhu*], ed. Chen Zhi (Nanjing: Jiangsu kexue jishu chubanshe, 1984), pp. 97 (preference for earlier Ming porcelain), 260 (brush pots), 317 (ideal characteristics), 352 (use of vases), and 419 (Potter Cui). The logic of the book is explored in Clunas, *Superfluous Things*; see in particular his comments on foreign objects on pp. 58–60, 85. The Beijing guidebook comment comes from Liu Tong, *Sights of the Imperial Capital* [*Dijing jingwu lüe*] (Beijing: Beijing guji chubanshe, 1980), p. 163. Reports of kraak porcelain in Chinese tombs appeared in the journal *Cultural Objects* [*Wen wu*], 1982, no. 8, pp. 16–28, and 1993, no. 2, pp. 77–82; my thanks to Craig Clunas for pointing out these references.

For a seventeenth-century comment on the European taste for gold and silver dishes, see Pascale Girard, ed., *Le Voyage en Chine d'Adriano de las Cortes S. J. (1625)* (Paris: Chandeigne, 2001), p. 253.

Descartes's comment of 1631 is quoted in Fernand Braudel, *The Perspective of the World* (London: Collins, 1984), p. 30. For Evelyn's comment on Paris in 1644, see *Diary of John Evelyn*, vol. 2, p. 100.

Pieter Isaacsz's 1599 painting, *The Corporalship of Captain G. Jasz. Valckenier and Lieutenant P. Jacobsz Bas*, is cited, among others, in A. I. Spriggs, "Oriental Porcelain in Western Paintings, 1450–1700," *Transactions of the Oriental Ceramic Society* vol. 36 (London: 1965).

For a quick sketch of the history of Delft tiles, see Bailey, *Vermeer*, pp. 173–77; the quote appears on p. 175. The Amsterdam satirist on Chinese art is mentioned in Edwin Van Kley, "Qing Dynasty China in Seventeenth-Century Dutch Literature, 1644–1760" in *The History of the Relations Between the Low Countries and China in the Qing Era (1644–1911)*, ed. W. F. Vande Walk and Nöel Golvers (Leuven: Leuven

University Press, 2003), p. 230. On the use of abandoned Delft breweries as potteries, see Richard Unger, *A History of Brewing in Holland: Economy, Technology and the State* (Leiden: Brill, 2001), p. 324.

Li Rihua's discussion with Merchant Xia appears in his *Diary from the Water-Tasting Studio* [*Weishui xuan riji*] (Shanghai: Yuandong chubanshe, 1996), p. 84.

Lam's exploits in 1617–18 were noted by the English factor in Hirado, Richard Cocks; see William Schurz, *The Manila Galleon* (New York: Dutton, 1959), p. 352.

CHAPTER 4. GEOGRAPHY LESSONS

Las Cortes's account of the shipwreck of 1625 has been published in French by Pascale Girard as *Le Voyage en Chine*. I have drawn particularly from pp. 37–55, 65–69, 85–87, 97, 106–9, 354–57.

On the concept of "Moor" in the seventeenth century, see Allison Blakely, *Blacks in the Dutch World: The Evolution of Racial Imagery in a Modern Society* (Bloomington: Indiana University Press, 1993), pp. 33–36; Kim Hall, *Things of Darkness: Economies of Race and Gender in Early Modern England* (Ithaca, NY: Cornell University Press, 1995), p. 12. The Chinese description of Spaniards in Macao is from Yin Guangren and Zhang Rulin, *A Brief Account of Macao* [*Aomen jilüe*] (1751; 1800), 2.8b. Li Rihua's description of *luting* appears in his *Diary from the Water-Tasting Studio*, p. 103; for his description of Red Hairs, see p. 43. Wang Shixing's account of blacks in Macao comes from his *Continuation of My Record of Extensive Travels* [*Guangzhi yi*] (Beijing: Zhonghua shuju, 1981), p. 101. The price of oxen (four taels a head) is noted in C. R. Boxer, *The Great Ship from Amacon: Annals of Macao and the Old Japan Trade* (Lisbon: Centro de Estudos Históricos Ultramarinos, 1959), p. 184.

Lu Zhaolong's memorials appear in the *Unedited records of the Chongzhen Era* [*Chongzhen changbian*], 34.42a–44a, 35, 41.13a–14b, and 43.29a–b; reprinted in *Compendium of Archives and Documents on the Macao question in the Ming-Qing Period* [*Ming-Qing shiqi Aomen wenti dang'an wenxian huibian*], ed. Yang Jibo et al. (Beijing: Renmin chubanshe, 1999), vol. 5, pp. 41–45. See also Huang Yi-long, "Sun Yuanhua (1581–1632): A Christian Convert Who Put Xu Guangqi's Military Reform Policy into Practice," in *Statecraft and Intellectual Renewal in Late Ming China: The Cross-Cultural Synthesis of Xu Guangqi*, ed. Catherine Jami, Gregory Blue, and Peter Engelfriedt (Leiden: Brill, 2001), pp. 239–42.

The account of Holland in the Veritable Records appears in the fourth lunar month of 1623, in *Veritable Records of the Tianqi Reign* [*Xizong shilu*], 33.3a–b.

The quote from Dai Zhuo is recorded in the fourth chapter of Wang Linheng, *The Swords of Canton* [*Yuejian pian*], quoted in Tang Kaijian, *Studies in the Early History of the Opening of the Port of Macao* [*Aomen kaipu chuqi shi yanjiu*] (Beijing: Zhonghua shuju, 1999), p. 113.

On the recruitment of Portuguese gunners, see Michael Cooper, *Rodrigues the Interpreter: An Early Jesuit in Japan and China* (New York: Weatherhill, 1994), pp. 337–51. The composition of the 1623 party is described in the Veritable Records of that year, *Veritable Records of the Tianqi Reign*, 33.13a. Yan Junyan's undated comment on Rodrigues appears in his *Case Summaries from Mengshui Studio* [*Mengshui zhai cundu*] (Beijing: Zhongguo zhengfa daxue chubanshe, 2002), p. 704. Lu Zhaolong's warm endorsement in his preface to Yan's book shows they were friends. I am grateful to Alison Bailey for introducing me to Yan's book. Rodrigues is mentioned in the *Veritable Records* of 1630 [*Chongzhen changbian*], ch. 44, reprinted in *The Macao Question in the Ming-Qing Period*, vol. 5, p. 45.

On Xu Guangqi, see Jami et al., *Statecraft and Intellectual Renewal in Late Ming China*. On Xu's interest in Japan, see my "Japan in the Late Ming: The View from Shanghai," in *Sagacious Monks and Bloodthirsty Warriors: Chinese Views of Japan in the Ming-Qing Period*, ed. Joshua A. Fogel (Norwalk, CT: EastBridge, 2002), pp. 42–62.

The classic study of Shen Que's attack on the Nanjing mission is Edward Kelly, "The Anti-Christian Persecution of 1616–1617 in

Nanking" (Ph.D. diss., Columbia University, 1971), key points of which have been revised by Adrian Dudink, "Christianity in Late Ming China: Five Studies" (Ph.D. diss., Rijksuniversiteit, Leiden, 1995). The Jesuit assessment of Shen Que's persecution as having failed is repeated in George Dunne, *Generation of Giants: The Story of the Jesuits in China in the Last Decades of the Ming Dynasty* (Notre Dame: University of Notre Dame Press, 1962), pp. 128–45. Semedo's description is taken from the 1642 English edition of his history of the Jesuit mission, *Imperio de la Chinae* [Empire of China], pp. 219–20; I am grateful to Gregory Blue for making this passage available to me.

On the early Dutch trade with China, see Leonard Blussé, "The VOC as Sorcerer's Apprentice: Stereotypes and Social Engineering on the China Coast," in *Leyden Studies in Sinology*, ed. W. L. Idema (Leiden: Brill, 1981), especially pp. 92–95.

The 1623 debate over whether the Japanese or the Dutch were the greater threat is discussed in the *Veritable Records of the Tianqi Reign*, 35.4a–b. For Li Zhizao's argument in favor of Portuguese cannon, see op. cit., 35.3a–b.

On the place of Macao in the Jesuit strategy to penetrate China, see George Souza, *The Survival of Empire: Portuguese Trade and Society in China and the South China Sea, 1630–1754* (Cambridge: Cambridge University Press, 1986), especially pp. 25, 37, 195–98. Rodrigues's letter of 1633 is reprinted in Cooper, "Rodrigues in China: The Letters of João Rodrigues, 1611–1633," in *The Path to a History of the National Language: A Festschrift in Honor of Professor Doi Tadao* [*Kokugoshi e no michi: Doi sensei shōju kinen ronbunshō*] (Tokyo: Sanseidō, 1981), p. 242. Ricci's popular reputation among educated Chinese as a spy for Macao is mentioned in 1609 in Li Rihua, *Diary from the Water-Tasting Studio*, p. 43. For subsequent charges of Jesuit spying in 1616 and 1623, see Dudink, "Christianity in Late Ming China," pp. 151, 258.

Pan Runmin is listed in the 1846 *Comprehensive Gazetteer of Guangdong* [*Guangdong tongzhi*] (Shanghai: Shangwu yinshuguan, 1934), p. 375; and the *Comprehensive Gazetteer of Guizhou* [*Guizhou tongzhi*] (1741), 26.8b. Pan earned his presented scholar degree in 1607. Yan

Junyan's comments appear in his summary of an undated case he heard in Canton, collected in his *Case Summaries*, p. 702.

The comments from Zhang Xie and his preface author Wang Qizong appear in his *Investigations of the Eastern and Western Oceans* [*Dongxi yangkao*] (Beijing: Zhonghua shuju, 1981), pp. 14, 19–20.

"You don't have to leave your house" is from Zhang Huang, *Compendium of Pictures and Writings* [*Tushu bian*] (1613), Ch. 29.

CHAPTER 5. SCHOOL FOR SMOKING

Yang Shicong's remarks come from his *Collected Writings from Jade Hall* [*Yutang wenji*] (repr. Taipei, 1968), p. 80. Fragments of his biography appear in *Gazetteer of Jining Subprefecture* [*Jining zhouzhi*] (1672), 5.19a, 56a; 8.49b; and Zhang Tingyu, *Standard History of the Ming Dynasty* [*Ming shi*] (Beijing: Zhonghua shuju, 1974), pp. 3658, 7942. For the cost of tobacco on the Beijing price list, see Shen Bang, *Miscellaneous Records from the Wanping County Office* [*Wanshu zaji*] (Beijing: Zhonghua shuju, 1980), pp. 134, 146.

On the history of tobacco, besides Kiernan, *Tobacco: A History* and Vigié and Vigié, *L'Herbe à Nicot*, see Sarah Augusta Dickson, *Panacea or Precious Bane: Tobacco in Sixteenth-Century Literature* (New York: New York Public Library, 1954); Jordan Goodman, *Tobacco in History: The Cultures of Dependence* (London: Routledge, 1993); Bernhold Laufer, "Introduction of Tobacco into Europe," *Anthropology Leaflet* 19 (Field Museum of Chicago, 1924). On the Dutch experience, see Georg Brongers, *Nicotana Tabacum: The History of Tobacco and Tobacco Smoking in the Netherlands* (Amsterdam: H. J. W. Bechts Uitgeversmaatschappij, 1964).

On Native smoking practices, see Ralph Linton, "Use of Tobacco Among North American Indians," *Anthropology Leaflet* 15 (Field Museum of Chicago, 1924); Johannes Wilbert, *Tobacco and Shamanism in South America* (New Haven, CT: Yale University Press, 1987). On *tabagies*, see Morris Bishop, *Champlain: The Life of Fortitude* (Toronto: McClelland and Stewart, 1963), p. 39.

On the association of tobacco with witches, see Dickson, *Panacea or Precious Bane*, pp. 161–62; regarding the papal bull of 1642, see pp. 153–54.

For the English commentator's remark that tobacco was "gretlie taken-up and used in England," see Laufer, "Introduction of Tobacco into Europe," p. 7, quoting William Harrison's *Great Chronologie*; the quotes from Camden and James I appear on pp. 10–11, 27–28. The quote from Thomas Dekker comes from the foreword to *The Guls Horne-Book* (London: R.S., 1609).

For the observation that "this herb prevaileth against all apostemes," see John Gerard, *The Herball or Generall Histories of Plantes*, quoted in Dickson, *Panacea or Precious Bane*, p. 43. Gerard based his claims on the earlier herbal of Rembert Dodoens.

On the role of the Dutch in the tobacco and slave trade, see Jonathan Israel, *Dutch Primacy in World Trade, 1585–1740* (Oxford: Oxford University Press, 1989), conveniently summarized in his *Dutch Republic*, pp. 934–36, 943–46. On the place of slavery in the economics of tobacco, see Goodman, *Tobacco in History*, pp. 137–53; also Kiernan, *Tobacco: A History*, pp. 13–19.

I have written about the culture of smoking in imperial China in two other essays: "Is Smoking Chinese?" *Ex/Change: Newsletter of Centre for Cross-Cultural Studies* 3 (February 2002), pp. 4–6; and "Smoking in Imperial China," in *Smoke: A Global History of Smoking*, ed. Sander Gilman and Zhou Xun (London: Reaktion Books, 2004), pp. 84–91. Still the best survey of Chinese smoking practices is Bernhold Laufer, "Tobacco and Its Uses in Asia," *Anthropology Leaflet* 18, (Field Museum of Chicago, 1924).

The expression "as fond of smoking as the Turks" is used by Julia Corner in her anonymously published *China, Pictorial, Descriptive, and Historical* (London: H. G. Bohn, 1853), p. 196.

Regarding Las Cortes's encounter with tobacco, see Girard, *Le Voyage en Chine*, p. 59.

Fang Yizhi's observations on tobacco are quoted in Yuan Tingdong, *A Popular History of Smoking in China* [*Zhongguo xiyan shihua*]

(Beijing: Shangwu, 1995) p. 35. The account of tobacco in Shanghai is from Ye Mengzhu, *A Survey of the Age* [*Yueshi bian*] (Shanghai: Shanghai guji chubanshe, 1981), p. 167.

On the history of smoking in the Ottoman Empire, see James Grehan, "Smoking and 'Early Modern' Sociability: The Great Tobacco Debate in the Ottoman Middle East," *American Historical Review* 111 (2006), pp. 1352–77.

A Japanese origin for the term *yan* is proposed by Li Shihong in his *Jottings from the Hall of Benevolence* [*Renshu tang biji*], quoted in Yuan Tingdong, *A Popular History of Smoking in China*, p. 52.

The "Great Western Ocean" is mentioned in Xiong Renlin, *The Woof of the Earth* [*Di wei*], quoted in Chen Cong *Tobacco Manual* [*Yancao pu*] (1773; 1 repr. Shanghai: Xuxiu siku quanshu, 2002), 1.2b. Chen's comment, "It originally came from beyond the borders," appears on 1.5b.

The French missionary who thought the Manchus had imposed smoking was Régis-Évariste Huc (1813–1860); see Huc and Joseph Gabet, *Travels in Tartary, Thibet and China*, trans. William Hazlitt (London: George Routledge and Sons, 1928), p. 123.

The idea of tobacco as native to Korea is mentioned in Liu Tingji, *Miscellaneous Notes from Zai Garden* [*Zaiyuan zazhi*], quoted in Chen Cong, *Tobacco Manual*, 1.3a. On the Manchu conduit, see L. Carrington Goodrich, "Early Prohibitions of Tobacco in China and Manchuria," *Journal of the American Oriental Society* 58:4 (1938), pp. 648–57.

Yao Lü's account comes from his *Dew Book* [*Lu shu*] (repr. Shanghai: Xuxiu siku quanshu 1999), 10.46a. On the quality of tobacco in Fujian, see Zhang Jiebin, *The Complete Works of Master Jingyue* [*Jingyue quanshu*] (repr. Shanghai: Renmin weisheng chubanshe 1991), 48.44b.

Wu Weiye's comment referring to the biography of Li Deyu in *New Dynastic History of the Tang* [*Xin Tang shu*] (Beijing: Zhonghua shuju, 1975), p. 5330, is approvingly cited in Wu Xinli, *Notes on Rare Historical Sources from the Ming-Qing Period* [*Ming Qing xijian shiji xulu*] (Nanjing: Jinling shuhua she, 2000), p. 225.

Zhang Jiebin's comments are from his *Complete Works*, 48.42b–45a;

his entry on betel nut appears on 49.30b–32b. One poet in Chen Cong's collection testifies that his taste for betel nut led him to smoking; Chen Cong, *Tobacco Manual*, 9.5a. On the Chinese medical understanding of tobacco in the mid-seventeenth century, see Laufer, "Tobacco and Its Uses in Asia," pp. 8–9. The idea that smoking counteracted environmental cold or dampness was popular also in the Philippines, where it was used to explain why children also smoked; Juan Francisco de San Antonio, *The Philippine Chronicles of Fray San Antonio*, trans. D. Pedro Picornell (Manila: Casalina, 1977), p. 18.

For the references to women smoking, see Yuan Tingdong, *A Popular History of Smoking in China*, p. 129, quoting Shen Lilong, *Pharmacopoeic Compendium of Edible Foods* [*Shiwu bencao huizuan*] (1681); John Gray, *China: A History of the Laws, Manners, and Customs of the People* (London: Macmillan, 1878), vol. 2, p. 149. On Suzhou women getting their hair done while asleep, see Chen Cong, *Tobacco Manual*, 3.3b. "Making Fun of my Long Tobacco Pipe" is quoted in Yuan Tingdong, *A Popular History of Smoking in China*, p. 71.

The poems appear in Chen Cong, *Tobacco Manual*, 5.8a, 9.3b. Chen Cong's family background is sketched in the *Gazetteer of Qingpu County* (1879) [*Qingpu xianzhi*], 19.43b–44a.

The quotes by Lu Yao are from his *Smoking Manual*, [*Yanpu*] (repr. Shanghai: Xuxiu siku quanshu, 2002), 3b–4b. The advice on writer's block is taken from Yuan Tingdong, *A Popular History of Smoking in China*, p. 128.

On the introduction of opium into China, see Jonathan Spence, "Opium Smoking in Ch'ing China," in *Conflict and Control in Late Imperial China*, ed. Frederic Wakeman and Carolyn Grant (Berkeley: University of California Press, 1975), pp. 143–73. For the references to opium in Ternate and the Philippines, see E. H. Blair and J. A. Robertson, eds., *The Philippines Islands, 1493–1803* (Cleveland, OH: Arthur H. Clark, 1905), vol. 16, p. 303; vol. 27, p. 183; see vol. 29, p. 91 for the doped assassin. Chen Cong deals with the early history of opium in China in his *Tobacco Manual*, 1.12b–14a, 3.4a. On the broader political impact of opium in the nineteenth and twentieth centuries, see *Opium Regimes: China, Britain, and Japan, 1839–1952*, coedited by Timothy Brook and Bob Tadashi Wakabayashi (Berkeley: University of California Press, 2000).

For the poem beginning "Swallowing dawn mist," see Zhao Ruzhen, *The Condolence Collection [Zhuai jí]* (1843), 4.13b.

Laufer's paean to tobacco appears at the end of his "Tobacco and Its Uses in Asia" on p. 65. The tobacco ballet of Turin is mentioned in Vigié and Vigié, *L'Herbe à Nicot*, p. 56. An illustration of a tobacco dance that could have influenced this ballet may be found in Theodore de Bry's *Americae tertia pars* (Frankfurt, 1593), reprinted as fig. 1 in Jeffrey Knapp, "Elizabethan Tobacco," *Representations* 21 (Winter, 1988), p. 26.

CHAPTER 6. WEIGHING SILVER

On Dutch coinage, see Posthumus, *Inquiry into the History of Prices in Holland*, vol. 1, pp. liv–lvii, civ–cxv. On the VOC trade in silver, see Bruijn et al., *Dutch Asiatic Shipping*, vol. 1, pp. 184–93, 226–32.

On the high price of Virginian tobacco and the satire of Thomas Dekker, see Knapp, "Elizabethan Tobacco," pp. 36, 42. The quote from Paolo Xu is cited in Richard von Glahn, *Fountain of Fortune: Money and Monetary Policy in China, 1000–1700* (Berkeley: University of California Press, 1996), p. 199.

Fluctuation in the population of Potosí is noted in Enrique Tandeter, *L'Argent du Potosi: Coercition et marché dans l'Amérique coloniale* [The Silver of Potosi: Coercion and Market in Colonial America] (Paris: EHESS, 1997), p. 96. On the riot of 1647, see Bartolomé Arzáns de Orsúa y Vela, *Historia de la villa imperial de Potosí*, trans. Frances López-Morillas, in *Tales of Potosí*, ed. R. C. Padden (Providence, RI: Brown University Press, 1975), pp. 49–50.

On the volume of silver flowing to China from Japan and Spanish America, see von Glahn, *Fountain of Fortune*, pp. 124–41; the current best estimates are summarized in the table on p. 140. For studies of silver production in Spanish America, see the chapters by Harry

Cross, John TePaske, and Femme Gaastra in *Precious Metals in the Later Medieval and Early Modern Worlds*, ed. J. F. Richards (Durham, NC: Carolina Academic Press, 1983).

The first contact between Chinese and Spaniards is described in Margaret Horsley, "Sangley: The Formation of Anti-Chinese Feeling in the Philippines: A Cultural Study of the Stereotypes of Prejudice" (Ph.D. diss., Columbia University, 1950), p. 106.

Information on Spanish-Chinese relations in Manila has been taken from Blair and Robertson, *Philippine Islands*: for Francisco Sande's remark, see vol. 4, p. 67; "all that the human mind can aspire or comprehend," vol. 6, p. 198; "all of this wealth passes into the possession of the Chinese," vol. 12, p. 59; descriptions of the Parián, vol. 22, pp. 211–12; vol. 29, p. 69; the obligation of Chinese Christians to wear hats, vol. 16, p. 197.

The description of Fujianese sailors comes from Zhou Qiyuan's preface to Zhang Xie, *Investigations of the Eastern and Western Oceans*, p. 17; "cramming winter" (*yudong*) appears on p. 89. "Cramming winter boys" appears in a poem by You Tong, in Yin Guangren and Zhang Rulin, *Brief Account of Macao*, 2.8a.

On the massacre of 1603, see Antonio de Morga's 1609 account in *Philippine Islands*, vol. 15, pp. 272–77; also vol. 16, pp. 30–45, pp. 298–99. The event is covered, with willful misunderstanding of the Chinese side, in Schurz, *Manila Galleon*, pp. 85–90; see also p. 258 on the galleon sinkings. More reliable, though still incomplete, is José Eugenio Borao, "The Massacre of 1603: Chinese Perception of the Spanish on the Philippines," *Itinerario* 22:1 (1998), pp. 22–39. Zhang Xie, *Investigations of the Eastern and Western Oceans*, p. 92, gives a higher estimate of twenty-five thousand killed. The figure of thirty thousand is cited from a 1637 report in Schurz, *Manila Galleon*, p. 81. The minister of war's estimate of the number of Fujianese going abroad appears in *Unedited Records of the Chongzhen Era*, 41.2b. The dynastic history simply says "tens of thousands"; Zhang Tingyu, *Standard History of the Ming Dynasty*, p. 8368.

Schurz's *Manila Galleon* is the authority on the galleon trade; the quotes come from pp. 265 (scurvy and starvation) and 91 (the 1643 comment on the lack of business causing the uprising). Regarding thirty ships arriving in 1639, see Souza, *Survival of Empire*, p. 84, table 4.8.

For the comment on the arches in Chaozhou, see Girard, *Le Voyage en Chine*, p. 103.

On pearl diving in south China, see Gu Yanwu, *Advantages and Disadvantages*, 29.126a–b.

Feng Menglong mentions the guarding of silver mines in his *Provisional Gazetteer of Shouning County* [*Shouning daizhi*] (1637) (Fuzhou: Fujian renmin chubanshe, 1983), pp. 36–37.

For "one man in a hundred is rich," see Brook, *Confusions of Pleasure*, p. 238. On the price of rice in Shanghai in 1639–47, see Ye Mengzhu, *A Survey of the Age*, p. 153; on selling two children for a peck of wheat, see Zhang Lixiang, *Supplement to the Agricultural Treatise, annotated edition* [*Bu nongshu jiaoshi*] (repr. Beijing: Nongye chubanshe, 1983), p. 174.

On junks, see Pierre-Yves Manguin, "The Vanishing *Jong*: Insular Southeast Asian Fleets in Trade and War (Fifteenth to Seventeenth Centuries)," in *Southeast Asia in the Early Modern Era: Trade, Power, and Belief*, ed. Anthony Reid (Ithaca, NY: Cornell University Press, 1993), pp. 197–213.

Francesco Careri's comment is taken from Schurz, *Manila Galleon*, p. 253.

For post-1644 Chinese polemics against silver, see von Glahn, *Fountain of Fortune*, pp. 219–22; Gu Yanwu's comment about "resorting to wine" appears on p. 221.

Andre Gunder Frank, *Reorient: Global Economy in the Asian Age* (Berkeley: University of California Press, 1998), pp. 237–48, sees the world monetary crisis of 1640 as caused by the overproduction of silver. For a contrasting interpretation, see Jan de Vries, "Connecting Europe and Asia: A Quantitative Analysis of the Cape-route Trade, 1497–1795," in *Global Connections and Monetary History, 1470–1800*, ed. Dennis Flynn, Arturo Giráldez, and Richard von Glahn (Aldershot: Ashgate, 2003), pp. 35–106.

The sinkings of the *Concepción* and the *San Ambrosio* are noted in Schurz, *Manila Galleon*, p. 259. The recovery of the *Concepción* is described in Eugene Lyon, "Track of the Manila Galleons," and William Mathers, "*Nuestra Señora de la Concepción*," both in *National Geographic*, Sept. 1990, pp. 5–37 and pp. 39–55. Excavated in 1987–88, the ship was the first Manila galleon to have its cargo retrieved through underwater archaeology.

The principal source for the 1639 uprising is the anonymous "Relation of the Insurrection of the Chinese," translated in Blair and Robertson, *Philippine Islands*, vol. 29, pp. 208–58. On the history of Chinese in the Philippines, see Ch'en Ching-ho, *The Chinese Community in the Sixteenth Century Philippines* (Tokyo: Center for East Asian Cultural Studies, 1968); also Edgar Wickberg, *The Chinese in Philippine Life, 1850–1898* (New Haven, CT: Yale University Press, 1965).

The Chinese-Franciscan conversation on silver is taken from Pedro de la Piñuela, *Questions and Answers on First Meeting* [*Chuhui wenda*], in Pascale Girard, *Les Religieux occidentaux en Chine à l'époque moderne* (Lisbon: Centre Culturel Calouste Gulbenkian, 2000), pp. 388, 472.

For "until recently has supported the full weight of the Monarchy," see Jeffrey Cole, *The Potosí Mita, 1573–1700: Compulsory Indian Labor in the Andes* (Stanford: Stanford University Press, 1985), pp. 52–53.

The story of Fulgencio Orozco is from Padden, *Tales of Potosí*, pp. 27–32. For Calancha's comment about Potosinos being "zealous in the pursuit of riches," see Lewis Hanke, *The Imperial City of Potosí* (The Hague: Martinus Nijhoff, 1956), p. 2.

CHAPTER 7. JOURNEYS

Van der Burch's *The Card Players* is discussed by Michiel Kersten in *Delft Masters, Vermeer's Contemporaries: Illusionism Through the Conquest of Light and Space*, ed. Michiel Kersten and Danille Lokin (Zwolle: Waanders Publishers, 1996), pp. 174–75. Two Dutch paintings of the period depicting African servants in the British Royal Collection are Jan de Bray, *The Banquet of Cleopatra* (1652), and Aelbert Cuyp, *The Negro Page* (ca. 1655), the former published in Christopher Lloyd, *Enchanting the Eye: Dutch Paintings of the Golden Age* (London: Royal Collection Publications, 2005), pp. 50–51. Note that de Bray includes a carrack porcelain on the table before Cleopatra.

On the Dutch slave trade, see Peter Emmer, "The Dutch and the Slave Americas," in *Slavery in the Development of the Americas*, ed. David Eltis, Frank Lewis, and Kenneth Sokoloff (Cambridge: Cambridge University Press, 2004), pp. 70–86. On the history of blacks in seventeenth-century Dutch society and art, see Blakely, *Blacks in the Dutch World*, especially pp. 82–115, 226–28. On the role of blackness in early modern European society, see Hall, *Things of Darkness*, especially pp. 1–15 and ch. 5; also Steven Epstein, *Speaking of Slavery: Color, Ethnicity, and Human Bondage in Italy* (Ithaca, NY: Cornell University Press, 2001), pp. 184–97. As Epstein points out, blacks were latecomers to the slave population of Europe.

Lobo's history is recounted in C. R. Boxer, *Fidalgoes in the Far East, 1550–1770: Fact and Fancy in the History of Macao* (The Hague: Martinus Nijhoff, 1948), pp. 149–53. On the end of the Portuguese trade to Japan, see C. R. Boxer, *Great Ship from Amacon* p. 155.

The Jesuit rector's objection to trafficking in children is cited in Souza, *Survival of Empire*, p. 195.

Bontekoe's voyage is described in his *Memorable Description of the East Indian Voyage,* pp. 57–59, 92–95, 105–13, 142–43. For Coen's rebuke, see Bruijn et al., *Dutch Asiatic Shipping*, vol. 1, p. 71.

The 1646–47 voyage of the *Nieuw Haarlem* is recorded in Bruijn et al., *Dutch Asiatic Shipping*, vol. 2, p. 96, and vol. 3, p. 52.

For "they behaved like a mouse does when it sees a cat" see Nishikawa Jōken, *Twilight Tales of Nagasaki* [*Nagasaki yawagusa*], referring to an incident in 1665, quoted in Boxer, *Jan Compagnie in Japan*, p. 121.

Weltevree's story is told in Gari Ledyard, *The Dutch Come to Korea,* (Seoul: Yaewon, 1971), pp. 26–37; the quotes appear on pp. 28, 36,

181–82, 186, 221; on Bosquet, see pp. 144, 204. A second VOC ship named *Hollandia* embarked from Goeree and arrived in Batavia on 29 August 1625, but as Weltevree said he sailed from Amsterdam, he was more likely on the *Hollandia* that departed from Texel. See Bruijn et al., *Dutch-Asiatic Shipping*, vol. 2, pp. 52, 56; vol. 3, p. 28. The fate of the *Ouwerkerck* is noted in Boxer, *The Great Ship from Amacon*, pp. 114–15.

Cocchi's story is told in Dunne *Generation of Giants*, pp. 235–39, and by Antonio Sisto Rosso in the *Dictionary of Ming Biography*, ed. L. Carrington Goodrich and Chao-ying Fang (New York: Columbia University Press, 1976), pp. 409–10.

On "women in between," see Sylvia van Kirk, *"Many Tender Ties": Women in Fur-Trade Society in Western Canada, 1670–1870* (Winnipeg: Watson & Dwyer, 1980), pp. 4–8, 28–29, 75–77. On the "middle ground," see Richard White, *The Middle Ground: Indians, Empires, and Republics in the Great Lakes Region, 1650–1815* (Cambridge: Cambridge University Press, 1991), p. 52.

The quotes from Caliban come from act 1, scene 2 of William Shakespeare's *The Tempest*. For "it is you who overturn their brains and make them die," see Penny Petrone, ed., *First People, First Voices* (Toronto: University of Toronto Press, 1983), p. 8. Armand Collard's poem, "Barefoot on the Massacred Earth," is quoted in Sioui, *For an Amerindian Autohistory*, p. 33.

Richard Trexler's comment comes from his *The Journey of the Magi: Meanings in the History of a Christian Story* (Princeton, NJ: Princeton University Press, 1997), p. 6; see pp. 102–7 on the black magus and the eccentric position of the third king.

CHAPTER 8. ENDINGS: NO MAN IS AN ISLAND

Donne's seventeenth meditation is found in John Donne, *Devotions upon Emergent Occasions* (Cambridge: Cambridge University Press, 1923), pp. 97–98; I have modernized some spelling and punctuation.

For Bontekoe's purchase of pigs, see his *Memorable Description*, p. 109.

For "today it is snowing in China," see Ledyard, *The Dutch Come to Korea*, p. 28.

On Corcuera's disputes with the Church and subsequent career, see Cushner, *Spain in the Philippines*, pp. 159–67; "for where shoes were worth two reals before," see *Philippine Islands*, vol. 35, p. 195.

For Catharina's comments on "the ruinous and protracted war," see Montias, *Vermeer and His Milieu*, p. 351. On the bodies buried in the Thins–Vermeer grave in the Old Church, see O. H. Dijkstra, "Jan Vermeer van Delft: drie archiefvondsten" [Jan Vermeer of Delft: Three Archival Discoveries], *Oude Holland* 83 (1968), p. 223.

Notes

Chapter 1. The View from Delft

1. The Ming dynasty, founded in 1368, was overthrown in 1644 when a rebel army captured Beijing and drove the last emperor to suicide, then was forced out in turn by a Manchu army invading from the northeast. The Manchu Qing dynasty lasted till 1911.

2. Europeans prized pearls that were large, which this pearl is, and round, which it isn't. Chinese valued size—a first-rate pearl had to be at least 3.75 centimeters in diameter—but preferred a pearl that was "slightly flattened on one side, giving it the shape of an overturned pot," to quote a formula used by all Chinese writers on pearls. A pearl of this quality was called a "pendant pearl" and used exclusively for earrings.

Chapter 2. Vermeer's Hat

1. The map depicts the coastal half of the new United Provinces, with west at the top of the map. Originally compiled by the van Berckenrode family of Delft mapmakers, it was published just after 1620 by the leading commercial cartographer of Amsterdam, Willem Blaeu. Vermeer may have included it to allude to, or mock, an earlier Dutch painterly tradition that used images of the world, such as maps, to disparage the worldly concerns of figures in a painting, particularly women.

2. The Montagnais are known in Canada today as the Idlu First Nation. The name, also romanized as Innu, means "the People."

3. The name *Algonquin*, meaning "relatives" or "allies," was applied to Algonkian-speaking tribes widely dispersed across present-day Québec and Ontario. Champlain's particular allies were the Onontchataronons, known today as the Petite Nation Algonquins.

4. The Hurons who fought with Champlain were the Arendarhonons, the People at the Rock, one of four tribes of the Confederacy. The name *Huron* appears to have been coined by the French as an abbreviation of *Arendarhonon*, punning on the French term for the hair on a boar's head (*hure de sanglier*). The Hurons called themselves the Wendats, the Islanders, referring to the cosmogonic myth that placed them

on the back of a turtle-island swimming in the cosmic sea. Their descendants today are known in Québec as Wendats and in Oklahoma as Wyandots.

5. The Iroquois Confederacy grew to six nations later in the century; the Six Nations now live in southwestern Ontario. The Iroquois called themselves the Rotin-nonhsionni, the House Builders (which the French turned into *Hodénosaunee*). To the Algonquins, they were known as the Naadawe, the Snakes. The Mohawks called themselves the Kanyenkehaka, meaning People of the Flint Site. "Mohawk" is an Algonkian insult meaning Eaters of Animate Things, by implication, Eaters of Humans. The French called them the Anniehronnon.

6. The name was given not by Champlain but by mockers of René-Robert de la Salle's attempt in 1669 to find a water route to China. When the explorers returned to Québec in failure, they were called "the Chinese," and de la Salle's fief, here at Sault St. Louis, was renamed Lachine. The place-name is still in use.

7. Jean Guérard's 1634 world map, *Carte universelle hydrographique*, includes this note beside Hudson Bay: "Grand Ocean descouuert l'an, 1612, par henry hudson Anglois, l'on croit qu'il y a passage de la au Japan" (The Great Ocean discovered in the year 1612 by the Englishman Henry Hudson; it is believed there is a passage from here to Japan).

8. The lake that Champlain put on his map, although in the wrong location, is Lake Nipigon, Nipigon being another version of *Ouinigipous*. The name would be adapted yet again for the first major settlement in Manitoba, Winnipeg.

9. The French also called them Gens de Mer, the People of the Sea, and also Peuples Maritimes, the Maritime Peoples. The desire to associate them with oceanic water was unshakeable.

CHAPTER 3. A DISH OF FRUIT

1. One bag of pepper weighed about 12 kilograms. At a retail price on the Amsterdam exchange of fl. 0.8 per old pound (0.494 kilograms) this cargo of pepper was worth 364,000 guilders.

2. In 1603, Gao Cai sent a semi-official delegation to the Spanish colony of Manila in the Philippines to investigate the truth of tales he had heard of a "gold mountain." It was enough to alarm the Spanish with fears of invasion and set off a massacre of Chinese residents in the city—an event that would be repeated thirty-six years later, the subject of chapter six.

3. The Dutch favored lion names for their ships, especially in the early days of the VOC. A *Red Lion* sailed to Japan in 1609, to choose one at random. The Dutch also used place names. The *Delft* was launched in 1607 and made three return journeys to Goa and Java; a new *Delft* was built in 1640. The *China* was lost in 1608 while riding at anchor in a storm off Ternate in the Spice Islands; in 1676, the Amsterdam Chamber launched another *China* two and a half times the size of her earlier namesake. By contrast, the Portuguese named their carracks after female saints, seeking their protection. The Chinese used bird names, wishing for their ships the power to speed across the water.

4. When a Dutch ship—also bearing the name of *White Lion*, as it happens—pillaged French ships in the St. Lawrence River in 1606, the king of France lodged a complaint with the Dutch government, declaring that the Dutch had no right to trade in territories under his jurisdiction. The Dutch agreed to compensate the owner of the ships for his losses, but they also used the inquiry as a platform to declare that the French had no right to block them from trading wherever they liked.

CHAPTER 4. GEOGRAPHY LESSONS

1. "Moor" is a European term that originally referred to Muslim traders from Morea on the Peloponnesian coast. Later it was expanded to include all Muslims around the Mediterranean, and eventually Muslims everywhere. Masmamut may well be a version of Mohammad. "Moor" was also used to name black Africans.

2. This was not the first time the Ming government had recruited Portuguese from Macao for military assistance. The previous emperor had made the same invitation after ascending the throne. Seven Portuguese gunners went north in 1622 with an interpreter and an entourage of sixteen. Court politics turned against them, so that when a gun exploded during a demonstration in 1623, killing the Portuguese gunner and wounding three Chinese, they were sent back.

3. Rodrigues was lucky to get back to Macao. Twelve of the Portuguese gunners died the previous winter in Shandong province when Chinese soldiers mutinied for back pay. As the mutineers stormed the city the Portuguese were defending, Rodrigues managed to escape by jumping from the city wall into a snowbank. Thanks to global cooling, he only broke an arm in the fall.

CHAPTER 5. SCHOOL FOR SMOKING

1. After leaving the Americas for France, the word "petum" returned with the French who, needing to name a Native tribe outside the Huron Confederacy who were the major tobacco dealers, called them the Pétuns.

2. Dekker is describing a cigar: tobacco leaves rolled into a cylindrical mass, inserted into a casing ("Pudding"), then smoked. Smoking this thing was part of Dekker's humor, "pudding" being Elizabethan slang for penis. "Trinidado" was the name for tobacco coming from Trinidad.

3. The Japanese abandoned *en* for *tabako* in the nineteenth century when they switched from pipes to cigarettes, but the word lingers on No Smoking signs: *kin'en*, "smoking prohibited."

CHAPTER 6. WEIGHING SILVER

1. Eight reals had the value of one peso, which was valued at 26.4487 grams of pure silver. Until 1728, the peso was refined to a purity of 0.931, giving the coin a

real weight of 28.75 grams. The English translated "pesos" as "pieces" (pieces-of-eight being pesos of eight reals).

2. The government imposed a state monopoly on pearl beds from the same anxiety that wealth in private hands threatens the dynasty. In the case of pearls, only Tanka, or boat people, of south China were allowed to harvest pearls under government license. But the best pearl divers in south China were ten-year-old boys who trained themselves to sink to the bottom undetected, break open a mussel, swallow the pearl, and then swim off.

3. The term "ghetto" was first used when Venetian Jews were moved in 1516 to a small islet of this name in the Cannaregio district. The ghetto, a Venetian word meaning "foundry," was an artisan district where glassmaking had been done until it was moved to the island of Murano to reduce the threat of fire. The gates to the ghetto were closed at night; whether they were locked depended on the political climate. The gates were removed after 1797, but rebuilt in 1815 during the Austrian occupation. Jews were granted freedom of residence in Venice only in 1866.

4. "Junk" came into European languages in the 1610s to transcribe *jong*, the Malay word for their large flat-bottomed boats. Europeans soon narrowed the word exclusively to designate the cargo vessels that Chinese merchants used in Southeast Asia, which incorporated elements of Malay design. The English synonym meaning "rubbish" derives from a different maritime origin: "junk" was a piece of old nautical rope too worn to serve as rigging and only fit for other uses, such as padding or stuffing.

CHAPTER 7. JOURNEYS

1. The *Mauritius*, on which Bontekoe's younger brother Jacob sailed to the East three years later, may have taken the same course on its outbound voyage, for its death toll was shockingly high. The *Mauritius* and its sister ship the *Wapen van Rotterdam* lost 275 men on the crossing. They abandoned the *Wapen* on the south coast of Java for want of manpower. Jacob was later sent back to recover the ship, which he did, and was made its captain (*Memorable Description*, p. 114).

2. Some of these garments may have been imaginary, but perhaps not all. According to the posthumous inventory of his possessions, Vermeer owned two "Turkish mantles," a "Turkish robe," and a pair of "Turkish trousers," as well as two "Indian coats." Did Bramer have his own collection of Oriental costumes in which to dress up his models?

CHAPTER 8. ENDINGS: NO MAN IS AN ISLAND

1. The desire to discover a common history for all humankind also motivated European scholars to build universal chronologies, usually by expanding biblical history into a global framework. Research of this sort led James Ussher in 1650 famously to determine that the history of the world began with its divine creation in 4004 B.C., an invented date that apparently still finds favor in certain fundamentalist circles.

INDEX

A Note on the Author

Timothy Brook holds the Shaw Chair in Chinese at Oxford University and is principal of St. John's College at the University of British Columbia. He is the author or editor of twelve books, including the prize-winning *The Confusions of Pleasure: Commerce and Culture in Ming China,* which has been translated into several languages. He is also the editor in chief of a six-volume series on the history of China published by Harvard University Press. He was awarded the François-Xavier Garneau Medal by the Canadian Historical Association in 2005 and a Guggenheim Fellowship in 2006.

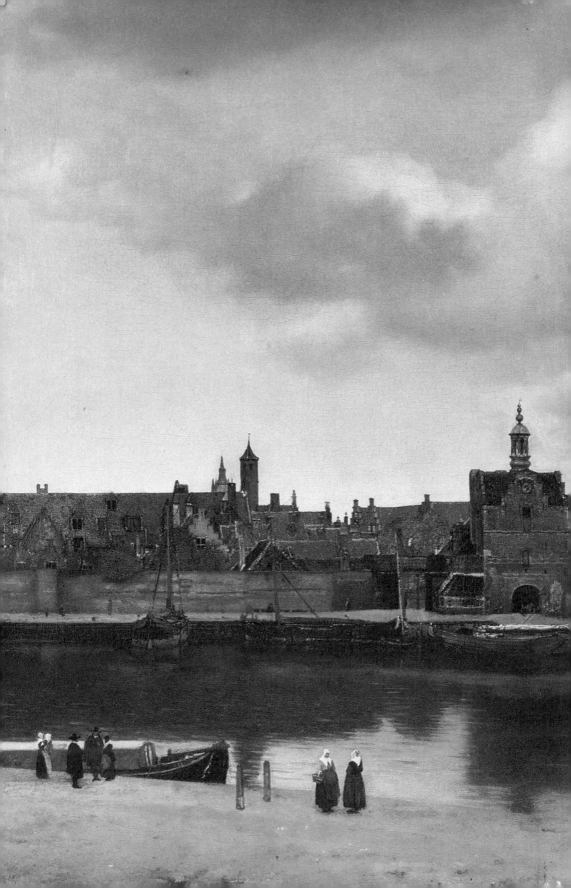